Seminary Papers
Part Two

Rev. Terrence S. Dwyer, MDiv, MBA

Copyright © 2017 Rev. Terrence S. Dwyer

All rights reserved.

ISBN-10: 1544104960
ISBN-13: 978-1544104966

DEDICATION

This book is dedicated to my wife Kathy and our children Kelly, Patrick, and Katharine. Their unconditional love, unwavering faith, and personal sacrifice enabled me the space to wholly answer God's call upon my life to enter into ministry. I am deeply grateful for your generosity of spirit. This work is dedicated to these four amazing souls.

CONTENTS

	Acknowledgments	i
5	Christian Ethics	1
6	Christian Formation	34
7	Evangelism	99
8	Apologetics	127
9	Systematic Theology	169

ACKNOWLEDGMENTS

I would like to acknowledge all of my teachers, mentors, counselors and colleagues along the way who continually encouraged me in my studies and affirmed my calling into ministry. The papers included here are a selection of some of the course work that I submitted during my theological studies at Fuller Theological Seminary between 2009 and 2012.

CHAPTER 5: CHRISTIAN ETHICS

A Brief Review of the Ethical Implications of the USA's Medical Industrial Complex

By: Terrence Dwyer, September 10th, 2010
Fuller Theological Seminary
ET513: Perspectives on Social Ethics-Sacramento
Professor: Ron Sanders

Introduction

A young woman in labor here in Alameda County is turned away by a local private hospital because she didn't have the appropriate medical insurance. A few hours later she lies distraught on a gurney as her baby is born dead in the local county hospital. In San Bernardino, a hospital surgeon in the emergency room sends away a patient who had been stabbed in the heart to a county medical center where he arrives exhausted and succumbs to cardiac arrest and dies upon arrival. Both of these patients were shifted to county facilities not for medical reasons but for economic reasons. These patients simply weren't good for business. The stories of catastrophic loss incurred by families in the United States are seemingly endless. Stories of families who have lost their homes and have had to file for bankruptcy simply to pay their exorbitant health care bills are common. The ethical implications of the growing commercialization of the health care system in the United States have become a heated debate in our society. I will seek here to briefly review the dire economic status of our current health care system and then review the healthcare debate from the point of view of the evangelical left, the evangelical center, and the evangelical right as respects their point of view with regard to the recently passed Affordable Care Act. I will then briefly introduce a biblical perspective of the issue and afterward propose what I think is an appropriate solution for the church in the midst of this continuing healthcare debate.

A Broken System

For those of us who are fortunate enough to have access to the American health care system we enjoy access to some of the finest health care in the world. But despite our technical advances in the field of health care our national system of delivering this health care to the masses is broken and with tragic consequences. The ever-increasing high cost of health care in the United States is caught in an unsustainable paradigm. Overall spending on health care in the United States reached an astronomical 17.6% of the GDP in 2009 which amounted to $2.5 trillion dollars or $8,160 dollars per person. The United States is unique among industrialized democracies as we continue to retain our exorbitantly priced, free market health care system. By contrast, Canada spent 10%, France 11%, Germany 10.6% and the United Kingdom spent 8.4% of their GDP's on their healthcare which each offer a combination of public and private care options. All of the citizens of these developed countries have full access to at least government provided healthcare while 46 million American citizens are uninsured and without access to decent or affordable healthcare. Yet the healthcare systems in these other countries consistently outrank the USA in several health categories. For example, the USA's infant mortality and obesity rates consistently exceed these other countries. Our healthcare system costs almost double per person as that of other major developed countries and yet our health is not better for it but in certain categories we appear to be worse for it. Additionally, it is estimated that 18,000 Americans die unnecessarily every year, many from low-income families, for lack of access to basic health insurance. It is also estimated that 60 percent of bankruptcies are due to medical bills with 75 percent of those declaring bankruptcy due to medical bills have health insurance. By 2018 it is projected that USA health care system spending will exceed $4.3 trillion dollars or $13,100 dollars per person annually, and climb to an economically crippling, 20.3% of the GDP. Clearly, our health care system as currently structured is economically unsustainable and increasingly growing in disparity of accessibility to the system between the rich and the poor.

The Evangelical Left

On March 23, 2010, President Obama signed into law the Affordable Care Act. This new law puts into place comprehensive health insurance reforms that will hold insurance companies more accountable and will guarantee more health care choices through health insurance coverage mandates for employers and additional public health insurance purchase options though a government sponsored health insurance system.

Led by Jim Wallis and Sojourners, the Evangelical Left came out strongly in support of the Obama Administration's Affordable Care Act which they see as a more equitable distribution system of accessible health care through the government sponsored health insurance system. The evangelical left initially sought to consolidate with the right on the issue of government funded abortions but abandoned these traditional evangelical pro-life convictions believing that achieving firm restrictions on government funded abortions were no longer possible. Wallis along with Ron Sider of Evangelicals for Social Action, Joel Hunter of National Association of Evangelicals, David Gushee of New Evangelical Partnership for the Common Good, and Glen Stassen of Fuller Theological Seminary, among others, sent a letter to Congress in support of passing the Senate version of the Affordable Care Act even though there was misleading language in the bill's abortion provisions. By contrast, the U.S. Conference of Catholic Bishops opposed the Senate's version of the bill pointing out that it lacked clear restrictions against government funded abortions.

The evangelical left felt that they could no longer win the fight for restrictions on government funded abortions so they threw their weight behind Obama's Affordable Care Act in hopes of pushing it through Congress. The evangelical left then was partially responsible for helping to bring about the new Affordable Care Act and its subsequent new system of greater access to health care.

The Evangelical Center

David P. Gushee eloquently establishes his case for the evangelical center in his brilliant work entitled, "For the Health of the Nations, An Evangelical Call to Civic Responsibility." He reminds us of the call of God's prophets to create just and righteous societies with fair economic systems that do not favor the rich or tolerate perpetual poverty for the poor. He says that economic justice includes both the mitigation of suffering and the restoration of wholeness with wholeness including the full participation in the life of the community. He includes health care and nutrition as important ingredients in helping people transcend the agony of poverty and re-enter the community. He urges Christians who work in the public, political realm to advocate for health care and social welfare that will protect and empower those who are trapped in poverty with the goal of providing them with health care support that would eventually restore them to community and to wholeness.

Gushee then, as a spokesperson for the evangelical center, came out publicly in support of the Obama health care plan and thus supported the

Affordable Care Act. As mentioned above, Gushee publicly supported the Senate version of the bill as it was working its way through Congress. Thus, the evangelical center then was also partially responsible for helping to bring about the new Affordable Care Act and its subsequent new system of greater access to health care.

The Evangelical Right
The evangelical right was fairly universal in its condemnation of the Obama health care plan. Their rallying cry was that the health care bill as proposed in the Congress would end up funding abortions unless they were specifically excluded. Tony Perkins from the Family Research Council came out against it publicly as did Ken Connor from the Center for a Just Society as well as James Dobson from Focus on the Family in addition to Wendy Wright from the Concerned Women for America. Wright said, "Make no mistake about it; abortion will be funded by the government through the new health care plan."

Harry Jackson and Tony Perkins stated in their book, "Personal Faith, Public Policy" that they favor a free market approach to the health care system in America and they attack the European system of combined public and private health care as a broken-down system. They go on to state, "Mandated coverage and taxpayer-funded services such as abortions, sex change operations, and other morally objectionable services simply ignore the moral complications and concerns that come with a government-run or funded health care system."

The Affordable Care Act passed and was signed into law by President Obama on March 23, 2010 despite the strong objections of the evangelical right.

A Biblical Perspective
In this biblical perspective we will look at two attributes of the kingdom of God. The first being the ministry of healing within the church and the second being the church's call to justice. In Matthew chapter five we see that while John the Baptist was in prison he heard about the deeds of the Christ and he sent word by his disciples and said to him, "Are you the one who is to come or shall we look for another?" And Jesus answered them, Go and tell John what you hear and see; the blind receive their sight and the lame walk, lepers are cleansed and the deaf hear, and the dead are raised up, and the poor have good news preached to them." Jesus' announcement and implementation of the kingdom of God is in line with the prophetic promises of the time of salvation as seen in the words of Isaiah which Jesus quoted above from Isaiah 29:18-19, 35:6, 53:4, 26:18-19,

and 61:1. One of the attributes of the kingdom of God as announced by both Isaiah and Jesus is the ministry of healing. Jesus performed numerous extraordinary healings from bringing the dead back to life, to curing leprosy, dementia, deaf, dumb and blindness, to curing paralysis and hemorrhage to curing cripples and invalids. Nowhere is it recorded where Jesus told his disciples that they were not to do the same regarding healing others. On the contrary, in Luke 9:1-2, Jesus called the twelve together and gave them power and authority over all the demons and to cure diseases, and he sent them out to proclaim the kingdom of God and to heal. Indeed, in John 14:12-14 Jesus the Lord of the universe proclaims; "Truly, truly, I say to you, whoever believes in me will also do the works that I do; and greater works than these will he do, because I am going to the Father. Whatever, you ask in my name, this I will do, that the Father may be glorified in the Son. If you ask me anything in my name, I will do it."

This extraordinary ministry of supernatural healing is still alive and present within the church today but it is a hidden ministry that has been pushed to the fringes of the church. I used to run long distances and suffered a debilitating injury and was diagnosed by an orthopedic surgeon with a torn ACL in my knee requiring surgery. I sought out a friend with the gift of healing and was subsequently prayed over and laid hands upon by this dear brother in Christ and I was instantly healed. I subsequently ran marathons on that miraculously healed knee. The church has countless stories of supernatural healings such as this. In my proposed solution to follow regarding the health care dilemma I will include a recommendation that we make this extraordinary ministry widely known, more visible and accessible to our brothers and sisters in need within the church.

God also calls us to create just and righteous societies. God insists on fair economic systems which do not give undue favor to the rich nor perpetuate poverty. In Isaiah 10:1-3 he warns, "Woe to those who decree iniquitous decrees, and the writers who keep writing oppression, to turn aside the needy from justice and to rob the poor of my people of their right, that widows may be their spoil, and that they may make the fatherless their prey! What will you do on the day of punishment, in the ruin that will come from afar? To whom will you flee for help, and where will you leave your wealth? In Jeremiah 5:28-29 he advises, "They know no bounds in deeds of evil; they judge not with justice the cause of the fatherless, to make it prosper, and they do not defend the rights of the needy…shall I not avenge myself on a nation such as this?"

We are called as a church to create just and righteous societies and to seek the welfare of the city wherein which we live. This would include our working as a church toward seeking access to health care for those who are in need both within the church and within the society in which we live.

A Creative Proposal

My creative proposal for the church toward the health care debate within our country is twofold. The first is my afore mentioned recommendation that we make the extraordinary ministry of supernatural healing widely known, more visible and more accessible to our brothers and sisters in need within the church. This ministry should not be a hidden and neglected ministry on the fringes of the church but it should be made know and a visible part of the everyday ministry of the church. I must add here that I come from a Presbyterian background where the ministry of healing is not openly talked about or even practiced. Other denominations within the church, such as Pentecostals, may have a more common experience with this gift. A more visible representation of this gift would not only relieve untold sufferings by our brothers and sisters in Christ in need but it would also lead others toward salvation in Christ as it would more visibly represent the kingdom of God.

Secondly, we are called to share each other's burdens as did the early church. Hebrews 13:6 advises, "And do not forget to do good and to share with others, for with such sacrifices God is pleased." Also in Galatians 6:2 we are reminded to, "Bear one another's burdens, and so fulfill the law of Christ." Mutual care within the church was simply a way of life for the church from the beginning well into the twentieth century. After, World War II, government programs and insurance companies assumed a much greater role that had been previously played by the church. The church then should go back to working toward sharing one another's health care burdens and especially those of the poor and those in need. One of the ways we can do this as a church is to intentionally and visibly participate in one of the few Christian non-profit medical sharing plans that are available. We also we need to create more of these non-profit medical sharing plans and improve upon them. As a church, we intentionally need to support these non-profit medical sharing plans which are not health insurance plans but are non-profit sharing agreements whereby Christians pay for each other's medical expenses thus sharing in one another's burdens. They work similarly to insurance as members pay a monthly premium into a pool and members then draw from the pool when they incur medical expenses. Because these medical sharing plans are a non-profit Christian ministry they are not regulated as insurance and they can restrict the kind of medical services they will cover. Additionally, because they are non-profit ministries they do not have to support ungodly or unbiblical lifestyles and their subsequent medical services such as abortions. Thus the church can fulfill its call to share in one another's burdens while at the same time support biblically directed healthy lifestyles. These Christian non-profit medical sharing agreements also incorporate a holistic care approach toward praying for one another, health education and strongly incentivizing healthy lifestyles. Through intentionally supporting and improving upon these non-profit medical sharing plans the church can be a more visible model to the world of life within the kingdom of God thereby drawing others toward their salvation in Christ.

Conclusion

Over twenty years ago, C. Everett Koop, the surgeon general wrote, "We have to acknowledge that there is something terribly wrong with a system that spends more and more but seems to serve fewer and fewer people. In a system where demands for service are often unrelated to price, the system is not freely competitive and has virtually no moderating controls working on behalf of the patient. We seem to have a system that is distinguished by a virtual absence of such natural marketplace controls as competition in regard to price, quality or service." The conservative Koop went on to conclude that a change needed to be made within the structure of our health care system. Twenty years later we can see that the dysfunctional system that Koop was writing about has grown substantially worse with real life tragic consequences, especially for the poor.

The prophet's voice continues to call out to us today in Jeremiah 22:13, "Woe to him who builds his house by unrighteousness and his upper rooms by injustice, who makes his neighbor serve him for nothing and does not give him his wages." What does the Lord require of us as a church? He requires us but to do justice, and to love kindness, and to walk humbly with our God (Micah 6:8).

In conclusion, we have seen in this brief review how badly broken and expensive our health care system is. We have reviewed how the evangelical left, right and center have entered into the debate over the passage of the Affordable Care Act. We looked at each of their views as they faithfully worked toward the welfare of the nation within which they lived. We then reviewed our biblical perspective and we looked at two attributes of the kingdom of God. The first being the ministry of healing within the church and the second being the church's call to justice. Finally, we reviewed my twofold creative proposal for the church. The first being my recommendation that we make the extraordinary ministry of supernatural healing widely known, more visible and more accessible to our brothers and sisters in need within the church. Secondly, we need to reclaim the church's original ministry of sharing one another's burdens by sharing in one another's health care burdens and especially those of the poor and those in need. The church should intentionally and visibly participate in one of the few Christian non-profit medical sharing plans that are available and work toward creating more and improving them. By doing so, I believe then we as a church are doing justice, loving kindness, and walking humbly with our God as we participate in the powerful healing ministry of the Holy Spirit and we share in each other's burdens and especially those of the poor and needy and those outside of the church will be drawn toward their salvation in Jesus Christ.

Bibliography

Bibles, Crossway. The ESV Study Bible. Wheaton, Illinois Good News Publishers, 2008.

Foundation, Kaiser Family. "Trends in Health Care Costs and Spending." Kaiser Family Foundation (2009). [accessed September 7, 2010].

Grant, Tobin. "Where the Health Care Debate Lies." Christianity Today (2009). [accessed September 7, 2010].

Gushee, David P. The Future of Faith in American Politics. Waco, Texas: Baylor University Press, 2008.

Perkins, Harry R. Jackson Jr. & Tony. Personal Faith, Public Policy. Lake Mary, Florida: Frontline, 2008.

Sharing, Medi-Share Christian Care Medical. "Medi-Share 2.0 Guidelines." 22. Melbourne, Florida Medi-Share Christian Care Medical Sharing 2010.

Velasquez, Claire Andre and Manuel. "A Healthy Bottom Line: Profits or People?" Issues in Ethics 1, no. 4 (1988). [accessed September 7, 2010].

"System Overload: Pondering the Ethics of America's Health Care System." Issues in Ethics 3, no. 3 (1990). [accessed September 7, 2010].

Wallis, Jim. "Three Moral Issues of Health Care." Sojourners (2009). [accessed September 7, 2010].

Walton, Jeff. "Evangelical Left Dismisses Abortion Concerns, Urges Obamacare Passage." Christian News Wire (2009). [accessed September 7, 2010].

ET 525: Ethics of Bonhoeffer
Essay #1; By: Terrence Dwyer, August 6th, 2012
Professor Dr. Glen H. Stassen

1. In what ways do you think Bonhoeffer's emphasis on community in Life Together correct the privatistic individualism in our churches?

The postmodern era has well established the rights of individuals in society with movements toward democracy and human rights securing the individuals legal position against the power of the state and other societal forces (Todt, p 59). Economic individualism has also been established in the postmodern era and is expected to yield the greatest benefit for all as competition would produce the most productivity. Religious individualism has also rapidly increased within this era and this privastic individualism has become integrated into our churches. Bonhoeffer criticizes this individualism directly. "The cool relationship between individuals that are isolated through economy and law is countered by the concept of community. Social philosophy, with its individualistic social atomism is mostly blind to the reality that is meant by the concept of community. The only fruitful relationship with human beings - in particular with those who are weak - is love that is the will to keep community with them." (Todt, p. 61)

In Life Together, Bonhoeffer addresses the essential communal nature of the church as one in Jesus Christ in part to correct the religious individualism within the church. Bonhoeffer saw the church as being silent and ineffectual against the tyranny of Hitler in part because of religious individualism. Bonhoeffer also saw that individuals are powerless against the vastness of cultures and governments and that this individualism was a weakness within the church. Bonhoeffer advocated for the church to make a difference in the world as coming together in initiative groups of people banding together in community to proclaim the Gospel of Jesus Christ and to do peacemaking. (Stassen, Lecture 3B).

Therefore, in Life Together, Bonhoeffer advocates for the church to come together as one in Christ in Christian discipleship with one another to form our Christian character. Bonhoeffer proposes this Christian character formation through the following:
a) Ministering to the poor - experiencing the life of the other with your life being impacted by the other
b) Prayerful mediation on Scripture - quiet time in listening prayer developing our relationship with God in Christ
c) Commitment to follow Jesus Christ - the way of the cross

d) Becoming an integrated part of church - discerning Christ's was vs. the alternatives

Bonhoeffer advocated that God is sovereign over all of life and that there is no split between the church and the secular. In order to resist the false ideologies of the world such as Nazism we must reject religious individualism and we must go deeper into community with each other serving Christ as we commune together in spiritual love for one another as one together in the world.

2. In what ways do you think Bonhoeffer's understanding of Christ helped him perceive Hitler's evil more clearly and speak against Hitler's evil more strongly than those theologians who actually gave their support to Hitler?

Bonhoeffer understood Christ as Lord over all of life in that all of life was created and redeemed through Jesus Christ. Any thought of two spheres was a profound contradiction to the teaching in the Bible and the teaching of the reformation. "There are not two realities, but only one reality, and that is the reality of God, which has become manifest in Christ in the reality of the world. Sharing in Christ we stand at once in both the reality of God and the reality of the world. The reality of Christ comprises the reality of the world within itself. The world has no reality of its own independently of the revelation of God in Christ." (Ethics, p. 195). Bonhoeffer quickly and clearly perceived Hitler as evil before Hitler even took power. The war mongering of Hitler's National Socialist regime, their disregard of the justice system and the constitution, and the fanatical anti-Semitism all led Bonhoeffer to reject Hitler and his party as evil before they even held power and Bonhoeffer immediately and courageously spoke out against Hitler right after his election.(Todt, p. 188). Bonhoeffer preached that Christ is peace and justice and he called for the resistance to the calls for war coming from the Hitler regime. These calls for war and these injustices of Hitler and his regime drove Bonhoeffer into resistance and drove him to implore the church to make a strong stand against these injustices and the calls for war.

However, the church had lost its credibility after WWI with the German people. Nazism re-established the church for Germany and appointed members of the church to important positions within German society and appointed members of the party to positions within the church which further established their control over the church. This meant that the Nazi party had a means toward controlling the church through a "nationalistic German-Christian Protestant ideology and its' party-servile churchmen." (Todt,. p. 194). Bonhoeffer immediately spoke out against this development within the German church but to no avail. As a result, Bonhoeffer was compelled to create Finkenwalde as a seminary for the development of preachers independent from the influence of the state.

Anti-Semitism was a core of the nationalistic world view in Germany at the time and certain German theologians and church leaders thought the anti-Jewish excesses of the time were a transitory phenomenon in a time of revolution. (Todt,. p. 191). These theologians and church leaders thus supported Hitler while Bonhoeffer immediately recognized these injustices for what they were and spoke out against them. By the time the extermination of the Jews was in full swing in Germany it was far too late for these other theologians and church leaders to come out against Hitler. "The church was mute when it should have cried out, because the blood of the innocent cried out to heaven. Joining the resistance outside the church was necessary for Bonhoeffer since the church as a whole did not act according to its confession, but left the task of crying out in protest to some boards of the confessing church and to some personalities." (Todt, p. 216).

1. In the two drafts of "History and the Good" in his Ethics, Bonhoeffer is trying to work out some guidelines for how we should interpret the Sermon on the Mount as guidance for our lives. Explain what in those guidelines made sense for you.

In the first draft of "History and the Good" in Ethics, Bonhoeffer's interpretation of the Sermon on the Mount is authoritarian in that he regularly interprets the sermon as what we're not to do. He has a hermeneutic of renunciation in his initial interpretation of the Sermon on the Mount. However such universal ideals cannot be applied to all situations throughout history as it just doesn't work for every situation. When faced with the overwhelming tyranny of evil in Hitler, Bonhoeffer realized his hermeneutic of renunciation wasn't sufficient as it didn't do enough in the face of such evil. He realized he needed a hermeneutic of love and not one of simply renunciation. This hermeneutic of love shifts the emphasis from self to others and in particular extending love to others in relationship thus becomes a transforming initiative in these relationships. In his second draft of "History and the Good", Bonhoeffer has taken out his material on the Sermon on the Mount and was intending on writing a full chapter on this new interpretation on the Sermon on the Mount but was unable to complete the re-write due to his death.

Bonhoeffer's second interpretation of the Sermon on the Mount with the hermeneutic of love and the emphasis on transforming initiatives makes much more sense to me than his initial authoritarian interpretation. The Sermon on the Mount are not just rules or general principles to live by as it is so much more than that. The Sermon on the Mount is the largest collection of teachings of Jesus in the New Testament and they are the Words of God as the revelation of God in Jesus Christ. These are the new norms for the Kingdom of God which has broken into the world in the revelation of God in Jesus Christ and they are the new ways forward for our interacting with each other. These are "Christ formed practices for being with others." (Lecture 14-A). These are not rules to live by of things we should not do but are instead the things we are now enabled to do because Christ has entered into our very midst enabling us to go and do something positive and constructive which are transforming initiatives.

Also, the Sermon on the Mount is not just for those who are the followers of Christ who are blessed but it is intended for the blessing of all people. Bonhoeffer interprets the Sermon on the Mount for all people both Christians and non-Christians. It's not about whether the other person is a Christian which causes us to do these transforming initiatives but it is because we are Christian that we do them because Jesus is telling us to do so. For example, in his discussion on conscience, Bonhoeffer said, "The conscience which has been set free is not timid like the conscience which is bound by the law, but it stands wide open for our neighbor and for his concrete distress. And so conscience joins with the responsibility which has its foundation in Christ in bearing guilt for the sake of our neighbor. Therefore, there is a kind of freedom from sin, and this shows itself precisely in the responsible acceptance of the guilt of others." (Ethics, p. 241)

2. Which parts of Bonhoeffer's interpretation of the Sermon on the Mount do you think he would strongly affirm after he has become a participant in the conspiracy to stage a coup against Adolf Hitler and his Nazi regime?

I believe that Bonhoeffer would strongly affirm his second interpretation of the Sermon on the Mount calling for a living out of the transforming initiative of the hermeneutic of love which would ultimately enable him to take the responsible action of confronting evil out of love of neighbor instead of simply renouncing evil. The Sermon on the Mount is not about the renunciation of rights but it is about transforming initiatives enabling one to confront power and injustice nonviolently. Stassen argues in Healing the Rift, "The Sermon consists of fourteen teachings each of which climaxes not in a renunciation, but in a transforming initiative. This transforms the interpretation, making it significantly more helpful in a time of confrontation of power." (Healing, p. 97)

Jesus calls us and makes us participants in what He is doing in the world. We are not passive participants receiving passive grace but we are active participants receiving paticipative grace. Jesus breaks though the barriers and enters into our midst (and shame) restores our relationship with God and with others and makes us participants in what God is doing in the world. (Lecture 12-B) Jesus was confrontational against evil and injustice but always in a non-violent manner. Bonhoeffer then would have affirmed his participation in the conspiracy to stage a coup against Hitler as a transforming initiative acting out of love for his neighbor to confront the evil of Hitler and his regime. He personally would not confront or act violently by evil means but he would use his skills and relationships in a non-violent manner to confront the evil of Hitler toward assisting the efforts of the coup.

Bonhoeffer confronted the evil cult of the Fuhrer by distinguishing between the authority that was being given to the Fuhrer by man and contrasting that to the authority that was given to the office by God. Bonhoeffer's ecumenical ethic of peace and his theological ethic of state denied the state the right to wage war and to usurp the constitution and called for the church separate from the state and to speak out against the actions of the state none of which it did. (Todt, Chapter 7) Without the support of the church and without seemingly any other recourse, Bonhoeffer was compelled to take action against the evil tyranny of Hitler to do something to make peace as he is called to do in the Sermon on the Mount in Blessed are the peacemakers (Matthew 5:9) Making peace is an initiative that must be taken and Bonhoeffer felt called by God to take the initiative toward making peace by confronting the evil of Hitler and to see that he was overthrown. Bonhoeffer's initial interpretation of the Sermon that you overcome evil through "just suffering" and thereby absorbing evil was insufficient in the face of the concentrated evil of Hitler. Thus, Bonhoeffer's second interpretation where he developed an ethic of initiative is far more appropriate toward confronting evil instead of just renunciation and absorbing evil somehow.

Killing Hitler was a sin but it was a necessary sin for the sake and the welfare of others. We are all unrighteous and there is no pathway of purity this side of heaven. The least sinful path may be the path of confronting and killing Hitler in the face of the evil tyranny of his regime which was in process of killing six million Jews. Grace is about God entering into the very midst of the messiness of our lives and God calls us to make peace in our day and time in history and in our circumstance. Being obedient to the call of Christ to make peace, Bonhoeffer acted out of love for his neighbor, and through God's grace he took the transforming initiative toward making peace by confronting the evil regime of Hitler and for him it was the way of the cross.

ET525 – Ethics of Bonhoeffer- Essay#3
By: Terrence Dwyer, September 8th, 2012

1. What does Bonhoeffer mean by religionless Christianity, deus ex machina (God of the gaps), and coming of age?

Bonhoeffer conceived that "religion" and "Christian faith" are actually at opposites with each other. Christian faith in the revelation of God through Jesus Christ cannot be contained by the modern concept of "religion" and that when religion disappears Christianity will change. Christian faith or the Church will not pass away but the close connection between the traditional concept of "religion" and the Christian faith and the Church will become disassociated. Thus Bonhoeffer speaks of a "religionless Christianity" with the eventual passing away of "religion". In describing the passing away of religion Bonhoeffer described that; (1) The time of theological or pious language is past, (2) The time of inwardness is past, (3) The time of conscience is past, (4) The time of metaphysics is past, (5) The time of human being's individuality is past, and (6) The time of the precedence of other-worldliness over this worldliness is past. (Todt, p.44-49). Bonhoeffer argued that the withdrawal from the real world into an inwardness or an other-worldliness is a pious godlessness that emaciates the Church and keeps the Church from engaging the world in and through and for Jesus Christ. Bonhoeffer was wrestling with how and why the Church was ineffectual in standing up against the tyranny of Hitler and he surmised in part that due to this turning inward and toward an other-worldliness that the Church was unable to engage the world and stand against this evil.

Religion is a belief system that is developed out of our human need and our human weakness. Humanity thus creates an all powerful God to shore up our weaknesses and those things that we cannot explain. A "god of the Gaps" where God is pushed to the periphery of our existence for explaining those things we cannot explain. Religion "a priori" is the idea that there is a direct connection between humanity and God in that our ability to become aware of God is inherent within us as a part of the creation of God. The Creator leaves his mark upon all that he creates. When religion is based upon such a premise our connection to God is inward and individualistic and as such then what is the purpose of the Church? What is our concern for one another when our concern is solely for our own individual salvation? Barth and Bonhoeffer argue that due to sin and the fall we are completely broken off and separated from God and that God must break in from the outside to connect with us. Bonhoeffer wrote that the door to freedom must be opened from the "outside". God does break through to us through the revelation of God in Jesus Christ and upon His ascension the Church is the very presence of Jesus Christ in the world. Thus as the Body of Christ standing together in the world the Church is able to stand against evil versus individuals standing alone before God.

Bonhoeffer wrote that humanity is coming of age in that humanity is learning and growing and maturing and is less dependent upon the god of the Gaps. Humanity is becoming more and more autonomous and Bonhoeffer argued that this is a good thing and that this is what God desires. God wants us to know and to understand the world and to stand strong in the world in our God given abilities in Christ. Christ did not come to make us pious as such as much to make us like Him. We are not to stand in the world in power but like Christ we are to stand strong in God but we are to engage the world as the suffering servant to the world through Christ. Through Christ, God is forming a people to ENGAGE the world. It is in this manner that the Church can make a stand against the evil tyranny of one like a Hitler.

Discipleship in Christ then is the suppression of our ego through our submission to Christ who is the unseen center of all of creation. Our strength is not necessarily a bad thing if it is used for the benefit of others. Religionless Christianity is a worldly Christianity engaged in the world through Christ. We (the Church) know what to do and what not to do in the world in Christ. Bonhoeffer argued that we should shed religion and live strongly in this world in and through Jesus Christ. (Lectures 18A&B).

2. What feelings is Bonhoeffer revealing in his poems and prayers? How do they relate to his theology of God's presence in our lives?

Bonhoeffer was wrestling in prison with the meaning and purpose of God for his situation. He was wrestling with the presence of God in the midst of his confinement. In "Letter and Papers" pages 33 to 35 Bonhoeffer begins working through poetry to express the cries of his heart that regular prose leaves wanting. Through the beginnings of his poetry he searches for God in the midst of his confinement as he finds himself separated from people, from work, from his past, from his future, from his longing for marriage to Maria, and even from God. (Letters, p. 33) Bonhoeffer however finds God within his midst through Scripture. In

Ecclesiastes 3 he finds the sovereignty of God and that there is a time under heaven for everything including his confinement. In Revelation 3 he finds hope and the assurance of is faith. In Matthew 6 he finds the intimacy of Jesus who reminds him not to be anxious about his life nor about tomorrow. In Psalm 31 he finds his refuge is in God alone.

Bonhoeffer lived out his theology in prison in the midst of a great evil. He found meaning and purpose in his seemingly meaningless existence within prison. He was renowned throughout the prison by guards and inmates alike for his cheerful and positive attitude. He stood up against the guards at times when they mistreated others and he ministered to many throughout his year and a half in prison. Bonhoeffer also continued to read and write and study and to produce under very dire and difficult circumstances. He even was able to finally lay down his life and suffer martyrdom in an honorable manner bringing even further witness to his testimony of Jesus Christ. Bonhoeffer was able to accomplish all these things for Christ and the Kingdom of God because he stood strong in Christ as he was deeply connected to the Body of the Christ. Bonhoeffer wrote that the New Testament often called us to "be strong" and that weakness is a greater danger than evil. (Letters, p. 392) Bonhoeffer acted responsibly for Christ even within his confinement as Christ was in his midst through the power of the Holy Spirit enabling him to do so. In one of his last letter he writes to Eberhard Bethge, "The key to everything is the "in him". All that we may rightly expect from God, and ask him for, is to be found in Jesus Christ. The God of Jesus Christ has nothing to do with what God, as we imagine him, could do and ought to do. If we are to learn what God promises, and what he fulfills, we must persevere in quiet meditation on the life, sayings, deeds, sufferings, and death of Jesus." (Letters, P. 391)

In his "Prayers for Fellow-Prisoners" (Letters, p. 139 - 143), Bonhoeffer wrote of his utter dependency upon God and of his lostness without God who knows him better than he knows himself. He finds comfort in knowing that God is with him in the midst of his struggle and he finds gratitude within his heart for God's presence. He prays to accept the hard things from God's hand and finds trust in knowing that God will not give him more than he can bear and that God will make all things work together for good. He finds his comfort in the sufferings of Jesus Christ who is present with him in the midst of his own sufferings and in the Holy Spirit who gives him faith, hope, and love. He finally rests in the knowledge of the justice and righteousness of God and the knowledge that he is under the care of the sovereign God who is over all.

The Politics of Jesus
Author: John Howard Yoder
William B. Eerdmans Publishing Co.
Second Edition 1994

A Summary of the Author's Argument
By: Terrence Dwyer, July 15th, 2010
ET 513 - Perspectives on Social Ethics
Professor: Ronald Scott Sanders

The author seeks to test the hypothesis that the ministry and claims of Jesus are best understood as presenting to hearers and readers, not the avoidance of political options, but one particular social-political-ethical option. He tests his hypothesis by reading the Gospel narrative with one constantly present question, "Is there a social ethic present here?" He concentrates his study largely in the Gospel of Luke. Yoder seeks to accomplish his proof through two distinct methods. The first method he uses New Testament research and biblical scholarship to establish an understanding of Jesus and his ministry as having a direct significance for social ethics. In the second method he states his case for considering Jesus to be not only relevant but also normative for a contemporary Christian ethic.

Firstly, Yoder states the problem that Jesus is simply not considered relevant in any immediate sense to the question of social ethics and he gives six reasons why Jesus is considered irrelevant. They are: (1) the ethic of Jesus is an ethic for an "Interim" period which Jesus thought would be very brief. (2) Jesus was a rural figure and thus had no ethic for complex systems. (3) Jesus and his followers lived in a world over which they had no control. (4) The nature of Jesus' message was not historical by definition. (5) Jesus was a radical monotheist. (6) Jesus came for the atonement. Yoder touches on other norms of social ethics out there other than Jesus and describes these as nature, reason, creation, reality, and he describes and ethic established by Paul in his epistles apparently apart from any input by Jesus.

Yoder then establishes through the Gospel of Luke that Jesus is commissioned to enter into history at a certain place and time as the messianic son and servant of God, the bringer of good news and the promise of God. Yoder demonstrates through Luke that a new regime is being implemented and this new regime is a visible, socio-political, economic restructuring of relations among the people of God through the intervention of Jesus Christ into history. Jesus' new kingdom represents an unavoidable challenge to the powers that be and a new beginning of a radically new set of human, social, and political relationships.

The author establishes the importance to the kingdom of God of the concept of the jubilee year or Sabbath year where a person of faith is to (1) leave their soil fallow, (2) forgive all debts, (3) liberate all their slaves, (4) and return to each individual his family's property. The practice of jubilee was a key to understanding and equating the concept of jubilee with the grace of God. The practice of jubilee was not optional but was a precursor on the path toward entering into the Kingdom of God.

The author next reminds us through Scripture from both the Old and New Testaments that God fights on behalf of his people. The only call to the people was to believe and to obey and God would win the victory on their behalf. Thus, when Jesus introduced the radical new kingdom without proposing violent techniques to achieve his ends, the people hearing his message already understood the concept of waiting on the Lord for their victory as Scripture had taught them that the Lord would fight for them. Yoder then introduces the kingdom idea of nonviolent resistance.

Yoder moves to his second method of proof and asks the question "Is this ethical-social-political Jesus relevant in this present age?" He answers by suggesting the following reformulation of the thought patterns that underlie moral choice: (1) The Jesus of history is the Christ of faith and through him the kingdom is within reach. (2) Through practicing jubilee we learn to be solely dependent upon the grace of God alone. (3) The kingdom of God is a visible social order, not a hidden one, in which grace and justice are linked. (4) Jesus modeled both the rejection of the sword and those who wield it and calls us to do the same. (5) The ethics of the Sermon on the Mount is for face to face personal encounters.

The author shows that the ethical tradition carried on by the disciples is that of Jesus in which the believer's behavior reflects the same nature as that of the Lord. Through Scripture Yoder demonstrates that the disciples sought to participate in the divine nature, forgive as God forgave, love indiscriminately as God does, walk in Christ, die to self, love as Christ loved, serve as Christ served and be subordinate. Additionally, the disciples sought to suffer with Christ, share in divine condescension, give of their life, and be a suffering servant even unto death. We are called to do the same today.

Yoder next turns his attention to the issue of Jesus breaking the sovereignty of the powers of this fallen world by living a free and human existence. Christ was subject to these powers but did not support them in their self-glorification and thus disarmed them and their powers and made a public example of them through his death and utterly defeated them in his resurrection. The church in turn does not attack these powers but concentrates on not being seduced by them and our task and our weapon is to stay close to Him in living out our lives in Christian community.

Yoder concludes his proof by reviewing the concept of revolutionary subordination of the people of faith in their relationships, where each person regardless of their station in life has a moral status and responsibility and a meaningful witness and ministry and that this radical new way of living comes directly from Christ. Similarly, the church is to participate in God's victorious plan by displaying submission and patience with the rebellious powers of creation even as Christ himself displayed submission and patience unto death. Christ conquered the rebellious powers of this world through peaceful, humble, non-violent submission to the will and plan of God and we, his church, are called to live out our lives in community in the same manner. This is the power of God, the cross of Christ, which is our social efficacy.

ET525 – Ethics of Bonhoeffer – Professor Dr. Gen H. Stassen
Fuller Theological Seminary
Final Paper – A journal in dialogue with the readings
By: Terrence Dwyer, September 13th, 2012

As I work through my reading journal with Bonhoeffer I am seeking to engage these texts in the theme of standing strong in community in the Lord as we engage the world we find ourselves living in. Bonhoeffer had an extraordinary ability and uncommon strength to stand strong in his faith in the Lord and in his witness for the Gospel of Jesus Christ. I will seek to explore this theme and certain others that come up as I engage these texts. Bonhoeffer wrote that humanity is coming of age in that humanity is learning and growing and maturing and is less dependent upon the God of the Gaps. Humanity is becoming more and more autonomous and Bonhoeffer argued that this is a good thing and that this is what God desires of humanity. God wants us to know and to understand the world and to stand strong in the world in our God given abilities in the Body of Christ. We are not to stand in the world in power but like Christ we are to stand strong in our faith in God and we are to engage the world as the suffering servant to the world through Christ. Through Jesus Christ, God is forming a community of people to engage the world and it is in this manner that the Church can make a stand against the evil tyranny of one like a Hitler. I will review my interactions with our readings in the order that they were assigned; Life Together, Ethics, The Cost of Discipleship, Authentic Faith by Tödt, and finally, Letters & Papers from Prison. I had not read very much of Bonhoeffer prior to this class.

Life Together

The only book of Bonhoeffer's that I had read prior to this class was parts of Life Together a couple of years ago when we planted a church and the lead pastor had us read sections of this book. I had no understanding at that time of the context within which Dietrich Bonhoeffer wrote this book. Gaining an understanding of that context within this class made all the difference in world to me in gaining a deeper understanding of this great work. As I understand the context in a nutshell; Bonhoeffer was convinced and adamant that the Protestant Churches must stand up and speak out against the rapidly increasing militarization of Germany and against the mistreatment of the Jewish people. The Confessing churches didn't respond to Bonhoeffer's challenge leaving Bonhoeffer essentially alone in his stand against the tyranny of the Hitler regime. Bonhoeffer withdrew to London in 1933 to pastor two German speaking churches there but returned to Germany in 1935 to take charge of a clandestine seminary at Finkenwalde for the training of young pastors. It was during this brief time here that Bonhoeffer wrote both Life Together and The Cost of Discipleship on what it means for Christians to live together in true fellowship in Jesus Christ. (LT, P. 10-11)

Bonhoeffer concludes that he could not withdraw from participating in the political and military resistance against Hitler and deemed such withdrawal as irresponsible cowardice and a flight from reality. Bethge said that Bonhoeffer "could see no possibility of retreat into a sinless, righteous, pious refuge. The sin of respectable people reveals itself in flight from responsibility. He saw that sin falling upon him and he took a stand." (LT, p. 11) It is here that Bonhoeffer "acted in accord with his fundamental view of ethics, that a Christian must accept his responsibility as a citizen of this world where God has placed him." (LT, p. 12)

In Life Together, Bonhoeffer addresses the essential communal nature of the church as one in Jesus Christ in part to correct the religious individualism within the church. Bonhoeffer saw the church as being silent and ineffectual against the tyranny of Hitler in part because of religious individualism. Bonhoeffer also saw that individuals are powerless against the vast and pervasive power of culture and government and that this individualism was a weakness within the Church. Bonhoeffer advocated for the Church to make a difference in the world as coming together in initiative groups of people banding together in community to proclaim the

Gospel of Jesus Christ and to do peacemaking.

Therefore, in Life Together, Bonhoeffer advocated for the church to come together as one in Christ in Christian discipleship and fellowship with one another to form our Christian character together in community. Bonhoeffer proposed this Christian character formation through such things as; (a) Ministering to the poor - experiencing the life of the other with your life being impacted by the other; (b) Prayerful mediation on Scripture - quiet time in listening prayer developing our relationship with God in Christ; (c) Commitment to follow Jesus Christ - the way of the cross – laying down our lives and following Jesus Christ; (d) Becoming an integrated part of the Church - discerning Christ's was vs. the alternatives.

Bonhoeffer advocated that God is sovereign over all of life and that there is no split between the church and the secular. In order to resist the false ideologies of the world such as Nazism we must reject religious individualism and we must go deeper into community with each other serving Jesus Christ as we commune together in spiritual love for one another as one body moving in unity together in the world. In practical reality and especially in our western culture today this is particularly difficult to achieve apart from withdrawing into a monastery. However, the leadership team of our church plant reviewed ideas for Christian fellowship from Bonhoeffer's Life Together a few years ago when we planted our new church. From this work we found it absolutely essential to integrate discipleship into the daily life of our church in as many ways as we possibly could. Some of the things that we came up with are:

1) Neighborhood Community Groups: We are an urban church plant here in Oakland, CA and we sought to establish Neighborhood groups where people from our church who live near each other could meet once a week for fellowship, Bible study, prayer, and for works of community service together.

2) We also implemented what we call 20/21 groups where small groups of three would meet to spend time in the Word together and to pray for each other. We've just expanded these to now include groups of people who share common interests together such as hiking, biking, sewing, etc. where we meet for the common interest but the relationships are clearly for discipling each other in Jesus Christ. We are currently training discipling leaders for these groups so that we are trained in speaking the Word into each other's lives as we fellowship with each other. Bonhoeffer said, "The Christian needs another Christian who speaks God's Word to him". (LT, p. 23)

3) We've also recently implemented a community "Care and Prayer" bulletin which we hand out each week at worship which connects our entire community together daily during the week for prayer for our city and for those within our community in need, for praises for our many blessings, for daily Scripture study together, and for updates on community events and happenings drawing our community closer together. It is safe to say that this "Care and Prayer" bulletin came into being partially as a result of reading Life Together and taking this class. We saw the necessity of binding our community together during the week in prayer and Scripture study even as we are separated from each other during the course of the week.

Personally, Bonhoeffer's teaching on spiritual love which comes from Jesus and which serves Him alone knowing that it has no immediate access to other persons and that spiritual love is bound solely to the Word of Jesus Christ to maintain our fellowship in love was an extraordinary insight for me which has transformed my relationships in Christ. It is this new understanding which enables be to stand united together in spiritual love with my brothers and sisters in and through Jesus Christ.

Ethics
I found again in Ethics the recurring theme from Bonhoeffer of standing strong in community in the Lord for engagement in the world. In his chapter on "Ethics as formation" he writes that the whole world is reconciled to God through Jesus Christ who does not reconcile the world to himself by overthrowing the world but who reconciles the world to himself through the Cross and the resurrection. Christ is alive and in the world today through the Body of Christ in his Church. "The love of God does not withdraw from reality into noble souls secluded from the world. It experiences and suffers the reality of the world in all its hardness. The world exhausts its fury against the Body of Christ. But, tormented, He forgives the world its sin. That is how the reconciliation is accomplished. Now there is no more reality, no more world, but it is reconciled with God and at peace. God did this in His dear Son Jesus Christ." (Ethics, p. 72-73)

Thus, as members of the Body of Christ we are participants in and with Jesus in this reconciliation as Jesus is using us to reconcile the world to Him. Therefore, we are participants in the world through the love of Jesus and we are not called just to "pocket" our gift of salvation and withdraw from the world in righteous piety and renunciation of the world. We are to be strong in the Lord, standing together in community within the Body of Christ wherein we take transforming initiatives of love into the world through the love of Jesus for the world. Bonhoeffer went on to conclude; "Ethics as formation is possible only upon the foundation of the form of Jesus Christ which is present in His Church. The Church is the place where Jesus Christ's taking form is proclaimed and accomplished. It is this proclamation and this event that Christian ethics is designed to serve." (Ethics, p. 89) In a later chapter on Christ, Reality, and the Good, Bonhoeffer picks up again the same theme; "In Christ we are offered the possibility of partaking in the reality of God and in the reality of the world, but not in the one without the other. The reality of God discloses itself only by setting me entirely in the reality of the world, and when I encounter the reality of the world it is always already sustained, accepted, and reconciled in the reality of God." (Ethics, p.193)

Personally, coming to a deeper understanding of this is extraordinarily freeing and empowering. The world is already wholly sustained, accepted, and reconciled by God in Jesus Christ therefore I have nothing to fear by taking transforming initiatives of love into the world – God is already there and has already reconciled the world to Him. As a relatively young church plant in north Oakland we are in the process of discerning where it is within the city that the Lord is directing our church community toward transforming initiatives of love within our neighborhood community. One initiative that we have taken to date is to come alongside Oakland International High School which is in our neighborhood and where we have undertaken several initiatives of support for the school in a variety of different ways. Another transforming initiative that we are participating in is joining with other churches in our Oakland community toward marching and rallying for peace. We are coming together as a widely diverse community of churches toward taking political action against the violence within our community. We are taking up the responsibilities of loving those within our community whose lives are deeply impacted by the maddening cycle of gangs and drugs and violence and retaliation. Having this hermeneutic of love from Bonhoeffer along with his encouragement to stand strong together in the Body of Christ while engaging the world is a deep encouragement to me at this particular time of my ministry here in Oakland.

Bonhoeffer went on to further state; "For it is precisely this disordered world that in Christ is reconciled with God and that now possesses its final and true reality not in the devil but in Christ. The world is not divided between Christ and the devil but whether it recognizes it or not, it is solely and entirely the world of Christ. The dark and evil world must not be abandoned to the devil. It must be claimed for Him who has won it by His incarnation. What is intended here is not the separation from the world but the summoning of the world into the fellowship of this body of Christ, to which in truth it already belongs." (Ethics, p. 201&203)

The Church has by and large abandoned to the devil those within our city of Oakland who have been caught up in the cycle of gangs and drugs and violence and retaliation. These young men and women who are caught within this cycle of destruction urgently need to hear the message of the Gospel of Jesus Christ. Bonhoeffer is totally relevant today for the Church on the streets of Oakland where the Church needs to engage these young men and women with the Gospel and not abandon them to the devil. The Church must take up our responsibility and actively engage these communities in transforming initiatives of love in and through Jesus Christ. I am greatly encouraged by the writings and teachings of Bonhoeffer here as they encourage me to move forward in ministry in community within the Body of Christ into areas within our city which I may have previously been hesitant to approach prior to reading Bonhoeffer.

Dr. Richard Mouw echoes the encouragement of Bonhoeffer to engage the world in his work; "When the Kings Come Marching In" wherein Mouw writes about engaging the culture; "We must train ourselves to look at the worlds of commerce and art and recreation and education and technology, and confess that all of this filling belongs to God. And then we must engage in the difficult business of finding patterns of cultural involvement that are consistent with this confession. If in a fundamental and profound sense; God has not given up on human culture, then neither must we." (Kings, Mouw, p. 42) "The earth is the Lord's and everything in it." (Psalm 24:1)

In his chapter on "History and Good" Bonhoeffer continues his theme but emphasizes responsible action here. He writes, "Only the selfless man lives responsibly, and this means that only the selfless man lives." (Ethics, p. 222) Bonhoeffer goes on to say that it is Jesus Christ who sets conscience free for the service of God and of our neighbor; He sets conscience free even and especially when man enters into the fellowship of human guilt. The conscience which has been set free is not timid like the conscience which is bound by the law, but it stands wide open for our neighbor and for his concrete distress. And so conscience joins with the responsibility which has its foundation in Christ in bearing guilt for the sake of our neighbor. For responsible action, therefore, there is a kind of relative freedom from sin, and this shows itself precisely in the responsible acceptance of the guilt of others." (Ethics, p. 241) Here again, Bonhoeffer reveals to me an even deeper understanding of our freedom in Christ to engage the world in ministry. If I am bound by the guilt of my conscience I am bound from freely and deeply engaging in ministry with others. However, if my conscience is free from guilt through Jesus Christ taking my guilt upon Him, then I am released from the guilt of my conscience and I am free to engage others in ministry in a much deeper way. Once again I am grateful to Bonhoeffer for this additional insight toward our freedom in Christ and this is in keeping with the general theme that I am seeking to engage here in my review and that is the theme of standing strong in community in the Lord as we engage the world. Having this deeper understanding of our freedom in the Lord I am better able to engage the world with the Gospel of Jesus Christ.

The Cost of Discipleship

The theme of standing strong in community in the Lord for engagement in the world is found throughout The Cost of Discipleship. In this work Bonhoeffer examines grace and discipleship and costly grace versus cheap grace along with obedience and the way of the cross. Bonhoeffer also examines the Sermon on the Mount and what it means for the Christian disciple as well as the hidden character of the Christian life. Bonhoeffer also goes on in this work to further examine the life of the disciple and the Church in the world.

Bonhoeffer's explanation of costly grace versus cheap grace resonated deeply with me as I all too often have found myself availing for cheap grace instead of the costly grace that my Lord Jesus is calling me to. I think it is critical to understand the distinction Bonhoeffer makes here in that the call of the disciples is an act of obedience by the disciples and is not a confession of faith in Jesus. It is Jesus who in his authority who calls us and demands obedience to his word. Our discipleship to Christ then means our immediate obedience to his calling and our continued adherence to Christ through time. Bonhoeffer writes, "Christianity without the living Christ is inevitably Christianity without discipleship, and Christianity without discipleship is always Christianity without Christ. It remains an abstract idea..." (Discipleship, p. 59) Living without Jesus is simply a fabricated Christianity and a way of our own choosing.

The essential nature of obedience in the life of the disciple was made quite clear to me by Bonhoeffer as he described only the one who believes is obedient and that only the one who is obedient actually believes. I may believe in Christ and I may have faith in Christ and I may even lay down great portions of my life to follow Christ but that is not the call or the way of the cross. I must lay down all of my life to Christ and remain obedient to Christ in all things. I cannot do this under my own power or strength but the Lord enables me to be obedient to him. Bonhoeffer states, "Christ must first call him, for the step can only be taken at his word. This call is his grace, which calls him out of death into the new life of obedience." (Discipleship, p. 66) The important thing to note here is that the step of obedience must be taken before faith can be possible and it is Christ who gives us the grace for our obedience within His very call to us.

In my ministry the ability to discern disobedience in myself and others through the power of the Holy Spirit will be an important element for ministering to people. Our disobedience and our insistence upon controlling parts of our lives is what prevent us from seeing and hearing Jesus and experiencing His grace. Our willful disobedience distances us from Jesus and it is in this space where ministry happens to call others back into obedience and into submission to the grace of Jesus Christ. We learn what obedience is and how to obey Jesus simply by being obedient. We must make that first step of obedience and Jesus meets us there and he graciously gives is the grace to be obedient we must simply do so. Bonhoeffer paraphrases Jesus in the parable of the rich, young ruler; "You know the commandments, do you not? Well then, put them into practice. You must not ask questions – get on with the job!" (Discipleship, p. 78) This was quite a helpful insight on obedience for me to glean here not only for myself but for ministry toward others. Bonhoeffer further emphasizes that our call from Jesus was the Word of God Himself and all that it required was single-minded obedience. Obedience to this call is never within our own power. Our salvation through following Jesus is not something we can achieve for ourselves but through God's grace we can follow Jesus and we can be obedient. (Discipleship, p. 84&85)

Bonhoeffer goes on to discuss the way of the cross in that the way of the cross entails suffering and being despised and rejected by men and that the "must" of this suffering that Jesus "must" suffer this path also applies to his disciples. Bonhoeffer states; "To deny oneself is to be only aware of Christ and no more of self, to see only him who goes before and no more the road which is too hard for us. It is not the sort of suffering which is inseparable from this mortal life, but the suffering which is an essential part of the specifically Christian life. It is not suffering per se, but suffering and rejection for the cause of Christ." (Discipleship, p. 88) I must admit that my walk with Jesus has had its' share of intense sufferings for the cause of Jesus Christ. But in reflecting back he did not give me more than I could bear and he carried me through those difficult times and balanced them in my life with times of intense blessing and grace. In ministry to others it will be necessary to acknowledge and affirm their suffering for the cause of Christ as it will be necessary to bear the burdens and to forgive the sins and transgressions of others.

While Christ does call us into community he also calls each one of us separately, individually, and alone as our eyes are to be fixed solely upon our Lord Jesus. Bonhoeffer adds; "We cannot establish direct contact outside ourselves except through him, through his word, and through our following of him. To think otherwise is to deceive ourselves. We must repudiate any direct relationship with the things of this world for the sake of Christ. The same mediator who makes us individuals is also the founder of a new fellowship. He stands in the center between my neighbor and myself." (Discipleship, p. 97&100) We are called away from our community to follow Jesus Christ and God gives us back our community in the Body of Christ – the Church. We see here again from Bonhoeffer the theme of our being in community and of our standing strong and responsible within that community as we exercise our God given gifts in community as we engage the world for the Gospel of Jesus Christ.

While I have read and studied some on the Sermon on the Mount; Bonhoeffer's discussion of the Sermon on the Mount was enlightening for me especially the perspective from him that the Sermon on the Mount is the only ground that we can stand on to blow up the great "phantasmal" of Nazism and to stand against the ideologies of Nazism. (Lecture 12A) The way of the Sermon on the Mount is the largest block of teachings by Jesus in the New Testament and this is the Word of God to us – this is the way of Jesus in which we are to live during our place and time upon the earth. Bonhoeffer made some interesting comments and observations here; "The meek show themselves by their every word and gesture that they do not belong to this world. Those who thirst after righteousness look forward to the future righteousness of God knowing that we cannot establish here for ourselves. Also that the merciful have an irresistible love for the downtrodden, the sick, the wretched, and the wronged, and the outcast and that we cast away our dignity and our honor in order to be merciful to them. The pure in heart must surrender their whole hearts to Christ and those who are called peacemakers actually work toward making peace." (Discipleship, p. 110-112)

In writing about the Church community Bonhoeffer said that the Church is to penetrate the whole earth and that through it the earth subsists. Bonhoeffer makes a keen observation here; ""You are the salt", Jesus does not say, "You must be the salt." It is not for the disciples to decide whether they will be the salt of the earth, for they are so whether they like it or not and they have been made salt by the call that they have received."(Discipleship, p. 116) I find this to be a particularly helpful insight in that we are not to strive to be the salt for the world – we simply are the salt for the world through the very call of Jesus which contains the very grace which we need to be the salt for the world. Similarly with the light, "You are the light in your whole existence, provided you remain faithful to your calling. And since you are that light, you can no longer remain hidden, even if you want to. It is the property of light to shine." (Discipleship, p. 117) I find these insights from Bonhoeffer to be freeing in the sense that I am simply to be who I am in Christ and I am salt and light to the world. Similarly in ministry I believe I am now better able to acknowledge and affirm those in the Church as salt and light to the world.

I also very much appreciate Bonhoeffer's keen insight regarding the law wherein he writes; "It was the error of Israel to put the law in God's place, to make the law their God and their God a law. The disciples were confronted with the opposite danger of denying the law its divinity altogether and divorcing God from the law." (Discipleship, p. 122) Personal communion with God is the law fulfilled and genuine adherence to Jesus Christ means adherence to the law of God. "If men cleave to him who fulfilled the law and follow him, they will find themselves both teaching and fulfilling the law. Only the doer of the law can remain in communion with Jesus. It is not enough to teach the law of Christ – it must be done." (Discipleship, p. 124&125) I find this insight from Bonhoeffer to be helpful for me in reconciling Matthew 5:18; For truly, I say to you, until heaven and earth pass away, not an iota, not a dot, will pass from the Law until all is accomplished. Jesus fulfilled the law and if we are in communion with Jesus then we are to be teachers and doers of the law and if we are not doers of the law then we break our communion with Jesus. We remain strong in community in the Lord by remaining in communion with Jesus by being doers of the law through God's grace.

Finally, Bonhoeffer's discussion of loving our enemies helped me to see that even our enemies are objects of God's love and that we both equally stand beneath the cross of Jesus. God's perfect love is an all-inclusive love which we as followers of Jesus are to exhibit as well through the power of the Holy Spirit. We are a peculiar people living in the world, who are called by Jesus to commune in him, and to live out the teachings of the Sermon on the Mount while being obedient to his calling as the salt and light for the world. In living out this life we are to hide our righteousness from ourselves and to focus only upon Jesus. We are to continually commune with Jesus through on-going prayer while letting Christ rule in our hearts by surrendering our wills to him completely. In this manner we can then pray that his will be done and he who knows our needs before we even ask him. (Discipleship, p. 104) I also greatly appreciated Bonhoeffer's insights on fasting in his discussion on spiritual disciplines as self-control and discipline are essential characteristics of the life of a disciple and fasting helps to discipline the strong desires of the flesh. The Lord has been working on my heart to embrace fasting and this reading in Bonhoeffer on fasting has greatly encouraged me and convicted me that fasting is a spiritual discipline that I need to incorporate into my spiritual practices.

Authentic Faith:

It is here in Authentic Faith by Tödt where the theme of standing strong in community in the Lord for engaging the world is fully expressed in Tödt's examination of Bonhoeffer's thesis of Religionless Christianity. Tödt's articulation of Bonhoeffer's thesis helped me to understand it and encouraged me to embrace it. I found this discussion to be challenging, liberating, and greatly encouraging toward moving forward responsibly in ministry into the world.

Christian faith in the revelation of God through Jesus Christ cannot be contained by the modern concept of "religion" and that when religion disappears Christianity will change. Christian faith or the Church will not pass away but the close connection between the traditional concept of "religion" and the Christian faith and the Church will become disassociated. Thus Bonhoeffer speaks of a "Religionless Christianity" with the eventual passing away of "religion". Bonhoeffer argued that the withdrawal from the real world into an inwardness or other-worldliness is a pious godlessness that keeps the Church from engaging in the world for Jesus Christ. (Authentic, p. 24) Bonhoeffer writes; "Free responsibility is grounded in a God who demands the responsible deed freely ventured in faith, and who promises forgiveness and consolation to the human being who in doing so becomes a sinner." (Authentic, p. 12)

All too often I find myself longing or striving to retreat into inward attempts at piety. I think that if I can just meditate enough or pray enough or fast enough then things will be made right. But God is not calling us toward an inward piety – our righteousness is as filthy rags (Isaiah 64:6) – God is calling us to engage the world just as we are for his Gospel and to be salt and light for the world. Tödt explains; "The Bible does not know the modern distinction between the external and the inner, and so prevents us from removing God from the realm of public human existence to the inward, private and other-worldly realm. There is no exit for the Christian into the eternal, or into other worldliness, but, like Jesus in Gethsemane, the Christian must consent to earthly life to the full, must stand fast in this world and must consent to being addressed and claimed in the middle of life, and the Christian must, by a strength bestowed by God, partake of what God suffers from this world." (Authentic, p.26) "God lives in us, and his love is perfected in us. God discloses himself as we are placed completely into the world-reality which is experienced in the love for our neighbors." (Authentic, p.31)

I often encounter Christians in my ministry who view the world as a place to be endured and tolerated while awaiting the return of our Lord Jesus Christ. The world is often judged and scoffed at and condemned and withdrawn from in self-preservation and therefore not actively engaged. As a minister to the Church I will need to work to edify and to encourage the Church toward engagement in the world for the Gospel of Jesus Christ. Tödt writes; "The Christian individualist whose whole concern is salvation in the beyond, can regard this world, in its relatively differing conditions, only as an insignificant transition stage to be endured patiently. Those who rely on inwardness imagine that eternity is already within themselves. But Christians see themselves, as whole human beings, first of all oriented toward this world wherein their lives are to be lived responsibly in faith amid the fullness of tasks, questions, successes, and failures. Human beings are addressed and claimed by God in their strength, in their power, and in their gifts, so that they will engage themselves in affairs that pain God in the world, such as injustice, misery, oppression, emptiness, and senselessness." (Authentic, p.49&52)

It is here where Bonhoeffer lives out his theology when he returns to Germany from the safe harbor of USA during WWII knowing that by doing so he would literally be laying down his life at the hands of the Nazi's. Bonhoeffer stated that he would have no right to participate in the reconstruction of Germany after the war if he was not standing with his countrymen in the midst of the greatest need. So Bonhoeffer returns and engages the great evil of the Nazi's with all of his God given strengths and gifts. This decision was the way of the cross for Bonhoeffer as it eventually caused him to suffer the indignities of prisons and the pain of execution by hanging. Bonhoeffer explicitly showed us through the living out of his theology in his life of what it means to stand strong in community and to engage the world for the Gospel of Jesus Christ. I have immense respect and admiration for the courage and the faith and the strength of conviction of Dietrich Bonhoeffer. Granted, Jesus is our Lord who calls us and bids us to follow Him on the way of the cross but it is saints and martyrs like Dietrich Bonhoeffer and Martin Luther King, Jr. who show us the way to stand strong in our communities of faith and n Jesus Christ and to actively and responsibly engage the world for the Gospel of Jesus Christ. They are our examples for the way of the cross and our encouragement as we walk the paths we are each called to walk upon by our Lord Jesus.

Letters & Papers from Prison:

It is in this great work by Eberhard Bethge where we become intimate with Dietrich and where I got to know him on a more human level and where I found I could relate to him better as he reveals himself though his letters to and from others. Here Dietrich is in the midst of living out his theology by standing strong with his community in Jesus and where he is using his God given strengths and powers to the very last moments of his life for the cause of the Gospel. Bonhoeffer exhorts the Church in the prologue After Ten Years; "Civil courage, in fact, can grow only out of the free responsibility of free men. Only now are the Germans beginning to discover the meaning of free responsibility. It depends upon a God who demands responsible action in a bold venture of faith, and who promises forgiveness and consolation to the man who becomes a sinner in that venture. We will not and must not be either outraged critics or opportunists, but must take our responsibility for the molding of history in every situation and at every moment, whether we are the victors or the vanquished. The ultimate question for the responsible man to ask is not how he is to extricate himself heroically from the affair, but how the coming generation is to live. We are not Christ, but if we want to be Christians, we must have some share in Christ's large heartedness by acting with responsibility and in freedom when the hour of danger comes. Mere waiting and looking on is not Christian behavior. The Christian is called to sympathy and action by the sufferings of his brethren for whose sake Christ suffered." (Letters, p. 6-14) Bonhoeffer is living out the grist of his theology in the mill of living under the tyranny of the Nazi regime. His life is an extraordinary example for the Church of the call of Christ and the way of the cross in living out our lives as Disciples of Christ in the time and place wherein we have been called to do so.

One of the things I found fascinating throughout Letter & Papers from Prison was the inside look we get at what life was actually like for the Germans in the midst of WWII. I have many stories from my family of what life was like for them here in the USA during WWII and find that their stories are similar to those of Bonhoeffer and his friends and family until the end of the war when circumstances changed dramatically for the people of Germany. I was repeatedly taken aback while reading these letters at the normalcy of life for the participants while they were in the midst of this Great War. The German people seemed to be carrying on with their lives as if there were no war at all. They were marrying and traveling about and vacationing, etc. Their lives seemed quite normal with the exception that several members of their families were conscripted into military service and certain rationing systems were beginning to take effect. These experiences are similar to what we were experiencing here in the

USA during the same time. However, nearer toward the end of the war and particularly after D-Day the tone of the letters changed as many friends and extended family members were being lost in battle and travel and rationing restrictions were becoming more severe. Having one close family member who flew bombing missions over Germany; I found it fascinating to read about the advancements of their missions over Germany although it was at the terrifying expense of Bonhoeffer and others who were trapped in prison.

Bonhoeffer felt that this season of his life in prison was from God and that God would bring some good out of it. Despite his difficult circumstances he had a sense of God's active involvement in his life. Through his submission to God for His will for Bonhoeffer's life we can see the martyr living out the Gospel in a seemingly meaningless and hopeless situation. Bonhoeffer lived out his theology in prison in the midst of a great evil. He found meaning and purpose in his seemingly meaningless existence within prison. He was renowned throughout the prison by guards and inmates alike for his cheerful and positive attitude. He stood up against the guards at times when they mistreated others and he ministered to many throughout his year and a half in prison. Bonhoeffer also continued to read and write and study and to produce under very dire and difficult circumstances. He even was able to finally lay down his life and suffer martyrdom in an honorable manner bringing even further witness to his testimony of Jesus Christ. Bonhoeffer was able to accomplish all these things for Christ and the Kingdom of God because he stood strong in Christ as he was deeply connected to the Body of the Christ.

Bonhoeffer wrote that the New Testament often called us to "be strong" and that weakness is a greater danger than evil. (Letters, p. 392) Bonhoeffer acted responsibly for Christ even within his confinement as Christ was in his midst through the power of the Holy Spirit enabling him to do so. In one of his last letter he writes to Eberhard Bethge, "The key to everything is the "in him". All that we may rightly expect from God, and ask him for, is to be found in Jesus Christ. The God of Jesus Christ has nothing to do with what God, as we imagine him, could do and ought to do. If we are to learn what God promises, and what he fulfills, we must persevere in quiet meditation on the life, sayings, deeds, sufferings, and death of Jesus." (Letters, P. 391)

In his "Prayers for Fellow-Prisoners" (Letters, p. 139 - 143), Bonhoeffer wrote of his utter dependency upon God and of his lostness without God who knows him better than he knows himself. He finds comfort in knowing that God is with him in the midst of his struggle and he finds gratitude within his heart for God's presence. He prays to accept the hard things from God's hand and finds trust in knowing that God will not give him more than he can bear and that God will make all things work together for good. He finds his comfort in the sufferings of Jesus Christ who is present with him in the midst of his own sufferings and in the Holy Spirit who gives him faith, hope, and love. He finally rests in the knowledge of the justice and righteousness of God and the knowledge that he is under the care of the sovereign God who is over all.

CHAPTER 6: CHRISTIANFORMATION

Christian Spiritual Formation
By: Terrence Dwyer, October 31st, 2009
SP520: Foundations for Spiritual Life
Professor: Susan S. Phillips, Ph.D.

I am deeply grateful for the gift of salvation that God so mercifully and graciously gave to me so many years ago, through the work of His Son my Lord Jesus Christ. On November 29th, 1982, the Holy Spirit dramatically entered into my life and into my being immediately transforming my life from one of utter destruction to one of eagerly seeking after the ways of the Lord. I distinctly remember that shortly after this experience of receiving the Holy Spirit I felt strongly compelled to sit down and to write out my obituary. Oddly, I remember writing and crying over the "loss" of our dearly departed "Terry Dwyer" such as he was and thus, my spiritual transformative journey began.

I believe that this process of spiritual formation in Christ is a lifelong process and one that involves the daily ongoing tension of living life in our physical bodies while aspiring to live life in and guided by the Holy Spirit and others. Paul laments this very struggle in Romans 7:19 where he says; "For the good that I will to do, I do not do; but the evil I will not to do, that I practice."

However, Paul also reminds us in both Romans 6: 1-8 and Colossians 3: 1-4 that if we died with Christ and were raised with Christ then we are to seek those things which are above. We are to set our mind on the things above and not on the things on the Earth. For we have died and our lives are hidden with Christ in God.

C. S. Lewis reminds us in "Mere Christianity" that the more we get ourselves out of the way and let Him take us over, the more truly ourselves we become. Until we have fully given up our self to Him we will not have a real self and it is when we give ourselves up to His Personality that we first begin to experience a real personality of our own.

The issue then becomes one of how do we as Christians set ourselves aside and how do we give ourselves over to Christ. How do we live as Christians these eternal spiritual lives which we are called to live inside of these terminal physical bodies which we find ourselves in. This has been an ongoing struggle for Christians from the Disciples to Paul to us today. Sheldrake shows us in Spirituality & History that 14th century Christians sought out the contemplative way of life over the active and the spiritual way of life over the material as the Way for Christians. The story of Martha and Mary resonated as the symbol of the contemplative way as the better way.

Christian spiritual formation for me then refers to all of the various ways and means and disciplines and practices that we as Christians use to further deepen our walk of faith and to further our spiritual growth. Christian spiritual formation then is an ongoing act of the will as we daily decide to live in the Spirit through faith and not in the flesh. Firstly, we must have a heart toward Christ and be obedient to Christ. Jesus tells us in John 14:21; "Those who have my commandments and keep them, they are the ones who love me. And they who love me shall be loved of my Father, and I will love them, and will manifest myself to them." We cannot walk in the Spirit with Christ if we simultaneously choose to go our own way. Jesus asks us in Luke 6:46; "Why do you call me Lord, Lord and do not do the things I say?" If Jesus is our Lord then we will desire to be obedient toward Him.

Secondly, there are spiritual practices and disciplines that have over time been seen to be common to all Christians who walk in the Spirit through faith. These practices and disciplines include seeking out the contemplative, solitary and quiet spaces in life where we can reflect upon God and listen. These common spiritual disciplines also include prayer and fasting and worshipping and praising in gratitude. It is also common to spend much time in the studying of the Bible and in hiding the Word in our hearts and in reflection upon the Word. It is also common to be in fellowship and in communion with other believers where we love and edify one another, confess our sins to one another and to hold each other accountable where needed. It is through these commonly held practices and disciplines that we as Christians are spiritually transformed toward a life of walking in the Spirit. It is in this communion and fellowship within the Body of Christ where we are formed and transformed by others within the Body.

God the Father, God the Son and God the Holy Spirit will at times directly intervene into our lives at various moments to directly shape us and mold us into their desired image as a potter shapes and molds clay. The Holy Spirit will guide us, teach us and comfort us (John 14:16). Jesus will at times manifest Himself to us (John 14:21) and God the Father will at times speak directly to us (Matthew 3:17). Additionally, angels can at times appear to us to guide us or to warn us and we can also at times have dreams that impact us (Matthew 1:20). All of these supernatural occurrences are an integral part of the process of our Christian spiritual formation.

Finally, as we live out a life of obedience to Christ in faith, God begins in us through grace, the process of our own spiritual growth and transformation. Through living out our lives in obedience to Christ we connect and fellowship with others within the Body of Christ where we are further transformed into the image of Christ likeness. We seek to practice certain spiritual disciplines that are common to Christians throughout our history who have sought to walk by the Spirit in faith. Simultaneously as we seek to reach out to God the Father, God the Son and God the Holy Spirit they are actively, persistently and intimately involved in our spiritual formation.

Bibliography

Lewis, C.S. Mere Christianity. New York: Macmillan Publishing Company, 1960.

MacArthur, John. The Macarthur Study Bible, New King James Version. Vol. 1. Nashville: Word Publishing, 1997.

Sheldrake, Philip. Spirituality & History. New York: Orbis Books, 1995.

Seminary Papers-Part Two

A Brief Review of Attachment Theory
By: Terrence Dwyer, May 23rd, 2011
Fuller Theological Seminary
CN522 Basic Counseling Skills
Professor: Laura Taggart, MA, LMFT

Introduction

The purpose of this research paper is to briefly review the general theory of infant attachment and how disruptions to the infant attachment process may manifest into disturbing adult behavior patterns which may require various forms of therapy and treatment. From this research I hope to better understand the issues surrounding attachment and how these issues may present themselves in a pastoral counseling role. With this better understanding I would hope to be able to recognize certain markers of attachment disorder and thus be better able to counsel appropriately and effectively and refer to the appropriate professional for ongoing treatment whenever possible.

Additionally, I hope to gain a better understanding about my own attachment issues and subsequent behavior disorders as a result of this study. My primary care giver was my mother who was sick for a period of time and then died when I was two and a half years old. My subsequent primary care giver was my working father who suffered from depression and alcoholism and ultimately committed suicide when I was eleven years old. Significant behavioral patterns stemming from certain attachment issues ultimately manifested in my life. I have earnestly sought and received both significant healing from our merciful Lord as well as significant guidance and understanding from professional counseling therapy. I hope to enhance this personal understanding through my research for this paper.

For the purposes of this brief review, I have principally limited my attachment theory research to the noted attachment theory work of Bowlby and Ainsworth as well as certain current articles concerning attachment theory. Additionally, I have included information gleaned from two very insightful interviews that I conducted of two professional therapists and their encounters in their practices with behavioral disorders stemming from attachment issues.

Attachment Theory

Attachment theory was originally developed by John Bowlby (1907-1990), a British psychoanalyst who sought to understand the distress experienced by infants who had been separated from their parents. Bowlby observed that separated infants would go to extraordinary lengths (i.e.

crying, clinging, frantic searching) to prevent separation from their parents and to re-establish proximity to a missing parent. Bowlby argued that these attachment behaviors were adaptive responses to separation from a primary caregiver who provides support, protection, and care. Bowlby argued that over the course of evolutionary history, infants who were able to maintain proximity to a caregiver through this attachment behavioral system were more likely to survive to reproductive age.

According to Bowlby, the attachment system essentially "asks"; is the attachment figure nearby, accessible, and attentive? If the child perceives the answer to be "yes", the child feels loved, secure, confident, and is more likely to explore their environment, play with others and be sociable. However, if the child perceives that the answer to this question is "no", the child experiences stress and anxiety and is likely to actively search and vocally signal to attempt to re-establish attachment. These behaviors will continue until attachment is established or until the child wears down. In these cases, Bowlby believed that these children experienced profound despair and depression.

Mary Ainsworth (1913-1999), a Canadian developmental psychologist and colleague of Bowlby, sought to better understand the individual differences in the way children determine the accessibility of the attachment figure and how they regulate their attachment behavior in response. Through her research procedure called, A Strange Situation, Ainsworth determined that these behavior patterns could be placed into three categories and a fourth was later added. These categories are:

Secure attachment: A child who is securely attached to its mother will explore freely while the mother is present and will engage with strangers. These children are generally more secure and confident and better able to adapt.

Anxious-resistant insecure attachment: A child with an anxious-resistant attachment style is anxious of exploration and of strangers even when the mother is present. This style develops when the mother is engaged but on her own terms as sometimes the child's needs are ignored until the mother can tend to the child.

Anxious-avoidant insecure attachment: A child with an anxious-avoidant attachment style will avoid or ignore the caregiver, will not explore very much, and will not treat strangers much differently from the caregiver. This style of attachment develops from a care-giving style which is more disengaged. The child's needs are frequently not met and the child comes to believe that communication of needs has no influence on the caregiver.

Disorganized/disoriented attachment: A fourth category was added by Mary Main, a colleague of Ainsworth's who accepted this addition. These children show behaviors of freezing or falling to the floor around their mothers, or of repeated rocking to and fro, or repeatedly hitting themselves. Main found that most of the mothers of these children had suffered significant loss or trauma shortly before or after the birth of the infant and had reacted by becoming severely depressed.

For the majority of individuals, the manner in which they learned to manage anxiety and stress from their insecure attachments early in life will continue on through adolescence and into adulthood. For many people, these coping mechanisms can become quite pronounced and will continue unabated unless treated. Adults determined to have an insecure state-of-mind with regard to attachment have greater difficulties in managing the challenges of life generally, and more specifically their interpersonal relationships.

Milan & Kay Yerkovich in their ground breaking work How We Love, build upon the foundation of attachment theory and they have categorized five behavior styles that people develop as a result of their insecure attachments. These behavior patterns or styles are: Avoider – emotionally unaware, self-reliant, expects others to be the same. Pleaser – unaware of own feelings and needs, gives and appeases to avoid negative emotions. Vacillator – preoccupied with how others hurt or anger them, angry but unaware of their own underlying emotions. Controller – anger covers awareness of all vulnerable emotions, all about having control so insecurities do not arise. Victim – significant pain, feelings are deeply suppressed, no abilities toward other awareness. While the underlying attachment disorders may be difficult to ascertain as a pastoral counselor, these behavior styles described by Milan & Kay Yerkovich may be more readily recognized in pastoral counseling where an assessment and referral toward additional professional treatment may often be made.

Professional Therapist Interviews

To get a better understanding of how attachment disorder and subsequent coping mechanisms manifest themselves in adult behavior, I interviewed two professional therapists for insights from their personal practices. The first therapist is Ms. Merritt Seidenberg, MFT who is a Christian and practices as a therapist at the John Muir Hospital, Behavioral Health Out-Patient Center in Concord, CA. Her responsibilities include group therapy and skills training for out-patients with moderate to severe psychological symptoms. Merritt reported that a significant proportion of her cases stem from untreated attachment disorders. Most of these cases manifest themselves in manic depressive, bi-polar, and severe anxiety disorders. Her patients range in age from 45 to 55 and have never received therapy for their attachment disorders. She reported that up to 75% of her cases are substance abusers but are mostly high functioning adults with jobs and medical insurance. Merritt reported that all of her patients are on some form of anti-depression or anti-anxiety medication which is helpful toward getting the patients to be somewhat functional. She reported that without medication many if not all of her patients would be unable to gain treatment in counseling therapy as they would either be way too high with anxiety or way too low in depression to be treatable.

Her case study example was of a 54 year old male with a lifelong untreated attachment disorder which manifested into major depression disorder, general anxiety disorder, and a substance abuser since the age of 12. His father was an alcoholic and his mother was a classic co-dependent, enabler, who wasn't emotionally present during his development. He has been married for 30 years to a substance abuser who is also an enabler and co-dependent and who also suffered from sexual abuse as a child. He has been very resistant to therapy but is required to attend for insurance reasons as he has been out of work for two years on disability due to his depression disorder. Merritt's course of treatment is to proceed with group and individual therapy and to give the patient some skills toward helping him deal with and avoid his behavior disorder.

The second therapist I interviewed is Mrs. Bo De Long Cotty, Ph.D. who is a research psychologist working for West Ed in Oakland, CA. doing research toward supporting a wide variety of programs in education. Cotty specializes in doing research and developing programs and policy in the area of resiliency development in youth and adults. Cotty also maintains an active clinical psychology practice at the Berkeley Christian Counseling Center in Berkeley, CA. Cotty was mentored by Mary Main who was a colleague of Mary Ainsworth mentioned above.

In speaking about attachment theory, Cotty emphasized that no one has a perfectly secure attachment and that we all wrestle with various degrees of attachment disorder. Cotty explained that it is common for people to be fully functional in a work place setting even with attachment disorder as no one is pushing their "attachment buttons" at their place of work. She went on to explain that your attachment experience puts you in a mindset that is your filter for the world and that you see things through your particular behavioral style established by your attachment experience. How you cope with stress, fear, and the unknown are very connected to your attachment experience in childhood.

Cotty, a Christian; sees attachment as part of the fall of original sin and that attachment disorders are a result of the fall. After many years of clinical practice, Cotty believes strongly that it is the Holy Spirit that does all of the healing over the course of therapeutic treatment. Cotty explained that you can't move people along through therapy as only God can do that. However, you can help people recognize, name, and own their own issues and you can help them identify and recognize parts of their self which she says the Holy Spirit uses in the healing process. Cotty advised that God is continually working on the patients and that the therapist gets to see them at various points throughout the healing process. Interestingly, Cotty said that bad theology is often a significant problem in her therapy which she often has to address in addition to the recognition of self and owning of issues work described above.

Personal Attachment History

I am the fifth of five children and my primary caregiver was my mother who was a stay at home mom while my father was often away working on the railroad. I most likely developed a fairly secure attachment to my mother during my first year of development. However, this bond was disrupted when my mother was diagnosed with ovarian cancer and she died when I was two and a half years old.

Because I had spent inconsistent time with my father over the first year of my life, I most likely developed an insecure, anxious-resistant attachment with him. Anxious-resistant infants usually have caregivers who ignore clear signals of distress and send incongruent messages about their accessibility. Infants go through five stages when forming attachment relationships and I was in the last stage when my mother died. After her death, I no longer had my mother available to fulfill my needs for physical contact, closeness, and love which were necessary to maintain my secure attachment in this final stage. Because of this disruption, I transitioned toward an insecure pattern of attachment which would reappear later in life.

According to Erikson's psychosocial theory, each developmental stage includes a psychosocial crises that results from increasing societal demands. In order to move to the next stage of development, this crisis must be resolved through either adaptive or maladaptive coping strategies. The psychosocial crisis faced in infancy is trust versus mistrust, which is revealed through a feeling of mutuality with the caregiver. When a mother-infant relationship is disrupted, such as mine, the infant is at risk for a maladaptive resolution of the crisis and an experienced sense of mistrust. According to Erickson's theory, an infant who resolves this crisis negatively also develops the core pathology of withdrawal.

True to form, my insecure attachment with my mother began to be revealed fairly early on in my life through behavioral issues of mistrust which manifested into truancy, anger, aggression and other resistant behaviors which are often displayed by children with mistrust and insecure attachment. Additionally, the coping strategy of withdrawal, which was my core pathology from infancy, manifested itself as early as kindergarten and continued on throughout elementary school when I would often skip school and play hooky after having been dropped off at school.

Conclusion

Through the readings from this course and through the research done for this brief review, I believe I now have a much better understanding of attachment theory and of some the issues surrounding attachment disorder, coping mechanisms, and resultant behavioral styles. I believe that the knowledge that I have gained in this study will allow me to better continue my further studies on this issue and to better understand attachment issues and behavioral styles that I may be confronted with as a pastoral counselor. I believe that I am now better equipped to assess and refer individuals to an appropriate professional therapist whenever the need may arise.

I also believe that this study has greatly assisted me in my own better understanding of the attachment issues in my own life, the coping mechanisms that I developed, the behavioral style through which I see the world and where I am in the healing process. I have experienced significant healing from the Holy Spirit and have benefited greatly from counseling therapy but my prayer as a potential pastor is; where Lord do I still need healing from you? It is deeply humbling to think, with all my brokenness, that I could be used by the Lord in the healing process of others. However, I must continually surrender and submit myself to the Lord for his continued healing and restorative work in me if I am to be used for the benefit of others.

Bibliography

Ainsworth, John Bowlby and Mary D. Salter. "An Ethological Approach to Personality Development
" American Psychologist Vol. 46 no. 4 (1991): 333-342.

Bretherton, Inge. "The Origins of Attachment Theory:
John Bowlby and Mary Ainsworth." Developmental Psychology 28 (1992): 759-775.

David R. Cross, Ph.D. "Infant-Parent Attachment and the Strange Situation." Child Psychology (2007): 50.

Newman, Barbara M. Newman & Philip R. Development through Life: A Psychosocial Approach. New York, New York: Brooks/Cole Publishing Company, 2009.

Yerkovich, Milan and Kay. How We Love. Colorado Springs, CO: WaterBrook Press, 2008.

CN522 Basic Counseling Skills
Professor: Laura Taggart
Book Review: Addiction & Grace by Gerald G. May, M.D.
By; Terrence Dwyer, May 9th, 2011

    I found this to be an exceptional work on the nature of addiction within the fallen human condition as well as a spiritually transformative guide toward healing and wholeness from the destructive power of addiction. Although May admits that he is no theologian, his work is well founded on principles from Scripture which he cites throughout his work. May's principal argument in his work is that humans are created by God with an inborn desire for God. This inborn desire is to wholly love God and to be wholly loved by God but our fallen nature has broken this desire. We therefore fill the emptiness of our broken and unmet desire with desire for other things resulting in the idolatry of addictions of repression and addictions of attachment. Our addictions force us to worship these objects of desire which prevent us from freely loving God and loving one another. The healing process is one of letting go and simply ceasing from doing the addictive behavior and of turning our desire back toward our Creator through faith and through God's grace freely provided by God through the work of Jesus Christ and through the power of the Holy Spirit.

    This is much easier said than done and May shows us why this is so by taking us through in detail the psychological nature of addiction and the deeply ingrained neurological nature of addiction. The author's work on cell dynamics within the neurological aspects of addiction was quite profound. May showed just why it is so difficult to recover from addiction because of the extensive multisystem involvement of our bodies seeking to maintain equilibrium from our destructive addictions. In spite of the catastrophic picture May paints neurologically, the author offers significant hope for a pathway out of addiction throughout his text. The pathway May offers is a journey away from addictions and homeward toward God through faith, prayer, Scripture, and community.

This book deeply resonated with me personally as I have suffered from multiple addictions throughout my entire life. My father suffered from multiple addictions which eventually caused him to commit suicide when I was eleven years old leaving me orphaned. Both my genetics and my early formative environment were pre-disposed toward addictive behavior patterns which manifested themselves in me at a very early age. Through God's grace I was very fortunately miraculously healed of major addictions to drugs and alcohol instantaneously one night several years ago. May's description of our wills working in unison with God's will and grace in the healing of our addictions is profoundly accurate. In fact, I found nothing in this book that I disagreed with in the manner in which we are healed from our addictions as my personal experience tracks entirely with May's descriptions.

However, the part of this book that resonates with me most deeply at this stage of my life is May's description of the idolatry of addiction and the pervasiveness of these idolatries in our life. Once being healed from significant addictions; one often feels that he or she has been "healed" and that it is now time to get on with the other aspects of life. The importance of May's work to me is the recognition of and the acknowledgment of the extent of the idolatrous addictions that remain in my life. This book has been a revelation to me of just how much addictive behavior still remains in me. May has challenged me to confront my addictive behaviors still present in my life and to continue to work through the process of healing and transformation.

This book will be a significant resource to me in the counseling work that I hope to do in my future ministry. Because of my recovery from significant addictions, I very much hope to do ministry in the area of addiction ministry and counseling as a part of my overall ministry. May's work in Addiction & Grace gives me a good foundation for understanding the scope of the nature of addiction. May's descriptions of grace and healing in his chapters on grace, empowerment, and homecoming are exactly what I believe Bonhoeffer was describing in his chapter on community in Life Together. We cannot heal ourselves and others cannot heal us but we must desire to be healed and that desire working in tandem with God's love and desire toward us is what inevitably heals us. In my addiction counseling work ministry I must always remember that I cannot fix or heal in any way the person that I am counseling. It is God alone who is the healer. Bonhoeffer says we are to, "meet the other person with the clear Word of God and be ready to leave them alone with this Word for a long time, willing to release them again in order that Christ may deal with them".

I am grateful for this text and the transformative process that has already begun in my life as a result of reading it. I highly recommend this text for others and I look forward to reading other works written by Gerald G. May, M.D.

Bibliography

Bonhoeffer, Dietrich. Life Together. San Francisco Harper Collins, 1954.

Gerald G. May, M.D. Addiction & Grace. New York: Harper Collins, 1988.

CN522 Basic Counseling
3 Generation Genome Chart
By: Terrence Dwyer, May 2nd, 2011

Patterns and Problems

The most significant problem that is passed consistently from generation to generation is alcohol addiction. Alcohol addiction and the pattern of alcohol abuse are consistent throughout each generation with varying effects on the individual's lives. James P. Dwyer (1913-1966) committed suicide as a result of his alcohol abuse, addiction, and depression. Tobacco addiction through cigarette smoking is another pattern seen passed from generation to generation consistently. Stuttering was also passed from one generation to the next in one instance.

Divorce was also a pattern showing up with my father remarrying and divorcing after the death of my mother. One of my uncle's divorced and two of my siblings divorced with the other separated but eventually kept the marriage intact.

Sayings and Beliefs

God, country, and family were very strong themes that were present from generation to generation throughout. The Catholic faith is the predominant faith practiced throughout with the exception of one uncle and myself who are born again Protestants. Faith in God was highly valued, practiced, and demonstrated but in a quiet way with matters of God or religion rarely talked about or discussed.

The theme of honoring and serving the country was also very highly valued with uncles and several cousins serving in combat in the various armed forces. Matters of politics and country were discussed frequently. Hard work and honor in your work was valued equal to or higher than education. Higher education was rarely pursued until my generation. The predominant occupation throughout most all of the males from generation to generation was railroad engineer which essentially stopped with my generation. However, we still have several cousins and one niece who still work for the railroad. The traditions and celebrations of Irish heritage remain strong throughout from generation to generation but may be waning with the generation of our children as they are of mixed heritage.

Conflict Resolution

Conflict resolution within the prior generations was not practiced skillfully or artfully. Passive aggressive behavior/communication was legend with stories of people not speaking to each other for decades over some seemingly minor disagreement. At the other extreme, loud arguments and even fist fights were not uncommon as a means of attempting to resolve conflict. However, conflict resolution within the latter generations appears to be less extreme and more articulate and sensitive.

CN522 Basic Counseling Skills
Professor: Laura Taggart, MA, LMFT
By: Terrence Dwyer; May 31st, 2011
Reading Log Book Reviews

Changes That Heal by Dr. Henry Cloud

I was originally introduced to the work of Dr. Henry Cloud and Dr. John Townsend several years ago through the Celebrate Recovery Ministry at First Presbyterian Church of Berkeley. We studied Changes That Heal over the course of several weeks through a video series produced by Cloud-Townsend Resources. This book was an extraordinary gift to all of us who struggled with addictions as it greatly enlightened us and gave us the tools necessary to move forward in our healing process. This book has had a significantly positive impact upon my life and I have referred it and given it to others countless times and have read and re-read parts of it several times. It was a pleasure to re-visit this old friend in this class.

Dr. Cloud introduces three ingredients that we all need for growth as grace, truth, and time. The author describes grace as the relational aspect of God's character and truth as the structural aspect of God's character. Too much or too little of either of these ingredients applied in our lives and we become imbalanced and the author gives us several examples of what too much grace or too much truth looks like in our lives. One of the gifts that this text gives is the idea of redemptive time wherein which we live to work out grace and truth together as we grow through time toward maturity.

Two other key areas examined by this book are bonding and boundaries. Dr. Cloud examines what bonding is and the importance of bonding in our growth and development and what happens to us when we fail to properly bond with others. Dr. Cloud then gives tools to move toward bonding with others. The other key area is boundaries and the importance of keeping healthy boundaries. Dr. Cloud goes into depth here in examining what boundaries are and what happens to us when we don't keep healthy boundaries. The author again gives tools for establishing and maintaining healthy boundaries. Dr. Cloud then reviews the importance of being able to accept both the good and the bad and then examines what is adulthood and what it looks like to be a mature adult.

The Wounded Healer by Henri J. M. Nouwen

Henri Nouwen is one of my favorite authors. I deeply respect his work and his life and I love the simplicity in the way in which he expresses profound spiritual truths. The Wounded Healer is a particularly relevant work in that he speaks to those of us who are ministering in today's dislocated world. Nouwen perceives that people today have lost hope in their futures which eventually depletes their creativity and breeds apathy, boredom, and despair. Nouwen contrasts the Christian way of hope with how people deal with this existential crisis through either mysticism or revolution. Nouwen goes on to argue that the Christian minister of the future will need to (1) be an articulator of inner events, (2) be a compassionate leader, (3) and be a contemplative critic.

Considering that I am beginning my CPE training in just a few days, Nouwen's chapter on Ministry to a Hopeless Man was particularly helpful as it describes an encounter between a CPE trainee and a man who dies while undergoing an operation. Nouwen examines the interaction between the trainee and the patient and offers depth, insight, and principles for Christian leadership in such situations. Nouwen chastises that we are not to remain aloof to people in their suffering but that we are to enter into their suffering and it is from there that we are to minister and to offer the hope of the Gospel.

Nouwen argues that ministry is a confrontational service for others in that it does not allow others to live within their illusions of immortality and wholeness. On the contrary, ministry keeps reminding others that they are mortal and broken and that it is with this recognition that liberation begins. As ministers, making our own wounds a source of healing does not call for a superficial sharing of our own pains but for a willingness to see our own pain and suffering as rising from the human condition that we all share. It is from this deep place of shared woundedness that we minister to others and share the Gospel of hope in Jesus Christ.

Care of Souls by David G. Benner

This was my first time reading anything from Benner and I found this work to be quite helpful in my own spiritual development. I had not previously read or studied much on the soul itself and had not therefore developed much of a soul theology toward the care and nurturing of the soul. I found this book to be extraordinarily helpful in developing my understanding of the soul and of soul care. Benner begins by placing the discussion in context by giving us the history and the components of Christian soul care along with its Greek and Jewish roots. The author then investigates the reasons for the decline of soul care in the twentieth century and for the rise in therapeutic soul care. Benner examines the pluses and minuses of these developments and then he examines the relationship between psychology and spirituality. Benner then gives us an in-depth review of the uniqueness of Christian spirituality which is rooted in the Holy Spirit and in our commitment to Jesus Christ and in our transformational approach to life.

The first part of the book is more focused on theory while the second part of the book is more focused on the actual practice of soul care. Benner then introduces the importance of dialogue as the core of soul care. Benner defines dialogue as shared inquiry that is designed to increase awareness, understanding, and insight. Through dialogue we expand our understanding of self, of others, and of the world. Benner then gives eight practical suggestions for providers of soul care on facilitating the practice of pastoral dialogue with others. I found this section of the book to be helpful and practical. Benner then looks at the role of the unconscious in Christian spirituality and the importance of dreams and how they may be used for our growth toward wholeness. I found this chapter of the book to be fascinating as I always suspected the importance of dreams but had not done much study of them up until this text. Benner then concludes his work by reviewing various forms of Christian soul care and the practical challenges involved in both giving and receiving soul care.

The Peace Maker by Ken Sande

This is my first time reading Sande and I found this text to be a wealth of information and a practical guide toward making peace. This text is also personally quite timely as I have been seeking to develop and teach a class on "Anger" within the east Oakland community and this text will be an essential part of my presentation. Additionally, I'm involved in a church plant in east Oakland and this text will be an excellent resource for our congregation as we grow and will inevitably run into personal conflict from time to time. This book gives us the biblical principles and guidelines for working through these conflicts.

Sande's work on peacemaking is based upon four core biblical principles. The first is to glorify God based on 1st. Corinthians 10:31; 31 "So whether you eat or drink or whatever you do, do it all for the glory of God". Sande explains that biblical peacemaking is at its' core guided by a deep desire to bring honor and glory to God through revealing the reconciling love and power of Jesus Christ. Through God's grace we can live out the Gospel in our lives thus bringing God all the glory. The second principle is to get the log out of your own eye based upon Matthew 7:5; 5 "You hypocrite, first take the plank out of your own eye, and then you will see clearly to remove the speck from your brother's eye". Jesus teaches us to look at our own faults before we focus on another's. When we practice this principle, we will be able to overlook the faults of another person and others will then often respond to us in a similar manner. Thus, the way is opened up for meaningful discussion, negotiation, and reconciliation. The third principle is to gently restore based upon Galatians 6:1; 1 "Brothers and sisters, if someone is caught in a sin, you who live by the Spirit should restore that person gently. But watch yourselves, or you also may be tempted". When we practice this principle we are speaking the truth in love to another toward gently guiding them to see their own part in a conflict. By doing so, we can encourage repentance and restore peace. The fourth principle is to go and be reconciled based upon Matthew 5:24; 24 "leave your gift there in front of the altar. First go and be reconciled to them; then come and offer your gift". Peacemaking involves be committed toward restoring damaged relationships. When we practice this principle we are to forgive other as Christ has forgiven us and we are to seek satisfactory solutions toward peace. Sande's work gives us the tools for conflict resolution that are biblically based and which give us the pathway toward peacemaking that is not based on worldly principles but on Godly peacemaking principles.

Bibliography

Benner, David G. Care of Souls. Grand Rapids, MI: Baker Books, 1998.

Cloud, Henry. Changes That Heal. Grand Rapids, Michigan: Zondervan, 1992.

Nouwen, Henri J. M. The Wounded Healer. New York, New York: Image Doubleday, 1972.

Sande, Ken. The Peace Maker. Grand Rapids, MI Baker Books, 2004.

CN522 Basic Counseling – Fuller Theological Seminary
Professor: Laura Taggart, MA, LMFT
By: Terrence Dwyer, May 14th, 2011
Resource Visitation Reports

I recently visited with three non-profit ministries in Oakland in response to an urgent need that has arisen during my internship at Oakland City Church. I received a call from one of our congregants who expressed that he was "at the end of his rope" and that he didn't know what to do. His name is Michael and he is a 26-year-old African-American who was recently released from prison after serving five years for a felony conviction for accessory to murder. He has no work and few, if any prospects for work. He has no money and lives day to day. He recently lost his housing and he is currently living out of his car. He was also arrested recently for a disturbance and is out on bail and his bail bondsman is now after him for the money owed and is threatening to have a warrant issued for his arrest. Michael is trying to turn his life around but his overall life skills are poorly developed. He turned to me for assistance and guidance and among other avenues I approached three organizations here in Oakland seeking to assist Michael in his predicament. The organizations I visited are among the organizations that I've included on my resource list for this counseling class. The following is a report from those initial interview meetings and the results for Michael.

Goodwill Industries

Goodwill Industries is noted for their success in securing work for felons who are seeking to re-enter the work force. They operate nationwide and have a large corporate office and a large retail used clothing outlet at 1301 30th Avenue in East Oakland. I visited the corporate offices at this site and interviewed the receptionist there. She gave me a hand out/flyer and advised that Goodwill – Oakland has a hiring orientation once a month. The next session is scheduled for June 2nd, 2011 and Michael has agreed to show up early to attend this session. The session is at this location in their education classroom and it begins at 9am. She advised that people begin showing up around 6am as space is limited to the first 18 people in line that morning. After an hour and half orientation that morning the attendees are assigned their jobs or work assignments if there is work available. If no work is available that day, the attendees are now enrolled in their system and are given instructions on how to access work assignments as they become available. In addition to the enrollment and work assignments, attendees are given information on additional resources within the Bay Area for accessing work.

Michael was keen on the idea of connecting with Goodwill Industries as the word on the street is that it is a good resource for someone who wants to turn their life around. Michael has had positive feedback about Goodwill and is looking forward to developing his connections within this community.

City Team Ministries

I met with David Walker of City Team Ministries located at 722 Washington Street in downtown Oakland for purposes of obtaining information regarding housing options for Michael. David is in charge of the food box distribution program at City Team and he was handling the front desk duties when I arrived. Mr. Walker advised that housing is on a per night basis for men who show up by 5pm to sign up for housing for the night. The cost is $5 per night and it includes dinner at 8pm and breakfast the following morning. There is no limit on the number of nights you can stay but arrangements are on a per night basis.

City Team seeks to provide hot meals, hot showers, and a safe place for people who are homeless. City Team also seeks to provide drug and alcohol recovery programs for men as well as an education center to assist men with their skills development. In addition to the hot meals for their overnight guests, City Team also provides additional food and nutrition resources to the homeless community.

Michael was grateful to learn of this resource but he was less than keen on utilizing their services. He doesn't see himself as homeless although he is. He stays with friends from time to time for shower and clean clothing access but he prefers to stay in his car for the privacy. He has some family locally but none that is willing to let him stay with them. City Team provides Michael with a good alternative to his current situation as well as another community of support for him to plug into. I will continue to encourage Michael to consider City Team to develop his support network within the Christian Community.

Harbor House Ministries

I met with Tiffany Sheih of Harbor House Ministries located at 1811 11th Avenue in Oakland. Harbor House Ministries provides resources to people of low economic means within the San Antonio district of East Oakland. My purpose for contacting Harbor House was to seek to provide Michael with free computer and internet access for purposes of supporting his search for employment. Additionally, I was seeking to broaden Michael's network of support within his Christian community.

Tiffany advised that Harbor House opens its doors to the public on Tuesday and Thursday mornings for free computer and internet access and that Michael would be able to utilize their services. In addition to free internet, Harbor House has a free/low cost retail clothing store on site as well as a free food distribution program that Michael would be able to access. The core of their ministry however, is a daily after school program for over 70 elementary school children from the neighborhood public schools.

Michael was grateful for learning of Harbor House and of the free internet and computer access which he doesn't have access to now. He is currently trying to access the computers of friends when available but the Harbor House option gives him more control and a place to do his employment research. In addition to Harbor House, I have also advised Michael of several secular career centers in the East Bay which also provide internet access for purposes of job hunting. However, I'm seeking to encourage Michael to actively develop his contacts within the Christian support community.

Comparative Book Review:
Jayber Crow and Erikson's Life Cycle
By: Terrence Dwyer, November 14th, 2009
SP520: Foundations for Spiritual Life
Professor: Susan S. Phillips, Ph.D.

Introduction

We will examine here the life of Wendell Berry's Jayber Crow though the developmental lens of Erik Erikson's psychosocial human development life cycle. Erik Erikson examines the psychosocial life cycle of Ingmar Bergman's Dr. Borg as Borg reflects on his life one day as he travels to Lund to receive an honorary degree. Erikson describes in remarkable detail the various stages of life Dr. Borg is forced to re-examine in this compelling

Bergman film. On the other hand, Wendell Berry gives us the intriguing life of Jayber Crow from infancy through old age but Berry's narrative does not neatly break out for us in such detail the various life stages as Erikson does for Bergman's Dr. Borg. While there is a blending and a revisiting of the various life cycles in Crow's life as there was in Borg's; we will seek here to break out each of these stages in the psychosocial development cycle of Jayber Crow and examine each of them.

Infancy

The period of infancy for Jayber Crow appears to be one of stability, safety and security. He was an only child born into a two parent household where his father worked nearby as a blacksmith and his mother stayed home to raise him and keep the house. Jayber appears to begin his life on a solid foundation here where he was nurtured and closely tended to by his mother. He states, "I remember sitting in my mother's lap in the rocking chair beside the kitchen stove, and the sound of her voice singing in time to the beat of the rockers." Erikson advises that during this period of infancy is where we develop our ability to trust and the corresponding virtue of hope. The description of the warm, melodic, rocking in his mother's lap would appear to give Jayber the nurturing environment that he needs to fully develop his ability to trust. We eventually see that this becomes evident in Jayber's life as he appears to have a fairly healthy sense of trust throughout his life with few exceptions. He doesn't trust Troy Chatham but this appears to be a healthy mistrust due to Troy's questionable behavior and character.

Early Childhood

Jayber's early childhood period begins on a solid foundation but ends tragically. His early childhood period starts off well as he says, "I remember walking from house to shop holding my mother's hand" and "I can remember my father's stance and movements at his work." This picture of a young toddler spending time with both of his parents even as they work appears to be a healthy and well integrated early childhood. However, Jayber's early childhood period ends tragically as both of his parents die from illness within a few hours of each other during a severe winter when Jayber was just three and a half years old. Autonomy vs. shame is learned in Erikson's early childhood period with the corresponding virtue of willpower developed here. While Jayber does develop a healthy autonomy in his life we do see him struggle with shame during his life. When he gives up the ministry and hitches a ride to Lexington from Sam Hanks we see that Jayber is reluctant to share with Sam who he really is. Jayber lies to Sam and says, "To have identified myself to him would have been like raising the dead." He later says, "Maybe because I was ashamed, I took

Sam Hank's advice and headed for the trotting track." Jayber was ashamed of his early life and didn't want to have to deal with his shamefulness with Sam Hanks so he lied about who he was.

Play Age

Erikson describes the play age as the preschool stage of psychosocial development where we learn to develop our initiative along with the virtue of purpose and direction vs. guilt. Jayber Crow appears to have had a remarkably rich play age period but it was a period filled more with "working" alongside adults than being at play with other children. After Jayber's parents died he was taken in by "Aunt Cordie" and "Uncle Othy" who "had a store of affection laid away and they now brought out and applied to me. Later I would know how blest I had been." Jayber stayed close to Aunt Cordie as he could. "When she moved I moved and I helped her with everything: keeping up the fires, maintaining the lamps, cooking, cleaning the fish, dressing the poultry, washing the dishes, washing the clothes, cleaning the house, working in the garden, putting up food for the Winter. We were in a way playmates." Jayber displayed a relatively healthy sense of initiative in his life which he developed within this early play age with Aunt Cordie. His remarkable work ethic and distinct lack of play in his adult life probably stems from this play age period where his "play" was "working" with Aunt Cordie. During one period of his adult life, Jayber simultaneously runs a barber shop business, works as the town gravedigger and the church custodian. It is interesting to note here that Jayber does not ever appear to work or play in a team which most likely also stems from this solitary working play period.

School Age

Erikson describes the school age period as the period where one learns industry and the corresponding virtue of competence versus inferiority. After Aunt Cordie died, Jayber Crow entered the Good Shepherd Orphanage and school at the age of ten which is well into the school age period. Jayber's life blends his earlier extended play age period with his late developing school age period so a portion of his development of industry is learned under the wings of Aunt Cordie and a portion is developed at the Good Shepherd Orphanage. The effects of the institutionalized life at the Good Shephard on Jayber were sudden and significant. Jayber enjoyed learning but refused to work at learning because it gave him a sense of power over the institution to not perform. Jayber says, "I was, they said, like a good horse who would not work; I was a disappointment to them; I was wasting my God-given talents. And this gave me, I believe, the only self-determining power I had: I could withhold this single thing that was mine that I knew they wanted." Jayber tries institutional learning again later in life where he attends classes at the university toward becoming a teacher but he doesn't complete the degree program nor does he care about his grades. His inability to fully develop this earlier stage of his life stunts his ability to move beyond the relatively unskilled labor of barbering. He says about this period, "The future was coming to me, but I had not so much as lifted a foot to go to it."

Adolescent Age

The adolescent age is the period of development in Erikson's model where we learn identity versus role confusion and the basic virtue developed is fidelity. Jayber Crow spent most all of his adolescent age within the confines of the Good Shepherd School and orphanage. Identity confusion was a common theme throughout his time at the Good Shepherd. Again, the impact of the Good Shepherd upon him was immediate and significant, upon entering he says, "I had no power…I had no thought…I was who? I was a little somebody who could have been anybody. We became in some way faceless to ourselves and to one another." At the very point in his development where his identity needed to be established and affirmed it was suddenly shaken and removed. He had no identity and needed to search for one. It was here at the Good Shepherd that he first learned his initial barbering skills. However, it was also during this period of identity development that Jayber heard preachers talk of being called into ministry and Jayber thought that he too might have been called into the ministry. Jayber received a scholarship to attend Pigeonville College where he was a pre-ministerial student. However, he had questions and doubts about his calling to preach. Jayber says, "I wasn't just a student or a going-to-be preacher anymore. I was a lost traveler wandering in the woods, needing to be on my way somewhere but not knowing where." He leaves Pigeonville College and his pursuit of the ministry at the age of 21 and steps out into the world, finally free of institutional life, but without a fully developed sense of identity.

Young Adulthood

In young adulthood Erikson advises that it is within this stage of our psychosocial development where we learn intimacy versus isolation and where we develop the virtue of love. Sadly, this stage remains undeveloped within Jayber Crow until much later in his life and even then is never really fully developed. Throughout this period Jayber says of himself, "I made acquaintances, but I didn't make any friends. I came and went without speaking to anybody. My solitariness turned to loneliness. Without a loved life to live, I was becoming more and more a theoretical person. I had no past that I could go back to and no future that I could imagine, no family, no friends, and no plans." Jayber was 34 years old before he finally met and began an intimate relationship with Clyda Greatlow whom he deeply liked and greatly enjoyed her company but whom he never fell into love with. Later in life Jayber fell into unrequited love with Mattie Chatham and his heart was opened to the ways of love but Mattie was married and he was unable to be intimate with his love save for a few brief interludes of walking in the woods together. The very last sentence of the book leaves us pining for Jayber's lack of intimacy as Mattie lies dying and they hold hands and she gives him a smile "that I had never seen and will not see again in this world, and it covered me all over with light."

Maturity and Old Age

We will combine these last two stages of development for purposes of our review here. Erikson describes these final two stages of development as where we learn generativity and integrity versus self-absorption and despair. The resulting virtues developed are care and wisdom. Despite the distinct lack of fully developed earlier psychosocial developmental stages in Jayber's life he nevertheless arrives into maturity and old age and must now address these additional developmental stages. Jayber gives back to his community by taking on the role of the gravedigger for the community. He also connects, participates and serves within the community by humbly serving as the janitor for the church. His very necessary and integral work within the community often goes unseen and is never heralded. Even after he retires from barbering he continues to barber his regular customers as needed by the community.

His integrity and wisdom are remarkably developed as he now approaches the end of his life. In speaking of his community and his church he says, "And yet I saw them all as somehow perfected, beyond time, by one another's love, compassion, and forgiveness, as it is said we may be perfected by grace."

Conclusion

In conclusion, we don't always smoothly progress along our psychosocial developmental paths from one stage to the next and if one stage is left undeveloped we may need to re-visit that stage at a later time in life to further our development. Just like Bergman's Dr. Borg, Jayber Crow was no exception. He progressed through his life nearly developing some of his stages, hardly developing others and needing re-visit others later in life to continue his development.

Bibliography

Berry, Wendell. Jayber Crow. Berkeley: Counterpoint, 2000.

Erikson, Erik H. Adulthood. New York: W.W. Norton & Company, 1978.

CF 500, Teaching for Christian Formation
Galindo/Wilhoit Response Paper
By: Terrence Dwyer, January 20th, 2010

A key issue for Galindo is that the context of Christian education takes place within the community of faith and that the methodology of teaching is mainly dialogical versus classroom instruction. It is through these relationships with other believers that the process of education and transformation takes place for the learner. It is here within this community of faith that the student learns the values, attitudes, practices, customs and culture of the community. Galindo emphasizes this by redefining curriculum for Christina education to be that of the life of the church. It is also within this community of believers where the Holy Spirit gives the gift of teaching to certain members of the community for the instruction of others.

A second key issue for Galindo is that the primary content of Christian education is the person of Jesus Christ. Traditionally, the content of most Christian education has been focused on the Bible. Galindo points out that the Bible points us to Jesus Christ and toward a relationship with Christ. Therefore the approach toward Christian education is to be relational as it is teaching about being in relationship with Jesus Christ versus an educational format that has been traditionally didactic or instructional. However, Galindo does point out that religious instruction is an important part of the community of faith as it perpetuates the very core teachings of the church. It is through religious instruction that key areas such as Scripture, theology, doctrine, and history are passed on to the learner.

A third key issue for Galindo is that the outcome of Christian education is the learner is changed by their relationship with Christ and that their relationship with Christ deepens. The learner becomes all that they are meant to be through their relationship with Christ. Christ taught obedience to God and the life of the learner therefore needs to display obedience to God. The life of the learner must reflect that a change has taken place within the heart of the learner and that the learner is putting into practice what has been taught. Galindo points out that the four components of feeling, knowledge, action, and will must all be operative within the learner for teaching to be effective in engaging an effectual faith within the learner (CCT 35).

One of the aspects that both Galindo and Wilhoit agree on is regarding the purpose of the Bible in Christian education. Both see the Bible as a critical tool in using it for instruction toward introducing the learner to a relationship with Jesus Christ. They agree that Bible instruction is not an end in and of itself but that Bible instruction is a means toward promoting fellowship with God. Additionally, they both agree that knowledge of God requires factual, cognitive knowledge but that this knowledge must also extend to an experiential relationship with God. God must be known to the learner not only in the head but also in the heart. Here again they both agree that obedience to God is a demonstration of the knowledge of God residing within the heart of the believer and that the learning process has been effectual. Finally, they both agree that the teacher must already be in obedience to God to model and demonstrate the life of obedience that the learner is moving toward.

Wilhoit suggests that the Holy Spirit fulfills a variety of roles for him theologically as an educator. First, the Holy Spirit equips certain Christians with the ability and the desire to teach others. This gifting includes spiritual insight, motivation to minister and the ability to communicate effectively (TCE 44). Second, the Holy Spirit is in the process of transforming from the inside out both the teacher and the student as they are both being transformed by the renewing of their minds. The Holy Spirit works to deepen the teacher's spiritual insight, compassion and goodness. Third, the Holy Spirit illuminates the teacher enabling them to comprehend the deeper truths of God's revelation. The Spirit provides the gifted teacher with spiritual insights and the abilities to receive these insights. The Spirit is also indwelling within the student and giving the student spiritual vision and receptivity along with conviction and guidance (TCE 46).

Wilhoit also suggests that the Bible was born through the inspiration of the Holy Spirit who enlivens his people so that we can hear the Word of God. Wilhoit suggests that the Holy Spirit is active today in testifying to us that the Bible is the Word of God. Wilhoit also advises that it is through Scripture that the Holy Spirit gives witness to and glorifies our Lord Jesus Christ. The Holy Spirit brings alive the messages and events of the Bible to believers throughout the world. Finally, Christian education takes place in a Spirit filled environment through the transformative work of the Holy Spirit throughout the church creating a positive educational environment for both teacher and learner.

In thinking through my teaching and learning experiences with the Holy Spirit I would concur with Wilhoit's theological stance on the Holy Spirit's place in education in every aspect that he mentions. It was Holy Spirit who dramatically entered my life several years ago and immediately began transforming me from the inside out. I immediately began ridding myself of harmful, sinful practices and habits as directed to do so by the Holy Spirit. Also, shortly after coming into my life the Holy Spirit introduced me to the Bible and it was the Spirit that made the words come alive to me off of the page giving me understanding and insight into their meaning. Additionally, it was the Holy Spirit who pointed me in the direction of Jesus Christ and introduced me into a relationship with my Lord Jesus. While all of these spiritually transformative things were happening in my life, the Holy Spirit also brought into my life an incredible array of gifted teachers. These teachers came to me in a wide variety of ways from mentors who walked along side to disciple me, to gifted radio and television preachers and teachers who taught me. The Holy Spirit also brought into my life various pastors, teachers, and authors within the wide church community who additionally taught, encouraged and nurtured my faith. The Holy Spirit was present in their gifted teaching and present in my receiving their teaching through the illumination of the Spirit in enabling me to understand what was being taught. It has also been the Holy Spirit who has further taught me lessons in life through experiences of living out my faith and learning deeper truths directly from the Spirit from these experiences.

I believe therefore that the Holy Spirit has gifted certain individuals within the Body of Christ with the gift of teaching. Illuminating them, motivating them and gifting them for the purpose of teaching and edifying the church. I believe that the Holy Spirit is active today in pointing us toward the Bible and in giving enlightenment and understanding to both teacher and learner regarding the Scripture. I also believe that the Holy Spirit creates an atmosphere conducive for learning within the church. I believe that the Holy Spirit is at work transforming both the teacher and the learner from the inside out. Finally, I believe that the Holy Spirit is active in pointing us toward and introducing us into a relationship with Jesus Christ.

CF 500, Teaching for Christian Formation
Palmer, 4-MAT Reflection Paper
By: Terrence Dwyer, February 18thh, 2010

STEP 1: Parker J. Palmer reveals to us through his remarkable work in "The Courage to Teach" what many professionals experience working in their fields whether it be teaching or otherwise. Teaching, as in any truly human activity, comes from deep within us. Teaching emerges from our inner self and as we teach or express ourselves through other professions, we project the condition of our soul onto our students, the subject matter, and our way of being together. Entanglements experienced in the classroom can be at times revelations of entanglements within our inner life. Knowing our inner self is crucial to good teaching. Good teaching comes from the identity and the integrity of the teacher. It is critical then for teachers to know their inner self and to bring this self honestly and unmasked into the learning experience. Our abilities to connect with our students, and to connect them with the subject matter, depends less upon our methods than on the degree to which we bring our whole self-made available and vulnerable to the experience of learning. Conversely, bad teachers distance themselves from their students and their subjects (CTT11).

Fear is a powerful feature of both the academic landscape and in our inner landscape of self for both the teacher and the learner. These fears can be healthy or unhealthy and they must be acknowledged, understood and addressed for a meaningful learning experience to occur. Teaching and learning can be vulnerable experiences and fears can wall us off from engaged learning experiences. To reduce our vulnerability as teachers we tend to disconnect from our self, our students and our subject matter. We tend to build walls between our inner self and our outward performance as teachers. When this happens, true teaching and learning cannot connect in the communal sense where it needs to for true learning to take place (CTT40).

To overcome this potential disconnect then, teachers need to take the time to spend time connecting and nurturing their inner self as well as connecting and nurturing vulnerable and trusting relationships with other teachers. This connects, strengthens and supports the inner self enabling the teacher to better bring their whole self into their teaching from the depths of their own truth. Additionally, the tensions of paradoxes in the classroom can be divisive and they need to be held in creative tension to expand our hearts. Through the higher forces of love, beauty, goodness and truth these opposites can be reconciled in the classroom when embraced in creative tension (CTT87).

STEP 2: Having been on both the teaching and the learning end of several learning experiences over the years I can readily connect with what Parker Palmer is expressing here. Relatively early in my business career I thought that it would look good within the marketplace and on my resume to be seen and to be known as a teacher within my industry. I was a horrific teacher but it certainly didn't stop me from teaching those classes for five years. Whatever portion of my inner self that made it into the classroom was safely hidden under deep, protective layers of false identity and distorted ego. Years later near the end of my business career, I started up a company for another group and was leading and teaching them how to go through the process of starting up a company. My entire self was present throughout the experience, including the part of myself that was yearning to answer the call into ministry. What a remarkably different experience for both myself and the learners in these two contrasting experiences. In the first experience I was fake and disconnected from the subject matter and the students and in the second I was totally living out my experience with the learners and was deeply connected with them, our subject matter and with my inner self.

Having raised and educated three children from nursery school through graduate school, my wife and I have experienced numerous teachers both great and not so great along the way. The great ones were those that Palmer speaks of who integrated their whole self into their subject matter and brought their students along for the ride as they enthusiastically engaged their subjects. Whenever our children experienced one of these wholly integrated teachers they were never the same afterwards. In each case it changed their lives and their learning experiences. Our children each chose their various majors of study at university having been impacted by great teachers in high school who brought their connected self into the learning experiences in the classroom. It was a joy to see our children become enthusiastic, energized and curious about learning thanks to these great teachers.

Conversely, having sent our children through the Oakland public school system, we also saw teachers who had become completely and pathologically disconnected from their students, their subject matter and just about everything else. We experienced one teacher who would actually just sit with his feet on the desk and read the newspaper during class leaving the kids to fend for themselves. Fortunately, he was an exception and not the norm.

STEP 3: Bringing my whole self into any learning experience at this stage of my life means to unabashedly bring myself, my faith and the Spirit, wholly into these experiences. It is not I who lives but Christ who lives in me that would be present in these experiences. This is what I experienced in my last days in business when I was wholly present in my teaching and leading and experienced the Spirit ministering to others through me as we worked through starting up another company.

One of the issues that bother me from the reading is in the area of practicing to embrace paradoxes in creative tension toward opening up the hearts of the learners. I don't know if I have the necessary confidences and teaching skills that this would seem to require. I greatly admire teachers who can do this in the classroom and have been particularly impressed with my seminary professors who seem to pull this off routinely on very complex issues. I think this is an area perhaps where the giftedness in teaching from the Holy Spirit may be required. However, perhaps through prayer and practice and support from others I could attempt to embrace these paradoxes in creative tension instead of avoiding them.

STEP 4: Clearly a method that I would need to embrace prior to and during any teaching experience would be to intentionally connect with other teachers in vulnerable and trusting relationships. It is a process that has already started in this very class through our team project presentations and I have seen firsthand the fruits of these relationships. We were truthful and vulnerable and supportive with each other as we prepared and presented our project and this process was enormously beneficial for each for us. I can't imagine going through any teaching experience in the future without this kind of a support group all throughout the process. As a result, I will begin further cultivating these supportive relationships here in seminary and would seek to carry these relationships with me throughout my ministry. There are two specific ways in which I can be held accountable to ensure that I follow through on this important commitment. The first being my wife who would gladly hold me accountable in this area as she knows me so well and the second would be my men's accountability small group at church where they too would support me and hold me accountable in this area.

CF 500, Teaching for Christian Formation
Richards Reflection Paper
By: Terrence Dwyer, February 4th, 2010

My wife asked me just a few weeks ago if I would lead and teach a Bible study at her place of work as she and her staff were feeling that they could use some regular Bible study during the week to help them remained focused. She is the Executive Director of Harbor House which is a Christian ministry to the poor in the San Antonio district of Oakland. I surprised both her and myself when I declined to do so because I felt a check in my spirit that I just wasn't ready yet to lead a Bible study. If she would have asked me ten years ago I would have jumped at the chance to lead a Bible study anywhere anytime. In fact I did lead Bible studies ten years ago and have off and on over the years and didn't really think much of it. However, since being in seminary I have a whole new perspective on God's word and the high standard of care that must go into any kind of teaching of scripture. Reading Richards these past several days has so affirmed the validity of my hesitation as I saw for the first time the standard of care that I was searching for in myself. What a wonderful gift this book has been to me as Richards has given me the framework and the tools that I needed to properly prepare.

I have also taught several classes and seminars over the years within my prior career and again I never really put much thought toward the structure of what I was doing. I believe teaching is a spiritual gift and one that I feel that I have not been blessed with. However, teaching is something that God has had me do over the years and may have me do again in the future. This book is such a blessing as it gives me the framework and the tools that I need not only to properly present God's word but also to teach it in such a manner as to have the learners respond by taking God's word into their hearts and minds for their own spiritual transformation.

I have not yet taken any exegesis or hermeneutics classes in seminary so section one on studying the Bible was just the framework that I was looking for in how to systematically approach and effectively present scripture to others. I found it interesting that my mind kept envisioning myself teaching the Bible to a diverse group of adult addicts, and alcoholics as I read through this book. Therefore, I greatly appreciated the introductory overview of this first section as it gave me excellent contextual tools for explaining who God is in relation to the other alternatives out there and what scripture is and why we study it. I so enjoyed the authors' metaphor that good Bible teaching is like building a bridge through time from the modern world back to the ancient biblical world and then back again into our modern world (CBT 14, 182). The framework given in this section for the inductive Bible study method was invaluable to me. This is exactly the framework I felt that I needed for systematically approaching the scripture in my preparations before ever stepping forward to teach it. I feel confident now that given this structure I can take some bit sized bits of familiar scripture and work them through this inductive Bible study method. Although I must admit that I am deeply humbled to be called toward this awesome task of presenting God's word. I pray that through God's grace and through the power of the Holy Spirit and the mercy of Jesus and through an encouraging community I am able to become worthy of such an enormous task.

I've done some prior reading on teaching but have had no formal training whatsoever in the methods and practices of teaching so I found section two of this text not only to be greatly informative and enlightening but also to be an essential reference for me going forward in any fashion regarding the ministry of teaching. Learning that there is order and structure to learning was not surprising but it was enlightening to me. The importance given to the structure of the teaching in the effectiveness of the learning experience for the learner was an awakening for me. I knew it was there I just never paid any serious attention to it previously. Teaching with the learner in mind toward that learner applying biblical truths to their daily life is our goal and to do so I now see requires an immense amount of careful preparation on the part of the teacher. The importance of teaching with the student in mind of their taking an active role in their own learning is clearer to me now. Starting with the aim of what do I want the student to learn from this teaching session and working backward to answer that question was helpful (CBT 133). Revisiting the needs hierarchies here was also a helpful reminder of the various needs driven distractions that may come into a teaching session especially in disadvantaged environments. Also, reviewing the three domains of learning of cognitive, affective and behavioral, toward structuring our lessons to reach these three areas within the learner was another essential for my lesson planning.

Again, with little formal training in teaching, I found section three of the text to be another critically needed framework and essential reference guide for me. The lesson planning worksheet given there is an essential tool to have and I know that it will take time for me to learn to work through this process of lesson planning. The hook, book, look and took approach toward teaching works very well for me. This is a method that I feel I can understand and follow through on. Oddly, reflecting back on my many years in sales and the various sales training classes that I have taken over the year's actually sound quite familiar and similar to the hook, book, look and took method. I so appreciated the section on the various ways for engaging student response through guided self –application as this is what it's all about really. We are seeking to have the students discover their own specific ways that they can change by taking action on the biblical principles taught in the class (CBT 175). The various methods given here for reaching the cognitive, affective and behavioral areas were fun to read as I've participated as a learner in each and every one of the methods discussed and I could relate to what worked well for me and why and what didn't work so well for me but perhaps did work well for others.

I don't want to overuse this analogy but the common practices of truly great teachers referred to in section four of the text is also remindful to me of the common practices of truly great sales people. Perhaps I'm reflecting back now having finished this text and am finding many similarities between the ministry of teaching and my previous career in sales. Admittedly, I am overwhelmed by the enormity of the task of teaching scripture well which this text has brought to light for me. However, reflecting back now on the many similarities between the tasks required in my previous career and the tasks required of my new calling I now feeling encouraged and up to the task.

I also found that the section on teaching for adults, youth, children, and preschoolers to be an essential reference guide for me. Each has different needs, patterns of learning, and varying motivations and strengths. Having access to the varying teaching strategies for hook, book, look, and took for each category of these learners is a wonderful resource to me for which I am very grateful to have.

Through God's grace and through careful and thoughtful preparation I feel that I have the abilities to teach scripture. I now have access to a wealth of tools at my disposal through this text and this class and I now also feel encouraged that God has shown me that my prior career may be redeemed into my calling going forward. Maybe I'll take my wife up on her request to lead that Bible study after all.

**Christian Spiritual Formation
Through Short Term Communal Works
Of Mission, Mercy & Justice
By: Terrence Dwyer, December 5th, 2009
SP520: Foundations for Spiritual Life
Professor: Susan S. Phillips, Ph.D.**

Introduction

It was my very first day ever on a Habitat for Humanity jobsite a few years ago, here in Oakland, California. Our church was preparing to send a Habitat for Humanity Mission team to Thailand and those of us interested in going were asked to spend a day working together on the local Oakland jobsite. We were a motley crew of seasoned individuals with most of our group well beyond the retirement years. I was in my mid Forties and the youngest person there on the team at that time and I was thinking to myself who in the world is going to do the work of building this house today? I remember thinking that there is no way these old men can do much work let alone these old women we have assembled here. My false assumptions were quickly and emphatically corrected as soon as the work day began and continued all throughout the day. These "elderly" men and women folk worked harder than anyone I had ever been around and their skills in a wide array of construction technique were extraordinary. I was astonished and deeply humbled by the Holy Spirit that day and I was taught to never underestimate any of God's magnificent creation. I was spiritually transformed.

An integral part of Christian spiritual formation takes place when we are in communion with other believers of various ages, backgrounds and experiences. When we are taken out of our comfortable environments and placed together with a diverse group of fellow believers all working together toward a common goal, we become a microcosm of the church. We learn from the Holy Spirit and from others as we are often stretched, grown and matured by these short-term experiences of working together in mission, mercy and justice.

I ended up going on that Habitat Mission trip to Thailand and that experience dramatically changed the course of my life. My older and wiser roommate on that trip had only been with me one day when he told me that I needed to begin attending Bible Study Fellowship as soon as possible which I immediately did upon my return home. He knew from spending just a short period of time with me that I needed the Word deeper in my life and he emphatically encouraged me toward that end. "As iron sharpens iron, so a man sharpens the countenance of his friend." I am deeply grateful for having had the opportunity to participate on that short-term mission trip and for the spiritual formation that took root in my life as a result of that experience. Remarkably, just a few short years after this encounter I find myself called into the ministry and attending seminary. I am deeply grateful for the prayers, patience and mentoring of the Mission's Pastor of our church who continually encouraged me to dig deeper to seek God's call upon my life. Her deep ministry of prayer and service toward others has been in itself a transformative work within me.

Relationship

Clinical psychologist Dr. Henry Cloud tells us that "God is a relational being, and God created a relational universe. At the foundation of every living thing is the idea of relationship. Everything that is alive relates to something else." God created us to hunger for relationship both with God and with other human beings. Nothing grows in our universe that is not connected to something else and our own souls cannot grow unless we are connected to God and to others. Jesus tells us in John 15:5, "I am the vine, you are the branches. Those who abide in Me, and I in them, bear much fruit; for without Me you can do nothing." Christian Spiritual Transformation then comes from our being connected to Jesus.

However, in addition to our being connected to Christ, we must also be connected to one another. "The idea of a solitary believer, united to Jesus Christ and filled with the Holy Spirit but not joined to a company of Christians, is never taught in Holy Scripture. The people of God as a company were chosen in Christ before the foundation of the world. God places a high value on the church." We are all in varying degrees of spiritual maturity and that is just the point as we need each other in our spiritual growth process. Christ tells us in John 13:34 to, "Love one another; as I have loved you, that you also love one another. By this all will know that you are My disciples, if you have love for one another." Christian Spiritual Transformation then is in part a process of being connected or in relationship to God and to others in love. Dietrich Bonhoeffer goes one step further and says that our love for one another should not simply be human love but that it should be spiritual love. "Human love desires the other person, his company, his answering love, but it does not serve him. Spiritual love, however, comes from Jesus Christ; it serves Him alone; it knows that it has no immediate access to other persons. Because spiritual love does not desire but rather serves, it loves an enemy as a brother."

For us to grow spiritually then, we must in part be connected to God and connected to each other and practicing to love one another with a deep spiritual love that does not desire its own but desires instead for Christ to love others through us with our only desire to be to abide within the love of Christ.

Doing short term communal works of mission, mercy and justice require us to be in relationship. We are in relationship with each other within the group performing the works, and with those whom we meet with and are serving as well as all those who are supporting our efforts. "We need to seek out spiritually enriching relationships of love and service. We should put ourselves in places such as small groups and service units where the formation and growth of these relationships is encouraged. We need to invest in community." The books of Hebrews tells us in 10:24-25, "And let us consider one another in order to stir up love and good works, not forsaking the assembly of ourselves together, as is the manner of some, but exhorting one another."

Relationships are our biggest source of joy, as well as frustration and discouragement. We go to build cross cultural relationships with people who are different than we are and yet our biggest relational problems are most often with our co-workers. "Suddenly we are thrust together with people we probably did not choose as our neighbors, friends, coworkers, counselors and even support group. No wonder tensions arise! Add to this the challenges of adjusting to a new language and culture, fatigue and jetlag, loneliness, homesickness, physical discomfort and spiritual conflict. Even excellent relationships are placed under severe stress." It is within this cauldron of strangeness, stress and fatigue where we are pressed into living solely by faith, trusting in God, trusting in those around us and where we learn to quickly forgive and to walk the pathways of spiritual love as we see Christ loving others though us in astonishing ways.

Servanthood

Within the church then there are an endless array of opportunities for our banding together into small communal groups to work together toward some work of mission, mercy or justice for others who are in such great need. For example, there are more than 143 million orphans living in the world today which is a number greater than the entire population of Russia. Each of these orphans needs to hear the Gospel and obtain food, clothing, housing, medical care, education, and eventually employment. Simply taking on that task alone could keep the church quite busy and yet there are a myriad of other needs such as starvation, crushing poverty, gross injustices and catastrophic disasters. Humans living on the inside of these dire situations need to know that someone cares for them. They need to know that God cares for them. We as a church need to go to them to connect with them and to share the Gospel with them. We need to be in relationship with them and to love them. So we band together into our small communal groups to tend to these works of mission, mercy and justice.

Jesus astonishes us and shows us the way in John 13:3-5, "Jesus, knowing that the Father had given all things into His hands, and that He had come from God and was going to God, rose from the supper and laid aside His garments, took a towel and girded Himself. After that, He poured water into a basin and began to wash the disciple's feet and to wipe them with the towel with which He was girded." Jesus is teaching us here to serve others. "One of the great secrets of Christian growth is learning to be a servant. When we learn that life consists of serving and not being served we have made a major step in growth. The towel is our symbol." St. Benedict also reveals to us, "I have discovered, you see, that the real Benedictinism requires us to pour ourselves out for the other, to give ourselves away, to provide for the staples of life, both material and spiritual for one another. The question is not whether what we have to give is sufficient for the situation or not. The question is simply whether or not we have anything to give."

One of my mission trips to Thailand was after the terrible tsunami in 2004 that killed over 250,000 people in a matter of minutes. The devastation was swift and catastrophic. There wasn't much I felt that we could do but I felt a strong tug on my heart that we had to do something to share God's love with these hurting people. We prepared and took a small team over there from our church to see what we could do. We went to the hard hit area of Khao Lak, Thailand and helped build housing there for two weeks with Habitat for Humanity. We walked along side and comforted many a broken spirit. We also attended a Habitat home dedication ceremony for a woman who had lost her parents, her husband, all of her children except the baby she was holding in her arms that day. She also lost her home and her business and all of her possessions all within a few minutes in that tsunami. We couldn't even hope to begin to restore what that woman had lost. But we could build her a house and that's what we were there for. To see her holding her baby and smiling in the threshold of her new house is a scene I'll never forget. She was in relationship with someone who cared about her plight and it gave her hope for herself and for her baby. God loved her through those who took the time to go and serve. This experience of seeing and hearing this woman's story also brought home to each of us the deeper realization of just how richly blessed we truly are in our lives which developed within us a deeper sense of gratitude toward God's tender mercies toward us.

We don't have to travel across the globe to serve others as there are more than enough works of mission, mercy and justice needing to be done right here in our own neighborhoods. For example, illiteracy in our local schools is still prevalent and young students need tutors and mentors to take the time to walk alongside them, teach them, and to encourage them. It doesn't matter where we serve. What does matter is that we serve. "In participating through the Holy Spirit in the body of Christ which was offered once-for-all on the Cross, the members of the church are stimulated and enabled by the same Holy Spirit to offer themselves in Eucharistic sacrifice, to serve one another in love within the body and ultimately to the needy world."

Transformation

The serving believer is transformed through the experience of serving others. Sometimes poor motives such as pride or self-righteousness can deaden our growth experience but for the most part service to others will shape our soul. Also, the sense of being a part of something so much larger than ourselves is a soul stretching experience. "Service draws the Christian closer to Christ as he or she senses the privilege of acting on His behalf. Service produces a sense of purpose that is eternal, even while grounded in the earthly and physical needs of those being served. Humans need a sense of significance, and being with and acting on behalf of Christ makes us sense something even larger than significance." We are transformed by God as we experience God working through us to unconditionally love those we meet along the way.

As we travel, live and work with our co-laborers on our short term communal works of mission, mercy and justice, we also become transformed through our relationship with each other. After having participated on and leading several such teams; I am convinced that it is the Holy Spirit who puts these short-term teams together specifically for the transformative work that needs to be done within the souls of those participating on the team. We had one young woman join our Habitat tsunami team at the last second. She seemed an unlikely candidate as she wasn't a member of our church, she had no real construction skills and she knew no one on the team. Our Senior Pastor however knew her story and encouraged her participation on the team so we took her along. We usually take turns doing morning devotions on these trips and when she presented her devotion one morning her whole story came out. She was recently engaged to be married but her young fiancé tragically died in an accident as he was moving his things out of his apartment and into their new home. He fell down the stairs carrying boxes and broke his neck and died just a few weeks prior to our trip. Moreover, the police treated her as if she was a suspect in his death. The whole experience deeply traumatized her and this very sad story came out of her soul in deep heaving wails and sobs that morning. We were able to come alongside her and pray over her and comfort her in a way that only the Holy Spirit could imagine. A traumatized and dispirited young woman at the beginning of the trip was an enthusiastic and engaging young woman who was full of life and promise by the end of the trip. It was an amazing transformation through the intricate work and power of the Holy Spirit. "We can gain insight into our own lives only if we are willing to pass over into the lives of others, for it is only in the moment of passing over into other lives that one has a glimpse of what full enlightenment could be. The authentic missioner is one who has the experience of passing over to other lives and discovering always some basis in his or her own life for understanding others."

While we were in Thailand on our tsunami rebuild, hurricane Katrina struck New Orleans back in the United States. We watched the events unfold on CNN and the BBC while in Thailand. Our hearts went out to the people of that devastated area and we felt led to immediately begin making plans for going to the Gulf Coast upon our return to assist with the rebuilding efforts there. True to form, the Holy Spirit assembled various teams of disparate believers and non-believers from all walks of life and with widely varying levels of spiritual maturity. We all had the common goal of helping the Gulf region rebuild from this immense disaster and through it all the Holy Spirit worked intimately within each of us to transform us toward further spiritual growth. Non-believers saw first-hand the love and joy of the Holy Spirit in our mature believer's unabashed expression of their faith and joy in Jesus. Believers openly shared their faith and patiently answered difficult questions from the non-believers among us.

I was quite skeptical of one elderly woman who joined our first Katrina team from another church. We had great difficulty communicating with her before the trip as she had no email or cell phone. She had no construction skills whatsoever and was fairly slow moving and deliberate and had certain medical and health issues. I knew this was going to be a challenge not only for me as the leader but for the entire team. She was however, from New Orleans and she wanted to help her people and therefore wanted to participate on our team. The Holy Spirit worked on each of us through her in amazing ways. Before going to work, we toured the devastation and ended up at her childhood home and neighborhood which was essentially destroyed. Her deep wailing and overwhelming sadness brought home to each of us the emotional impact this hurricane had on the people in this region. We tenderly and lovingly approached the people of the region we were serving knowing just how emotionally raw their own hearts must be seeing it first hand from our own elderly teammate.

Near the end of that trip our elderly woman wanted to share with us some of her Cajun culture and she arranged for a Cajun dinner for our team at a relative's house. It sounded like a good way to wrap up the trip so I agreed. She never really said how far away it was she just said it was "down the road apiece". Our team ended up traveling almost 100 miles at night in a terrific thunder and lightning storm. People began fearing for their safety and were questioning the wisdom of our decision. However, we each learned to have faith, to trust in God and to have patience through this experience as on the other end of that road trip was a Cajun feast beyond description. In addition, people came from all around to thank us for being there for them and to tell us their stories. We were once again spiritually stretched and transformed as a team.

Conclusion

In conclusion, the short term communal experience that we have as believers has at its core an emphasis on the transformation of the participants through their living together and learning to love one another and others together as a group. However, no matter how much we may want to, we can't really change much about the places we may visit during these short term works of mission, mercy and justice. We may build a house, paint some school rooms, or distribute some food and medicine. We may listen to the stories of orphans or refugees from war or victims of atrocities. We may visit grave sites, or prisons, or places of worship and pray for God to step in and heal these places of great pain and suffering. But on the whole, the changes we may effect, if any at all, as a small band of believers traveling together are quite small in comparison to the overwhelmingly great need.

But the fact that we go does matter. The people that we meet with there and connect with repeatedly tell us that it does matter. They tell us that we actually do make a difference because they are given hope and encouragement seeing that somebody else cares about their plight and that they are not alone. They are in relationship in the midst of their plight with somebody who cares. My dear friend in Christ, Abraham Bagalya from Jinja, Uganda took me aside on my last night there during one of my recent visits to Uganda. He sternly admonished me to return to Uganda. He said that our being there gives people hope and that we must continue to come back to show people that we truly do care. Our willingness to go and to connect with people individually and in groups matters. The giving of our time and of our resources and of our giftedness matters. During that particular trip to Uganda we built a Habitat home for a large family in need who were previously living in a small, dark mud hut. During the dedication ceremony the homeowner took me into a small room within his new house. We didn't speak each other's language so we couldn't talk to each other. However, he grabbed me and hugged me harder than I had ever been hugged before. He wouldn't let go and tears flowed down his face. What price do you put on that kind of an experience?

These short term communal work trips matter because it is we who are transformed the most through these experiences. The going is about our coming home. We come home transformed, spiritually stretched, grown and matured. We see the world and each other and God with new eyes and a new heart. We come home ready to change our own lives as a result like my immediately enrolling into Bible Study Fellowship upon my return from my first mission trip. We also share our experiences with others who may be moved in such a way as to take action and to change their own lives as a result. One of my recent co-workers is now sponsoring a young man from Gulu, Uganda through seminary after hearing me tell his story of captivity by the LRA rebels. These short term communal works of mission, mercy and justice are about our own transformation and as such are thus transformative to the world. Gandhi was once asked what it would take for India to become a Christian nation and he said that it would simply take the Christians to be Christian. These short term communal works are where we learn how to be just such a Christian through our relationships with God and with each other as that is where we learn to travel into the deeper pathways of spiritual love.

Bibliography

Bonhoeffer, Dietrich. Life Together. San Francisco: Harper Collins, 1954.

Cloud, Henry. Changes That Heal. Grand Rapids, Michigan: Zondervan, 1992.

Coote, James M. Phillips and Robert T. Toward the 21st. Century in Christian Mission. Grand Rapids, Michigan William B. Eerdmans Publishing Company, 1993.

Dearborn, Tim. Short-Term Missions Workbook. Downers Grove, Illinois: IVP Books, 2003.

Hitt, Russell T. How Christians Grow. New York: Oxford University Press, 1979.

Joan D. Chittister, OSB. Wisdom Distilled from the Daily. San Francisco, CA: Harper Collins Publishers, 1990.

Lawrenz, Mel. The Dynamics of Spiritual Formation. Grand Rapids, Michigan: Baker Books, 2000.

MacArthur, John. The Macarthur Study Bible, New King James Version. Vol. 1. Nashville: Word Publishing, 1997.

Wilhoit, James C. Spiritual Formation as If the Church Mattered. Grand Rapids, Michigan Baker Academic.

CF 500 Winter 2010
Willard Reflection #1 – WIDP Chapters 1 through 7
By: Terrence Dwyer, January 8th, 2010

I often struggle with the Kingdom Life described in the New Testament as it does appear to describe a divine life that I have yet to completely enter into. Although I am a born again, spirit filled believer in Jesus Christ that has spiritually grown and matured substantially over the years, I still struggle with the content of my own heart. I do know a few people who rejoice in the Lord with an indescribable and glorious joy but that joy only seems to come in fits and starts for me. At times I have genuine unconditional love pouring from my heart but at other times I am appalled at what is present in my heart. Getting rid of all malice, guile, insincerity, envy and slander is my fervent desire but no matter how hard I try I can never seem to actually totally rid myself. It seems as if these maladies are encoded into my DNA and into my heart. The timing of reading and working through "Renovation of the Heart" is perfect and I am grateful to God for this next step in my spiritual formation.

What a relief it is to hear Willard say that the life that God holds out to us in Jesus is not meant to be an unsolvable puzzle. This rings true to me as does the idea that spiritual formation is an orderly process. This is the God I know. It has been my experience that God is abundantly gracious and my spiritual growth over time has come in what appear to me to be sequential steps. It doesn't always seem to me to be the case that the yoke of Christ is easy or that His burden is light. But I am seeing a new understanding of this message at least in regard to my spiritual transformation. It is not through my efforts that I can rid myself of my hearts' maladies. Sometimes I fast as a means of trying to rid myself of my "worldliness" and to try to attain a higher spiritual plateau. This works for awhile but eventually I revert to the same person as before. I now understand that it is only through my complete surrender, my complete relinquishing of my heart to God to allow God to do the work necessary in my heart for the transformation of my heart. My efforts at spiritual transformation are futile. I am however to humbly cooperate with God in the work that God chooses to do in my heart.

So much of my spiritual growth has come to me at times through very dramatic episodes or periods of my life where God stretched and grew me beyond what I thought I was capable of. Some of these events were great trials and tribulations where I learned deep lessons in forgiveness and unconditional love that now permeate my spirit. It now seems that God is seeking to work microscopically in my heart and I so welcome this work as my dreadful heart has so anguished me over the years. As I pray for the renovation of my heart and work through the Daily Practice God seems to be continually reminding me of my lack of patience and my lack of gratitude which often leads to frustration and then to anger. It seems staggering and exhausting to me that I have been struggling with these issues for as long as I have with such little progress. I am light years ahead of where I was as a young man but not where I need to be as a humble and grateful follower of Jesus Christ.

My Prayer

"Lord please forgive my self-centered prideful heart. Please forgive how I have repeatedly sinned against you through my heart. I completely and totally surrender to you my Lord. I surrender my heart to you my Lord Jesus. I turn it over to you for your workmanship upon it and through it. Please show me that which is in my heart that displeases you and please show me where I must work with you now to grow into the man that you want me to be. Thank you and praise you Lord for your forgiveness, patience, graciousness and love. Amen."

I now see how futile it was for me to attempt to establish a "Christian Business" several years ago. I attempted to set up a business in this world based upon Christian principals but ran into great difficulty in implementing and maintaining certain Christian policies. Certainly justice and mercy rained down throughout our organization due to the Christian leadership of the organization but ultimately the organization did not last. At the time I thought I was establishing a "beach head" for Jesus in the business world and that He was blessing me and enabling me to do so. My understanding is so different now. It is not the system or the organization of the business that Jesus is seeking to establish as that is not the Kingdom of God. The Kingdom of God is in our hearts. Jesus tells us in Luke 17:21 that "the Kingdom of God is within you." It is there that Jesus must reign and it is there that I must surrender to Him fully.

Choosing to love is an act of the will. Today I chose to love as God gave me opportunities to love throughout the day. Today I chose to smile and my smile was recognized and acknowledged by others which encouraged me to smile more. Today I chose to do something unexpectedly kind for my wife and it was such a joy to see how incredibly happy it made her that it greatly encouraged me to explore how I can continue to unexpectedly bring her joy. Today I chose to give unexpectedly to a person who reacted with great joy and it encouraged me to keep on giving to others. Today I chose to be grateful instead of impatient. Today I chose to be grateful instead of critical and judgmental. Today I chose to be patient and kind in helping a friend. These are small steps within my heart today and I am grateful for the opportunity to learn from them.

Of the six basic aspects of a human life it is the thought life and feelings that give me the most consternation. They are interdependent and are not found apart from each other. It is here where I find at times too many distractions and too much conflicting input. My thoughts and my feelings are barraged by our western culture and at times I find it difficult to remember to quiet my spirit and to listen for the Holy Spirit. I start and end each day quieting my spirit and listening and praying but it is throughout the course of the day that my thoughts and feelings become engaged in the world. I often think that having more scripture memorized would help me greatly in aligning my daily thoughts with God's own heart. I seek to always remember the Lord and that He is at my right hand and that I shall not be moved.

My Prayer
"I seek Lord to surrender to you my thoughts and my feelings. I seek Lord that your will is my will. I surrender my choices to you. I surrender my body, my personality and my relationships to you. You are the Lord of who I am, you are the Lord of my soul. Please help me to honor you in all my thoughts, feelings, choices, actions and interactions with others."

CF 500, Teaching for Christian Formation
Willard Reflection #2 – WIDP Chapters 8 through 25
By: Terrence Dwyer, January 21st, 2010

What a blessing it has been for me to enter into and to work through this book by Dallas Willard. I continue to experience deeper understandings of God and who I am in relation to God as I work through these exercises. I was under the assumption that since I had been filled with the Spirit and had put my faith in Jesus Christ and was "saved" that all was right with the world. All I had to do was to try and be a good person, try to follow Jesus as best I could, persevere through the trials, enjoy the blessings, and try not to do anything stupid to spoil it all. What I didn't understand was just how badly ruined my heart truly was and that my trying to do anything to fix it was useless. God is the only one who can heal my heart and only in the manner which God alone chooses to heal it. Complete and total surrender of my ruined heart to God for God to heal and to repair according to his sovereign plan is the only hope for my heart such as it is.

I also didn't understand that when Jesus said that the Kingdom of

God is within you that he also meant that our eternal life with him begins now. I understood that the Kingdom of God is here now in the Body of Christ here on this earth but I had always understood eternal life to begin after we died. This changes everything. My whole perspective has changed. My life is no longer as finite as it once felt and the true hope of eternal life now dwells so much more richly in me. This deeper understanding humbles me further toward submission to God for his healing of my heart and it also gives me a greater sense of urgency to share the good news of the Gospel with others.

Participating with God in the further restoration of my soul through dying to self has been an ongoing and arduous process for me. It is a theme that God has woven richly into my life while at the same time weaving in significant challenges. When the Holy Spirit entered my life I had a profound experience of death to self and that it was the Spirit who lived in me. My life was immediately and radically altered. Then again, just before entering seminary, I had another profound experience of choosing to demonstrate my willingness to lay down my life for Christ. Yet throughout my faith life I have not consistently demonstrated that I completely and totally surrender to God's care and that I at times look out for myself. It seems that the early loss of both of my parents has impaired my ability to trust at times. For me then, dying to self is a daily process of remembering God and to put my trust in him daily. I so appreciate Willard's guidance here toward seeking out humility and his admonition that we never really spiritually attain. As long as we are in the body we are to seek God's grace each and every day like the manna God gave to the Israelites in the desert. Willard profoundly states, "The greatest saints are not those who need less grace, but those who consume the most grace, who indeed are the most in need of grace – those who are saturated by grace in every dimension of their being. Grace to them is like breath" (ROH 93). Taking these words into my soul has changed how I live. I seek to pray now about everything to seek God's grace about everything before I do anything. It seems right to me. It seems that this is where I need to be in my utter dependence upon God to move forward into my eternal life.

Revisiting and meditating on Psalm 23 in the exercises helped immensely in my visualization of my complete contentment under the total care, provision, and protection of God. I had always read Psalm 23 with myself in mind as a person. I had never read it from the perspective of a contented sheep which Willard asks us to do. This new perspective opened up a deeper meaning of this Psalm and God's care for me. I recently returned from Patagonia where I saw very fat, contented sheep just sitting peacefully in lush green pastures. They didn't have a care in the world as everything they needed was right there surrounding them. Exactly the picture that Willard was asking us to call into mind! This picture totally relaxes me into God's care.

Willard prefaces his introduction to VIM (vision, intention and means as the general pattern for personal transformation), by using Alcoholics Anonymous as an illustration of the concept. I understand what Willard means by a desirable state being envisioned and that an intention to realize it is actuated in a decision with means being applied to realize the vision (ROH 84). Having suffered from alcoholism and having personally been through both Alcoholics Anonymous and Celebrate Recovery, I have an understanding of the importance of vision, intention and means in bringing about transformation in one's life. We cannot attain sobriety unless we have a vision of what a life of sobriety would be like. We cannot become sober unless we actually intentionally make a decision to move toward sobriety with the means to carry it out. Without this vision and this decision we are forever stuck in a life of endless pain. I thank God for this opportunity in my life now to work toward envisioning what life would be like in the Kingdom. I have God's word as a means to draw upon to richly develop my vision of the Kingdom. I also have my relationships with others within the Body of Christ as additional means to mentor me toward what my community holds as a Kingdom vision. It is my intention to step into that vision of the Kingdom and to live a life of total obedience and dependence upon Christ. A life of complete submission and trust in God through complete obedience will be the outward expression of my life within this vision. I envision this much like the mental picture I have of the contented sheep lying in the rich pasture in Patagonia.

Parts of my current life simply cannot be a part of the vision I am beginning to hold for a Kingdom life. Willard states that the ultimate freedom we have as human beings is the power to select what we will allow our mind to dwell upon (WIDP 66). Much of my television watching simply cannot be a part of where I choose to allow my mind to dwell. One of my mentors and a man I greatly admire has a mind chock full of God's word. This is the kind of mind I seek. I seek a mind that is filled with Scripture where my thoughts are aligned with the ways of God.

The implication for ministry in general from what I am learning from reading this book is a much deeper realization of the state of the human heart and our utter dependence upon God to initiate change within our hearts. The importance of holding a vision of life in the Kingdom along with intentionally moving toward that vision with means would be a part of my ministry and a part of any teaching that I may be called upon to do. This deeper understanding also draws me deeper into Scripture to better grasp a vision of life in the Kingdom which would even further deepen my understanding for my ministry and my teaching. This understanding also better guides how I would both approach and pray for others in both ministry and in teaching.

My Prayer

Lord please have mercy on me a sinner. I am but dust but it is my heart's desire to live within your Kingdom. It is my heart's desire for all of me to completely obey you and to do your will at every moment of my being. I surrender all of myself to you my Lord. I trust you and I love you and thank you for how you have provided for me at every turn. Your graciousness toward me is overwhelming. I seek Lord to call upon you at every turn. I seek to live by your grace alone. Please forgive me for how I have so disappointed you by going my own way so many times. Show me Lord where I am not in your will and please transform my heart Lord toward your heart. Please give me wisdom to walk in your ways and please direct my mind toward the study of your word. Amen.

CF 500, Teaching for Christian Formation
Willard Reflection #3 – WIDP Chapters 26 through 37
By: Terrence Dwyer, February 5th, 2010

These passages and practices in Willard these past two weeks have been somewhat of a bittersweet experience for me upon reflection. I so greatly appreciated the wisdom and insight gained from reading these passages and working through these exercises. However, one nagging thing that stays with me is the lost years of the life behind me knowing what I know now at such a deeper level. As a young man new to Christ I would at times try to memorize various passages of scripture and I have of course diligently read the Bible over the years. Unfortunately, much of my thinking was still worldly thinking and in reflecting back I could have done so much more in my spiritual disciplines. Ingesting the recommended passages from Corinthians, Colossians and Romans this past week almost made me cry for the time I have wasted. My spirit rejoiced in taking these passages in and I now know what I must do to move forward. Hopefully, through God's grace, this remorse I carry may be redeemed perhaps by pointing others toward the importance of ingesting scripture into their minds and spirits. God please forgive me for my slothfulness with your precious word.

Willard reminds us that the single most important thing in our mind is our idea of God and the associated images (ROH 100). While I seek to rest in God and to trust in God's care for me I also must seek to have intentional and clear thinking about God. I cannot simply rest. I must willfully focus my mind to seek the Lord and toward understanding him through scripture and community. Ingesting passages of the scripture focuses my mind on God and who he is and better enables me to remember God throughout the moments of the day. Through God's grace my mind will be healed from my previous destructive thought patterns as I replace these destructive thought patterns with whole passages of scripture embedded into my mind and into my heart. As I practice this spiritual discipline Willard assures me that God will meet me and will enable the renovation of my mind (ROH 80). This new mind filled with whole passages of scripture is my vision of what my kingdom life is to be.

A wonderful revelation came to me as I worked through these passages on the mind. Several years ago my wife and I were having a very difficult time in our marriage and we were in a complete stalemate in or relationship. The situation was not good and was quickly heading toward divorce. Through God's grace I was brought to a place of deep humility enabling me to make the first move of love toward my wife in an attempt to salvage our relationship. It worked. She responded to my initiation of love and our relationship was saved and we now have a wonderful marriage of 25 years.

Likewise, God made the first move of love toward me in our relationship through the sacrifice of his son for my sins. I must simply respond to his deep love for me by loving and trusting him in return and to move toward him and abandon myself to him. I need to trust deep into my mind and deep into my heart that he who loves me is love itself. I live beyond harm in his hands and there is nothing that can happen to me that will not turn out for my good (ROH 135). God wholly knows who I am and accepts me and loves me just as I am. Too often I have failed in my complete trust in God and have taken matters into my own hands with my worldly mind. God knows and understands how the significant early trauma to my ability to trust has hindered our relationship and his grace continues to sustain me and yet he continues to call me toward an even deeper relationship of trust and of an abiding love.

The passages on the four movements toward perfect love were some of the most spiritually transformative passages that I have read since being in seminary. This is my hearts' desire and this is what I have experienced in varying degrees throughout my life as a follower of Jesus Christ through loving him and others. However, this is a kingdom way of life that I have not wholly abandoned myself to the degree to which Christ is calling me to.

Self-sacrificial love and living wholly by the spirit each moment of each day is my vision of who I am to be in the kingdom. The humility and self-sacrificial love that I expressed to my wife when we were heading toward divorce is the same place where I need to live in every moment toward others. Love is to will to do good toward others and is assured that our good is taken care of without self-will (ROH 132). Thus love is made perfect or complete and perfect love casts out all fear. Being filled with love and being absent of all fear we are filled with peace, joy and love and with the fruits of the spirit. This is exactly what attracted to me to Christ in the first place when I saw peace and joy in the spirit of a believer and I reached out to God for this same peace and joy and subsequently received my salvation as a result.

A deep part of my not wholly entering into a kingdom way of life has been my trying to justify myself before God and others. This is a burden that I simply must lay down and have in large part been doing so for some time now. I must simply accept God's love and trust that all things will work toward my good and stop striving to justify myself to him. God's peace will permeate my being as a result of simply abandoning my spirit to God (ROH 134).

A couple of the daily experiments had us thinking through some issues that may be holding us back from moving forward on our path toward spiritual transformation. Over the past few years there have been two significant issues that I have had to let go to God to enable me to move forward and these were again brought to mind during these exercises. One was being called out of my almost 30 year career culminating with the sale of my business that I dearly loved. The other was being called out of the Habitat ministry at our church and into ministry and into seminary. I struggled with the loss of both of these works which I dearly loved and greatly enjoyed. I feel like I have been placed on the sidelines and am no longer participating in accomplishing God's will in our world. These have been hard to let go of and hard to endure their loss. However, I am gradually seeing God's wisdom and purpose in this new call. I'm astonished that he counts me worthy of this path and that is actually another of the things I had to let go of in working through the exercises - my destructive thought patterns regarding my intelligence and abilities. This path is so challenging and difficult for me that I simply must abandon myself completely to God wholly trusting that his perfect love is working to will toward good for me. My purpose is now to move forward in my spiritual transformation and toward a more intelligent, prepared and thoughtful participation in accomplishing his will in our world.

My Prayer

Lord I pray that you please open my heart and my mind toward learning whole passages of your word. I pray that you please not only renovate my heart but my mind and my emotions by your spirit and your word. Implant into my heart and into my mind your vision of whom I am to be in your kingdom. Please enable me Lord to live by the spirit and not by the flesh and to seek you at all times. Please remind me toward a humble and self-sacrificial love toward others at all times. Please show me those things that displease you and those things that please you. Please encourage me in my studies and remind me that you have more in store for me yet toward participating with you in working toward accomplishing your will in this world. Amen.

CF 500, Teaching for Christian Formation
Willard Reflection #4 – WIDP Chapters 38 through 49
By: Terrence Dwyer, February 17th, 2010

Probably the single most important sentence in this book study for me to date occurred in the prior reading assignment but its' message carries over and resonates throughout this reading assignment as well in relation to sin residing within our bodies. Willard advises that love is when we are concerned for the good of others and assured that our good is taken care of without self-will (ROH132). On my path toward spiritual transformation it has been at times a struggle for me to rest in the complete and utter defenselessness of trusting wholeheartedly in God that my good is taken care of without any of my own self-will. Putting others first through self-sacrificial love and seeking ways to bless others has been a much easier and readily acceptable spiritually transformative process for me through the power of the Holy Spirit. However, as an alcoholic and as a son of an alcoholic, attempting to control my environment for my own self-preservation is a deeply ingrained pattern of sin that is rooted into my mind, body and spirit and must be regularly dealt with. I have been dealing with this sinful pattern and releasing all control over to God for several years now and have experienced wonderful release and blessing from God as a result of my wholeheartedly trusting in him. However, it is an old sin pattern whose residue resides within my body and from which I continue to seek deeper levels of healing and transformation.

Willard writes that our will alone cannot carry us to change but that our will implemented along with changing our thoughts and feelings can result in our becoming the person we are meant to be in Christ (ROH143). Our putting on the mind of Christ and being transformed by Christ through spending time in the Word and with the Holy Spirit transforms our will and our character. This then transforms and governs our personality, our character, our decisions and our behavior for Christ as we become more and more like Christ. I now have a deeper understanding of the dignity God afforded us in his gift of free will to us and therefore our free will choices for him. It is my hearts' desire to always choose for God and I pray that our Lord forgives me for those times when I have chosen not to do so. Willard discusses the role of spiritual disciplines such as mediation, fasting, worship and service as a means for making room for the Word and the Spirit to work in us (ROH155). These disciplines permit destructive thoughts and patterns to become more clearly evident to us and then to be dealt with. We have buried these destructive patterns under layer upon layer of deception and denial and these spiritual disciplines help us to remove these layers so we can perceive them and address them.

I so enjoyed Willard's description of our being in the "grip" of grace and therefore sin does not exercise control over us except insofar as we allow it (ROH165). At times I have felt in the "grip" of sin and powerless as I felt that the body was fallen and destined for decay but at least my soul was saved and destined for glory. Willard's description of the spiritual formation of the body resonates so true to me as the Spirit resides in my body and all parts of my body must be transformed toward Christ likeness. Fully realizing and surrendering to the understanding that I have died with Christ and that I am only alive in and through Christ enables me to tap into that "grip" of grace and to become a slave of righteousness. Willard writes that the force of the Spirit of life that is in Christ Jesus is now also a real presence in my body and it opens the way to liberation from the force of sin in my bodily parts (ROH166). By not walking in the flesh but instead by walking wholly in the Spirit we come to a complete freedom from even the thought of any kind of evil (ROH171). It broke my heart to read where Willard reminded us that our bodies and our whole beings were literally bought back from evil by God through the death of his Son (ROH170). It saddens me to admit that I have willfully sinned knowing this price that God paid to express his unconditional and relentless love for me in buying me back from evil through the grievous death of his only Son. Father God I am so, so sorry.

I enjoyed the spiritual discipline of lying on the floor and formally surrendering my body to God (WIDP117). It felt wonderfully freeing to release all the various parts of my body and to ask God to take charge of each part and to fill it with his life and to use it for his purposes. It was also wonderfully freeing and uplifting to accentuate the positive throughout this practice instead of dwelling on the negative. It is uplifting to believe and to feel that God will work his purposes for good in my members. I now seek to share this with a pastor and to ask for his or her blessing and perhaps even ask for an anointing.

Personally, perhaps the greatest misuse of my body in my life had been through relentlessly overworking my body in my prior career. My competing in business in the world while seeking to provide well for my family was a great misuse of my body and my precious time. I believe that I am now in a place in my relationship with God in my body, mind and spirit where I trust him wholeheartedly and can rest in his safekeeping and provision for myself and my family. Learning to Sabbath properly was a key breaking point for me in ridding myself of compulsively overworking and simply resting in his provision. Willard writes that the body must be weaned away from its tendencies to take control, to run the world, to achieve and produce, to attain gratification (ROH175). I found that this weaning process began for me through deep Sabbath rest and worship which ultimately transformed my life away from working in the world altogether.

The two basic forms of evil in our relation to others in assault or attack, and withdrawal or distancing, resonated deep within me as I reflected over my relationships. It was painfully obvious to reflect upon one relationship where I initiated a withdrawal and the Spirit has been reminding me to initiate toward repairing that important relationship which I have begun to do. Another has been deeply painful to experience as I have recently felt the withdrawal of my son in our relationship. Willard advises us that we must break away from these patterns and reverse them by a calm but firm non-cooperation with those poisonous elements, and then by taking initiatives of goodwill and blessing in the midst of them (ROH190). It is so critical here for me to unconditionally love my son in his withdrawal and to continue to uphold him in prayer.

Finally, experiencing shared love for one another within the body of Christ consistently is my heart's desire. Realizing that my primary "other" in experiencing this shared love is always God is an important reminder for me here in my relationships. Resting in God and in his vision of me as a whole person and trusting and knowing that he is working toward bringing me toward that whole person is encouraging and reassuring.

My Prayer
Father God, I am deeply grateful for your gift of free will and all that it means. I freely choose you and all of your ways. I am so sorry for all of those times that I have willfully not chosen you. Please forgive me. I surrender to you all the various parts of my body and I look forward expectantly to see how you may use them for your good. I also surrender to you all of my relationships and especially the two you have recently brought

to mind. Please repair and bless each of these dear relationships by the power of your Spirit. Amen.

CF 500, Teaching for Christian Formation
Willard Reflection #5 – WIDP Chapters 50 through 61
By: Terrence Dwyer, March 5th, 2010

Willard reminds us that we are "fearfully and wonderfully made" (Psalm 139:14). "That the human soul is a vast spiritual (nonphysical) landscape, with resources and relationships that exceed human comprehension; and it also exists within an infinite environment of which, at our best, we have little knowledge" (ROH 202). Reflecting back upon my spiritual encounters and experiences over the years, I'm astonished at my cavalier attitude toward these miraculous encounters at times. When I share these spiritual experiences with others they are often taken aback by them but to me they are just another day in the life with Christ. Walking by faith is walking in spirit and one would and should expect spiritual encounters when walking by faith. It is wonderful to think of the many miracles and amazing occurrences that I have experienced in my own life as well as the others that I have heard and read about in other people's lives. The spiritual universe is a powerful, awesome, and vast matrix at the ready for our access anytime we wish.

However, having accessed and tasted the magnificence of these sweet spiritual experiences it troubles me that I do not pursue them all the more through regularly practicing my spiritual disciplines. My slothfulness is convicting me here it seems. However, since having been in seminary now for just a few months I have steadily begun incorporating into my life and begun practicing certain spiritual disciplines. My prayer is to continually set more of myself to the side and to continually relax more into the Spirit who lives in me and loves others through me.

My soul so enjoyed reading the passages in Willard about acknowledging our soul, caring for our soul, resurrecting our soul language, and continually taking care to place our soul under God's daily care. Willard writes, "We simply have to rest in his life as he gives it to us" (ROH 210). This is such a simple yet profound sentence. When I take control of my life and sin and pull away from God my soul is no longer are at rest in God. Thankfully, God's precious laws convict me of my sin sending me back to God seeking his forgiveness. He again restores my soul to him and gives my soul rest.

Willard's passage in Chapter 11 on antinomianism was a real affirmation and further revelation for me on the magnificence of God's laws. Through this class and our work in Willard, and in our earlier work on teaching the Numbers passage regarding the Tallit and the Tzitzit, I have come to a deeper understanding of God's laws from his relational perspective. In my immaturity, I hadn't recognized how much the spirit of antinomianism had tarnished my faith. I encounter this spirit so frequently in this culture and in my faith community that it is disturbing to me. In reading Willard's passage on Law and Grace Go Together, I was reminded of my favorite healing books which is "Changes that Heal" by Dr. Henry Cloud. In his book he speaks of the importance of equal measures of grace and truth in restoring our lives toward health and wholeness. My soul so welcomes and gladly wears all 613 of God's laws knowing full well that I cannot obey them without his full measure of grace enabling me to freely do so. Praise God for his abundantly loving heart!

I so enjoyed reading Willard's passages on Children of Light. He writes, "Children of light will be empowered by God in eternity to do what they want, as free creative agents. Spiritual formation in Christ likeness during or lives here on Earth is a constant movement toward this eternal appointment." I so love to create and build. Often, the times that I have felt closest to God were the times that I was walking by faith, trusting solely in his provision, as I created and built businesses from scratch. He gave me a vision one time of a magnificent enterprise that I would so love to create with him but it doesn't seem likely that this will occur in my lifetime here on this Earth. Reading these passages in Willard reminded me of this vision again and gave me hope that perhaps one day in eternity I could once again freely create with God this beautiful expression of his heart. I actually found my soul panting after God as I reflected briefly again on this.

Once again Willard convicts me in his reminding us that we are to be discipling others for Christ. He writes, "The call of Christ today is to be his apprentices, alive in the power of God, learning to do all he said to do, leading others into apprenticeship to him, and teaching them how to do everything he said" (WIDP 160). There are a number of men in my life that God has placed it upon my heart at times to mentor and disciple. I need to pay more attention to this and to regularly lift these men up to God in prayer and to be ready and available for them as God connects us together.

Lastly, Willard writes further about transformation, "God's plan for the growth and prospering of local congregations has to do with immersing the apprentices into the Trinitarian presence. God's intent is to be present among his people and heal them, teach them, and provide for them"

(WIDP 173). How critical it is therefore to stay connected to a congregation of believers to be immersed into this Trinitarian presence of God. Willard goes on to say, "The ministers with time and experience expect to receive from the Christ-with-them profundity of insight, sweetness and strength of character, and abundance of power to carry out their role in the local group" (ROH 247). This is comforting to read and to know that the enormity of the task that lies ahead will be more than adequately met by God if ordination into ministry is finally someday realized. From where I sit now the task looks so overwhelming that I often times wonder why I am even pursuing this. But I need to remember that this is not my plan but that it was God who called me into the ministry and that he will meet me and abundantly provide for me whatever may be needed to carry our his intended role for me.

My Prayer

Father, I am grateful for the amazing gifts that you have given me by your Spirit. I pray for wisdom to remember to always walk in the spirit, always trusting in you in gratitude. I am grateful for your laws and how they remind me to always return home to you. Thank you for your mercy, your love and your forgiveness. Thank you for restoring my soul. I look forward to the day when I can once again be free to create with you in eternity. I am humbled by your calling me into ministry and daunted by the task that lies ahead but I trust that you will meet all my needs through your glorious riches in Christ Jesus. Amen.

FE 501 A - Field Education Internship
Fuller Theological Seminary
Advisor: Gwen Ingram
By: Terrence Dwyer, May 31st, 2011

Reflection Paper on the Cultural Context of my Internship Site

I have been blessed to be able to serve my internship this past quarter at Oakland City Church (OCC). OCC is a church plant of City Church of San Francisco and is an RCA denominational church. There is no membership into the church at this point in its' development but there are currently about 70 to 80 people attending the Sunday evening service. This is an urban church which is temporarily located in Laurel Elementary School in an East Oakland boundary neighborhood. Prior to relocating to Laurel the church was temporarily located at an Evangelical Free church location near Mills College which is another boundary location. This is a traditional church plant of the RCA denomination but it does have some elements of emerging church in its ethos of coffee shop neighborhood groups which we will address later. There are currently three staff positions including the founding pastor, a co-pastor, and a pastoral assistant. The church is seeking to add another staff position for music and worship in the near term.

OCC's slogan is that it is a new church in Oakland for purposes of gathering people who don't belong together around Jesus for the sake of those who don't belong. It is intentionally a church for the convinced and the unconvinced. Oakland is a divided community between the rich who generally live in the hills surrounding Oakland and the poor who generally live in the flats of East and West Oakland. The vision of the founding pastor, my supervisor Rev. Josh McPaul, is to plant a church in a boundary neighborhood of Oakland that would unite these disparities in Christian community through the power of the Gospel of Jesus Christ and through the Holy Spirit. The hope is for this Christian community to be a light for the Gospel by working together toward peace and unity within the challenging and diverse communities of Oakland.

The church is currently conducting a "summer tour" of the Oakland boundary neighborhoods by actually locating itself within each boundary neighborhood for one month over the summer before settling upon a final location at the end of the summer. OCC began for several months located near the Mills College area and then recently relocated to the Laurel District for the month of May. In June the church is relocating to the Dimond District of East Oakland and then on to the uptown area of West Oakland before finally settling into the Temescal boundary area of Oakland.

Given the vision and mission of the church and the fact that this is a new church plant, the culture of this church is very fluid and very much a work in progress. The church has already experienced the expression of its vision in the economic diversity of the people attending on Sunday. There is a good mix of upper middle class attendees from the hills and the wealthier neighborhoods in the area. In addition, there is a good mix of economically disadvantaged that are attending from the nearby boundary neighborhoods that the church has intentionally located itself into. There is also a large mix of those who are in between those two extremes and who may be considered middle class to lower middle class economically. The educational mix of this congregation also varies dramatically with several highly-educated professionals with medical degrees and PhD's to adults with felony convictions and no high school diplomas.

Additionally, the church has already experienced cultural diversity in the attendees at the Sunday service. Some of this diversity may in part be attributable to the intentionality of the founding pastor who is Caucasian and is already co-pastoring with an African-American. Possibly as a result of this intentionality, the church has a relatively balanced mix of whites and African-Americans. Additionally, the founding pastor has been intentional in bringing diverse cultural representation from the community into the leadership team of the church. The church is therefore well represented in both its leadership and in its attendees by a diverse cultural mix of Asians, Latinos, African-Americans and whites. The church also regularly celebrates its cultural diversity through experiencing together a different cultural meal at the end of every Sunday service. One Sunday for example will be an Ethiopian meal and the following Sunday will be a Mexican meal and so on.

Finally, the church has a good mix of age ranges from young children to mostly young adults to some middle aged and some young seniors. The pastoral staff and the young adults drive the unwritten very casual dress code for the church community. The potential merger with the more senior African-American congregation in a few months will likely balance the age range of this predominantly younger congregation. There also seems to be a wide mix of both churched and un-churched backgrounds of the attendees with the churched being mostly from the Protestant denominations of Presbyterian, Reformed Church, or Baptist. The experiences and the expectations of worship, while culturally diverse, may actually be somewhat denominationally similar. Therefore, while creating a meaningful worship experience for this diverse community is challenging, there is enough common ground and common worship experience among the attendees for the worship team to create a meaningful worship experience for the attendees.

The church is a theologically reformed church and its worship embodies the traditions of worship and sacraments of the reformed tradition. The sacrament of communion is practiced at every Sunday service and is open to all who confess and trust in the Lord Jesus Christ as their Savior. The sacrament of baptism by sprinkling is also practiced and the church has baptized one adult new believer and one toddler since beginning. The worship is contemporary with a contemporary band but it also has a solid African-American style from time to time. The worship service itself mixes in African-American elements of dance and poetry and music along with traditional hymns and testimonies. The preaching is the focus of every service and it is gospel centered and powerfully delivered and Scripture is lifted up as the ultimate authority in all matters for our life.

I have been collecting the cultural artifacts for some time now from this church and have collected a surprising amount of material for such a young church. There are monthly and weekly bulletins, post cards, t-shirts, a robust web-site and an excellent blog. There also is signage posted throughout the communities in which the church is relocating throughout the summer. The culture surrounding the communication dynamic within the church is predominantly through texting, email, web-site and blogging along with cell phones. One must be completely plugged into each of these means of communication to fully participate in the church's communication.

The neighborhood groups that I mentioned earlier are an integral part of the culture of this church. The church has begun three separate and distinct neighborhood groups located in three different boundary neighborhoods within Oakland. Each of the groups encompasses fellowship, prayer, and discussion stemming from a biblically based teaching that is a follow-up on the previous week's sermon. The groups are also seeking to integrate works of mercy and justice within their various communities within Oakland. In this way, these small groups will minister to each other and to their communities and thus achieve the vision of the founding pastor of the church as being a light within the communities of Oakland working toward the peace and unity of the city in Christ.

It has been a terrific learning experience for me to have participated in such a diverse and dynamic church this past quarter with Oakland City Church. I have learned of the difficulties and the delicacies of cross-cultural communication and of the importance of carefully tending to such communications. Communications from one cultural context with a clear and certain meaning can be received within another cultural context with a totally different meaning and understanding. The challenges of clear and culturally sensitive communication within a culturally diverse community are extraordinary. Praise God for the Holy Spirit who helps us with not only our communication but also with our understanding of what is being communicated. I now better understand why so many churches are culturally homogeneous because achieving meaningful cultural diversity is significantly challenging and requires extraordinary skill and spiritual maturity.

I believe that I have just scratched the surface of learning better cross cultural communication in my time here at Oakland City Church and I look forward to serving here in the future to continue this process of cross cultural growth and development. Learning to better communicate cross culturally enables me to be a better minister to our Lord's diverse church. Learning to minister better cross culturally enables me to serve our church better as it seeks to be a light within this challenging community at this most difficult time. I believe that my overseas training in cross cultural communication in Thailand and Uganda have prepared me for this task and has developed my sensitivities toward carrying out this learning task locally. I look forward to serving our Lord and his church wherever he calls me to do so and I look forward to serving his church in all of its rich diversity of people.

FE 501B – Field Education Internship
Fuller Theological Seminary
Advisor: Gwen Ingram
By: Terrence Dwyer, December 5th, 2011

Reflection Paper on my Personal Spiritual Discipline

The spiritual discipline that I have chosen to participate in is journaling at regular intervals on a weekly basis. The reason I chose this particular spiritual discipline is because it causes me to cease from my daily activities, to set aside time to rest, to spend time in the Word and to reflect and mediate upon it and then to process my thoughts through the act of writing them down on paper. I tend to express myself better through the written word when I have had time to reflect and to organize my thoughts and to express them to God.

It has been a remarkable season of growth and maturity over the months as I look back and reflect back on some of my past journal entries. The angst and worries and concerns that I wrestled with seem trivial now as I reflect back upon how the Lord led me through the process of going through each pathway toward growth. It is also a delight and an encouragement to remember and to recall the Lord's faithfulness throughout each of these times. My reflecting and remembering his faithfulness elicits from me my deep gratitude and my worship. My ceasing from daily activities is a way of practicing Sabbath.

The spiritual discipline of journaling has also been a means for remembering my calling at some very difficult junctures along the path. There have been several times throughout the process of letting go and answering my calling and entering into and through the seminary process where I have wrestled with my calling. There have been moments of difficult academic struggle particularly through the languages where I have seriously doubted the sanity of my calling. However, the process of ceasing, reflecting, and remembering my calling enables me to proceed again with faith that the Lord knows what he is doing and has his plans for my life. My task is simply to follow and to prepare for whatever he has in store for the next season of my life.

It has also been in part through the process of this spiritual discipline that I have grown into my pastoral identity and my pastoral authority. This process of growth has begun to develop and connect with my internship. Over the past months I have been enabled to step into the roles of preacher, teacher, and minister which have affirmed my pastoral identity and authority. As I continue to grow toward maturity in these roles I will continue to seek to practice the spiritual discipline of journaling among others to continue to remember, to reflect, to examine, to process, to worship and to express my gratitude.

In the process of opening myself up to God with this spiritual discipline I can better take the time for self-examination and for confession before God. God knows all so there is no reason for keeping anything hidden from him. By bringing things onto paper and into the light I can better examine them with him and with the clarity of his Word and in the presence of the Spirit guiding me. This process teaches me humility and submission to his will and his authority and rule in my life. It is a time for learning and a time for pruning and a time for seeking new growth.

One of the lessons learned in part through the process of this spiritual discipline has been the importance of self-care. The academic demands of seminary and other responsibilities had caused me to put off self-care for extended periods of time. The results of putting off or neglecting self-care were not a good witness for the Lord as I would not be at my best physically, mentally, or emotionally. In part through repeatedly seeing this thread run through my reflections, I initiated change into my daily disciplines and elevated self-care to a higher priority in my daily routine. This has resulted in a significant improvement in my over-all well-being which enables me to better serve the Lord throughout the day.

This spiritual discipline also allows me to better reflect upon my relationships with others and to remember them and how much their relationship means to me. It is a way of honoring them and remembering them for how they have poured their lives so richly into mine. It reminds me of the importance of honoring and deepening my relationships with others and the necessity of not only responding relationally but also the importance of initiating relationally. By reflecting upon my relationships I can also lift them up in intercessory prayer before the Lord. I have certain mentoring and discipling relationships that I can also remember and reflect upon and seek words of wisdom for at times. I also have accountability relationships with other men and my journaling helps me to reflect and remember what I need to discuss and share with my accountability partners. By looking back over journal entries I often see a thread of something that I will need to share with my accountability partner.

One of the practices I learned this past quarter from my senior pastor in my internship is the practice of writing out all of the thoughts that come to me as I spend time in the Word that I will be preaching prior to seeking out any other resource material. This was a significant change and improvement in my sermon preparation as prior to this change I would read the text that I was going to preach on and then seek out commentaries and begin building my sermon from there. However, the process of spending time in the text and writing out what the text means to me personally and what it brings to me and how it interacts uniquely with me is a terrific first step in my sermon building practice now. This practice helps me to sit and live more deeply with this Word in me until such time it needs to be preached. I still go to the commentaries to continue to build my sermons but the commentaries no longer drive my sermons. I've found this journaling practice to be affirming in a way that I hadn't expected. God has uniquely created me and given me a unique set of life experiences which is the lens through which I am to meet and preach his Word. I then turn to my community to test and verify that my experience, my understanding, and my interpretations are valid and true. It is only then after this process of reading, writing, sitting with the Word, verifying my understandings, and editing am I finally able to proceed with standing before the community to preach the Word of God. I am deeply grateful to my pastor for sharing this insight with me and for the growth that this insight has given me.

Throughout my internship we have also spent time together in community in the study of certain texts as the Gospel of Luke, Isaiah, and Psalms among others. Studying the Word in community gives differing perspectives which always adds richness and depth to the Word for me. It is important for me to remember these different perspectives and to write them down and reflect upon them. We also did book studies such as Bonhoeffer's "Life Together" among others and again it is the interaction in community with the richness of the different perspectives that adds a depth to the understanding of the material. Here again, It is an important spiritual practice for me to write down these thoughts to remember them and to reflect upon them along with my own experiences. At times, I will incorporate a devotional reading into my daily discipline and there are times when the devotional will spur something that I will want to write about to process the thought more fully.

My prayer life is often times "prayer on the run" as I'm going throughout the day. However, the spiritual discipline of journaling better focuses my prayer life. As I cease from the daily activities and spend time with my journal, I am better able to focus my prayer life as I have there written down various prayer needs and concerns that I might otherwise forget. One of the prayer practices that may be beneficial for me would be to seek out a prayer partner where we could spend time in prayer together. A spiritual discipline that I have neglected and have noticed a common thread that is on my heart lately is the practice of fasting. It is a spiritual discipline that I used to practice as a younger man but have fallen away from the spiritual practice lately. As returning to this spiritual practice has been on my heart I will seek to incorporate fasting into my spiritual discipline practices going forward.

In conclusion, in reflecting back over the course of the past several months I feel that I have grown and matured and am beginning to realize and step into my calling and into my pastoral identity and authority. The spiritual discipline of journaling has allowed me to remember, reflect, and process the ups and downs of the journey along the way. It has given me touch stones where I can look back and see where the Lord was with me and speaking to me and walking with me during the difficult times. This greatly encourages me which better enables me to proceed along the pathway ahead. There are moments of frustration not knowing where the Lord is leading me but those moments are fleeting as I can look back and see just how far he has led me every step of the way to this point.

FE 501C – Field Education Internship
Fuller Theological Seminary
Advisor: Gwen Ingram
By: Terrence Dwyer, February 29th, 2012

Reflection Paper on my Leadership Development Goal
1. Personal Leadership Development:

A. Restate your personal leadership development goal from your Learning Agreement, Section IID.

My personal leadership goal throughout my internship was to develop my experience and abilities toward mentoring and discipling young leaders within the congregation. We learn from Matthew 28:18-20 that Jesus commands us to go and make disciples.

18 Then Jesus came to them and said, "All authority in heaven and on earth has been given to me. 19 Therefore go and make disciples of all nations, baptizing them in the name of the Father and of the Son and of the Holy Spirit, 20 and teaching them to obey everything I have commanded you. And surely I am with you always, to the very end of the age."

We also learn from the Apostle Paul in Ephesians that we are to use our gifts toward the building up of the body of Christ.

11 So Christ himself gave the apostles, the prophets, the evangelists, the pastors and teachers, 12 to equip his people for works of service, so that the body of Christ may be built up 13 until we all reach unity in the faith and in the knowledge of the Son of God and become mature, attaining to the whole measure of the fullness of Christ. 14 Then we will no longer be infants, tossed back and forth by the waves, and blown here and there by every wind of teaching and by the cunning and craftiness of people in their deceitful scheming. 15 Instead, speaking the truth in love, we will grow to become in every respect the mature body of him who is the head, that is, Christ.

My leadership goal was to use what gifts that Jesus has equipped me with for the building up of his body the church of Jesus Christ. My prayer was to use these gifts toward mentoring and encouraging young leaders within the church in their walk with Christ.

B. Using a leadership situation, or a series of situations from your internship, discuss how the leadership situation(s) formed you as a Christian leader.

A recent event offers an example of a leadership situation in my internship that formed me as a Christian leader and which worked toward the building up of the body of Christ through all who participated in the event.

I and three others were tasked by our pastor to create and host an Ash Wednesday service combining the congregations of Oakland City Church and Faith Presbyterian Church. Our pastor clearly wanted our team to step forward and lead this service which we did. Our team began exchanging emails about ideas for the service and we set up a time to meet to go over our ideas. I being the choleric melancholy that I am, researched the history of the service, interviewed another minister that had done many Ash Wednesday services for ideas on what worked well and what didn't work in these services, and then wrote out a detailed suggested Ash Wednesday service plan for our group which I attempted to email to our team prior to our meeting.

Thankfully, praise God, the Lord stymied or blocked the ability to send the attachment with my email and I felt a strong impression from the Spirit that I should hold off and wait which I did. If my plan had been sent out, it would have dampened the spirit and creativity of our younger team members. Three of our four team members met the next day to discuss our ideas for the service and we together prayed over and put together our collective plan for the Ash Wednesday service which turned out to be a very nice Ash Wednesday Service for our combined congregations utilizing all of our ideas and suggestions. I never presented my previously written plan for the service to the team but instead worked collaboratively with the leadership team to encourage and affirm their ideas as we collectively created our service plan in community for our communities. As a result, I believe both I and the younger members of our team were edified in this experience thanks to the gracious intervention of the Lord.

C. How did you make theological sense of the leadership situation(s)?

It is Christ who is the head of the church and it is Christ who leads and who builds up his church. When we move too forcefully and not wait on the Spirit to lead and guide us in our planning and in our decision making then it is us who leads and not Christ. As I was walking in and working in my giftedness I lost sight of the community within which I was working and wasn't sensitive toward how I might dampen and quench the spirit and creativity of others who needed to express their own giftedness in community. Thankfully, the Lord graciously intervened and allowed me to prayerfully correct my behavior back toward walking and working in the Spirit in community with others.

D. How did your handling of the situation(s) reflect your growth as a leader?

This was a good learning experience for me in ministering to the church in community with others in community. On the one hand, I learned again about how my personality type can get in the way of ministering in community as I tend toward taking charge almost without noticing at times. Thankfully, the Lord graciously reined me in where I was able to meaningfully collaborate with other leaders in our prayerfully planning out this service. I learned that I was able to clearly articulate my ideas and theology for ministry without having to take control. I believe I learned and gained added sensitivity and receptivity toward ministering in community through this experience. On the other hand, I also learned that I was able to go to my ecclesiastical community for a wealth of resource on how to minister in areas where I have little or no experience. This experience also gave me confidence in my abilities to draw upon my collegiate community as a resource for ministry.

E. If applicable, what could you have done differently to improve your effectiveness as a leader?

Ideally, I would not have to be preemptively corrected by the Lord in a situation such as this but would know better to work in community with my brothers and sisters in Christ where all of the giftedness of the Spirit can be brought together collaboratively. As a leader I can improve toward fostering and encouraging the giftedness of others without quenching their giftedness with my own.

2. Future Ministry: Reflect on how this internship has shaped or influenced your call to ministry. How do you feel your participation in this internship will affect your future ministry (e.g. readiness for ministry, vocational choices, life balance in ministry, leadership capacity, etc.)? What has God revealed to you throughout your internship about yourself and your ministry?

When I reflect back on where I was at the beginning of this internship almost a year ago, to where I am today the growth and development has been significant. Granted there was my CPE experience over the summer which greatly solidified my pastoral role and pastoral identity. However, this church internship has also greatly shaped and influenced my call to ministry by further affirming my pastoral role and pastoral identity within a congregational setting. Although the opportunity to preach was limited here the experience of preparing the sermon with my supervisor was developmentally significant as well as affirming.

When I began this internship I really felt quite clueless about the work of ministry but believe that I have grown in my understanding of the shepherding work of ministry. I feel giftedness for and my heart is drawn toward a pastoral care ministry including the preaching and teaching of the Word. On more than one occasion the Lord has spoken into my heart the words from John 21:15-17;

15 When they had finished eating, Jesus said to Simon Peter, "Simon son of John, do you love me more than these?" Yes, Lord," he said, "you know that I love you." Jesus said, "Feed my lambs." 16 Again Jesus said, "Simon son of John, do you love me?" He answered, "Yes, Lord, you know that I love you." Jesus said, "Take care of my sheep." 17 The third time he said to him, "Simon son of John, do you love me? "Peter was hurt because Jesus asked him the third time, "Do you love me?" He said, "Lord, you know all things; you know that I love you." Jesus said, "Feed my sheep.

Where the Lord will lead me next in ministry I do not know but I trust that he already has the work prepared in advance for me to do. I look forward to following Jesus into the next step that he has prepared for me in ministry to his church and am deeply grateful for this experience.

CHAPTER 7: EVANGELSIM

EV525 Contemporary Culture and Evangelism
Short Paper #2: Interview
By: Terrence Dwyer, November 17th, 2011

For purposes of this paper I interviewed Alex, a non-Christian Asian male in his late twenties who works with a member of my family. Alex and I have had prior theological discussions as he knows I'm in seminary and he approaches me from time to time to ask theological questions. He readily agreed to participate in this interview. I find Alex to be somewhat typical of a person in their twenties today as someone who is very interested in spiritual things but who is not much interested the old meta-narratives. Alex has no interest in attending church.

Alex' understanding of what it means to be a Christian is closely tied to his understanding of the Bible. He believes that Christians are essentially people who follow the teachings of the Bible and that Christians believe that the Bible is inerrant. He vaguely ties Christianity to the historical teachings of Jesus Christ but seems to more closely align Christianity with the teachings of the Bible. He articulates fairly well what Christians believe about Jesus in that he is the Son of God, and is God, and that he died for all of our sins and was resurrected from the dead. I believe Alex is closer to a conversion to Christianity than most people I've talked to in part due to Alex's ability to clearly articulate the Gospel. He understands it but he has not yet put his full weight and trust into Jesus. A significant stumbling block for Alex is the Bible and the fundamentalist interpretation of it. Alex needs to hear a softer voice and an alternative to the fundamentalist voice when it comes to the Bible.

Alex believes that Christianity for the most part has been positive for society as people need to believe in something and Christianity does teach kindness toward others. He also gives Christianity the benefit of the doubt when it comes to the negativity surrounding Christians as there is always a negative side to everything and after all we're all sinners. I found Alex to be quite forgiving and understanding concerning much of the negative images of Christianity. However, he also doesn't seem to have experienced much negative personal contact with the faith other than the fundamentalist voice he picks up from the media. On the contrary, it appears that parts of his life have been blessed by his personal contact with those of the Christian faith. The term Gospel really didn't resonate at all with Alex as music was the first thing that came to mind regarding the term but then upon further reflection thought perhaps it referred to stories in the Bible. The Bible on the other hand was a topic of concern for Alex as he continued to press the inerrancy issue. He astonishingly concludes that because he doesn't believe that the Bible is inerrant (his terminology) that he cannot be a Christian. He believes that the Bible is a compilation of stories from the believers in Jesus and that these stories teach noble moral lessons which all societies should follow. He finds however, that the Bible is often taken of context by those who are trying to get others to believe in their way of thinking or to prove arguments which he finds offensive. Again, for Alex to become a Christian, I believe Scripture will need to be presented to Alex in a significantly different voice than the one he is currently hearing.

His reaction to the Christian belief that Jesus is the only way to God was interesting. In his analytical mind, he concludes that if Jesus truly is God then he would be the only way to God so he has no problem with this belief. This understanding and logical articulation of Jesus as the only way to God leads me again to believe that Alex may actually be close to his salvation. However, he goes on to argue that the Jewish and Muslim faiths all share the same God and that it seems impossible to argue one God over another as human interpretation of God is simply fulfilling the spiritual needs of various diverse groups of people.

What Alex likes about Christianity are the essential teachings of the faith (his words) such as being kind to others, caring for others, giving to those less fortunate than yourself. He also likes the idea that you can pray to God and ask forgiveness for sin in the name of Jesus. He also has a great deal of respect for people who find solace and comfort and a community of friends who share in their beliefs. What Alex doesn't like about Christianity is the Christian view on homosexuality. He believes same sex couples should be allowed to marry. He also doesn't like how Christianity is used in politics to gain power and control over others and how people are often slandered for not living a Christian lifestyle. He also thinks that Christians hold to archaic literal translations of the Bible where modern science has proven otherwise such as evolution for example.

Alex seems to have a relationship with God and this belief and relationship seems to govern his moral behavior. He prays to God and he says that God often answers his prayers through others. He asks God to forgive him when he does wrong and he says he often invokes the name of Jesus when he does this. Yet he believes he is not a Christian and doesn't call himself Christian nor has he given his life or put his faith in Jesus. He is not connected to any faith community but he does have many Christian connections in his life. He doesn't read the Bible and really has some strong opinions against the Bible and against certain Christian practices. Yet he can articulate the Gospel without being able to define the word Gospel. He's interested in things spiritual and he continues to remain quite curious about Christianity. I believe the Holy Spirit is working in this young man's life and I believe he is close to putting his full faith and trust in Christ.

Alex believes in God and he has an understanding of who Jesus is but the idea of a relationship with God is still foreign to him. I agree that having another conversation with Alex about our relational God through Jesus Christ would be helpful at this stage. My thought is to explore the relational God found in Genesis in the Garden of Eden before the fall and how God through His grace, mercy, and love restores this relationship through Jesus Christ. I would hope to explain to Alex that we can gain access to this relationship with God through the work of Christ and through the power of the Holy Spirit.

This could naturally lead us into a discussion on Scripture and the authority and inspiration of the Bible. Alex seems to have his strongest reservations about Christianity concerning the Bible. Alex says there are positives and negatives to everything and I would use this insight of his to explain how the Bible is often used inappropriately by people for power or control and that this is not the intention of Scripture. I would explain general and special revelation and how God through illumination uniquely revealed Himself to us through Scripture. I would go on to explain that Scripture speaks to us and guides us through the illuminating power of the Holy Spirit.

I would then like to discuss our lost state of being through sin and our inability to remedy the situation ourselves. The questions I would ask Alex here would be concerning sin and our inability to remedy sin on our own. I would explain that God, through His overwhelming love for us, provides the grace and the means for remedying the situation and that all we have to do is believe in His gift to us which is Jesus Christ. By believing we are not only forgiven, but our relationship with God is restored, and we are given the gift of eternal life.

Finally, the idea of going to church is difficult and foreign to Alex. I really like the video in week #9 of the class about a diverse group of people attending church by just being themselves and bringing their doubts with them. I would like to share this video with Alex and I believe it would open up a discussion about attending church. In this discussion I could share with him about fellowship and community and learning and doing works of compassion, mercy, and justice together as community. I believe Alex would warm to the idea of church when seen in this context.

EV525 Contemporary Culture and Evangelism
Short Paper #1
By: Terrence Dwyer, October 28th, 2011

I was raised in a practicing Catholic family so my first exposure to the Gospel was through the eyes of a child as I experienced receiving the sacraments of the Catholic faith and experienced participating in the Catholic liturgy. These early life experiences seemed to indicate to me that salvation through Christ was something that was administered upon me by others. I was then to try and live my life by a certain moral code of conduct as best I could. My experiences later life eventually altered this early formed perception of the Gospel.

In my mid-twenties, I had an encounter with an uncle who cornered me rather provocatively and preached the Gospel into me. I didn't much appreciate his method of sharing the Gospel but I was strongly attracted to the fruits of the Spirit that were evident in his life. A few years later when I was near suicide I reached out at the last moment for the hope of that Gospel message from my uncle and I immediately had a powerful and dramatic spiritual experience of re-birth. It was through the guiding, leading, and teaching by this Spirit that I learned of Scripture and through Scripture of Jesus and of the Gospel. I then subsequently had encounters with this living Jesus as I continued to grow along my journey of faith.

In my early thirties, the Lord led me to 1st. Presbyterian Church of Berkeley where I encountered strong Biblical teaching and preaching and a loving community of faithful believers. Here my experience of the Gospel was one of an intelligently reasoned through faith which was intelligently presented in careful and compassionate ways and often through life long committed Christian witness.

In my mid-fifties I find myself being called by the Lord into ministry and into seminary where the weight of the Gospel is not only being revealed to me in ever more expanding ways but the responsibility of preaching this Gospel message to others is settling further onto my shoulders.

All of these lifelong experiences of receiving the Gospel message in various forms have influenced how I view and practice evangelism. The most powerful influence I would say is the manner in which I received the Gospel message from my uncle. While I greatly respected the man, the manner in which he shared the Gospel message with me was provocative which left me feeling challenged and uncomfortable. However, his life earned my respect and therefore I listened to his Gospel message and it ended up saving my life in a sudden and dramatic fashion. I found that when opportunities did arise for me to share the Gospel, I tended to do so unapologetically and with a sense of urgency. I tended to not couch the Gospel message but to be rather straight forward and matter of fact when presenting the message.

However, my experiences with the Gospel message at 1st. Presbyterian Church of Berkeley and here at Fuller Seminary have given me a much deeper and wider understanding of the Gospel message. I therefore am now able to present the Gospel message in a much more reasoned through manner with perhaps a greater understanding and answer for some of the potential arguments that I may encounter. But this reasoned through approach toward sharing the Gospel still carries within it the sense of urgency that I inherited from my earlier experience with my uncle. Less of an influence on my manner of evangelism would be my Catholic upbringing. However, these earlier Catholic experiences have given me an understanding and appreciation of the faith experiences of Catholics, and others such as Episcopalians, where I am able to speak the Gospel message "in their own language".

My generational and cultural backgrounds have also influenced how I practice evangelism. I am a white, middle class, American male in my mid-fifties. I come from the generation of street corner and tele-evangelists and from the culture that hijacked the Gospel message into mainstream politics and war. Both my culture and my generation are largely responsible for the demise of the Western Christian church. I believe these realities impact my ability to connect with and to reach many postmodern people. I am however keenly interested in contextualizing the Gospel into postmodern culture through attempts at creating more culture. "Culture Making" by Andy Crouch speaks toward creating more culture while David Kinnaman's "Un-Christian" shows us example of "Building a coffeehouse instead of a church" (Page 145). These possibilities for contextualizing the Gospel message into postmodern culture excite me and I look forward to the possibility of the Lord perhaps someday utilizing my prior business skills in this manner.

Finally, because of the deep influences that so many well lived Christian lives have had on mine, I think that perhaps my best method of evangelism at the end of the day is a well lived Christian life. It was the evidence of the fruits of the Spirit in the life of my uncle that warranted my listening to and reaching out to the Gospel message he shared with me. It was the well lived out Christian lives at 1st. Presbyterian Church of Berkeley and elsewhere that deeply wove the Gospel message into my own life. So, my approach is to depend upon the Lord to enable me to live a life worthy of the Gospel and a life where the fruits of the Spirit shine through. Then as the Lord brings opportunities for sharing the Gospel message, I will seek to bring all of my life experiences and gifts to bear in the sharing of the Gospel message with others.

An Evangelism Project Plan for Oakland City Church
By: Terrence Dwyer, December 5th, 2011
Fuller Theological Seminary
EV525 Contemporary Culture and Evangelism
Professor: Dr. Kimberly Thacker

Introduction
I am currently serving as a pastoral intern at Oakland City Church located in the Temescal neighborhood of Oakland. I served on the original launch team for this one year old church plant and also currently serve on the Executive Committee as the church Treasure. As a pastoral intern, my responsibilities are to participate in weekly staff meetings and to support the pastoral team wherever possible in a variety of supporting roles. We have two lead pastors, a music director, an administrator, and two pastoral interns.

We are a new church plant for the city of Oakland and it is our vision to plant a new church within a boundary neighborhood of Oakland seeking to bring the diversity of the city together around Jesus. Our mantra is that we are gathering people who don't belong together, around Jesus, for the sake of those who don't belong. We are seeking to bring together people of different economic, social, cultural, ethnic, and religious backgrounds together around Jesus. We find our common identity in the grace of Jesus and in his authoritative word. We currently have around 80 regular attendees on Sunday. After worshipping in three different boundary neighborhood locations during our initial year, we have now finally settled into the Temescal neighborhood where we share space with Faith Presbyterian Church. It is our desire to reach out deeper into this community to serve, to minister, to preach, to worship, and to evangelize.

The Vision

The Temescal neighborhood is a widely diverse neighborhood which has been experiencing the process of gentrification for the past few years. There are three elementary schools, one middle school, and two high schools within walking distance of the church representing over 3,000 students from numerous cultural backgrounds. Oakland International High School for example is just one block away and has immigrant students from all around the world attending the school. Our vision is to reach out to these students and their families within our neighborhood with the Gospel of Jesus Christ. We are seeking to evangelize our non-Christian neighbors well by loving them well evangelistically as we seek to love, serve, and worship God well.

Our Strategy

We have a variety of strategies for reaching the community with the Gospel message such as neighborhood BBQ's and volunteer work days at school campuses, neighborhood Bible studies and church meetings in local café's, etc. However, for purposes of this final project paper we are going to focus on just one strategy that we are currently planning on implementing. Our strategy is to develop a unique and inviting community meeting space from an existing under-utilized space within our church facility. This is a rather large space (2,000 sq. ft. with adjoining kitchen) that we would make available to the students and their families and the neighborhood for their use. We are not starting with a blank slate but we are starting with what has been handed down to us from the previous generation which is currently under-utilized and seeking to create something new to add to the surrounding culture. During the course of our interactions with those utilizing the space we will meet them with the Gospel of Jesus Christ in a variety of different ways.

Our Goal

Our formation goal is to have this community space designed, remodeled, and introduced to the neighborhood by the end of the first quarter of 2012. Our evangelism goal for the remainder of 2012 is for a 25 % growth in regular church attendees by the end of the year as a result of the addition of the ministry of this community space for the neighborhood.

The Plan

The practical and organizational details of proceeding with this plan and achieving our goals can be broken down into the three main categories of creating, sustaining, and ministering.

-Creating: The organizational plan for the creation of this ministry has a number of steps that need to take place in both a chronological and a concurrent order. During the creation phase we will need buy-in and approval to proceed with the plan from both Oakland City Church and Faith Presbyterian Church from whom we are sharing this space. We will need to go through an interior/exterior design phase incorporating as many of the visions for the space from the various ministry and community stakeholders. We are particularly interested in the vision and ideas for the space from our high school and college age group stakeholders and are seeking to have this group lead the development of this project. A capital budget for the cost of the design and remodel of the space will need to be developed along with fund raising accomplished to cover at least the initial cost of the new space. Concurrently with these tasks we will need to be interacting with our existing and new relationships within the community toward sharing and marketing our vision for the space and eliciting their input, ideas, and feedback from the community.

-Sustaining: The organizational plan for sustaining the ministries within the new space will need to be developed within the creation phase. A monthly operating expense budget for the new space will need to be developed along with recommendations on obtaining adequate funding to meet these monthly expenses. Church and volunteer staffing needs for each of the ministries within the new space will need to be reviewed and addressed by each ministry. Regular means of communication to and from the community regarding the use of the space will need to be established and sustained. Examples of community members with whom communication will need to be sustained with are neighbors, schools, businesses, community groups, etc.

-Ministering: Our means and methods of communicating the Gospel to our postmodern culture community must contemplate and contend with the powerful conflicting messages currently being sent out by over $400 billion spent annually on advertising. We also must contend with the conventional Gospel message often rejected by post moderns which in effect says that the Good News is such that if you want to escape eternal punishment in hell for your sins you must repent and believe Jesus was punished in your stead for you to get into heaven. All those who don't believe will be banished to hell and the earth will be destroyed. To reach post moderns our Good News message will need to contemplate the more emergent view that God loves humanity even in its' lost state and that God graciously invites all to turn from their current path and to a new way of following him which will transform you and the world around you.

The essential use of the actual space will be a gift to and for our neighborhood community. The design of the space will incorporate a variety of areas for small group meeting and discussion to take place. From comfortable seating around a fireplace, to a large table for at least twelve people, to an outdoor patio seating area, etc. It is in these settings that church members can engage and participate in one on one and in group dialogue where the Gospel can be discussed in an open and non-threatening manner. Post moderns perceive Christians as being unwilling to engage in genuine dialogue and only wanting to engage in proselytizing. In seeking to become genuine conversation partners with those utilizing the space we will need to have the perspective that we are all on a spiritual pilgrimage together and that we are each at different points on this journey. We each have our own issues that we are wrestling with and we each need to move forward on our journey and we need to be able to lovingly express what the Gospel means in our spiritual journey with God.

In addition to places for engaging in dialogue where the Gospel message can be shared, we will have our music ministry integrated into the space expressing the Gospel message in a variety of engaging and contemporary music styles. In addition to our music ministry, we will engage a variety of contemporary art mediums from drawings to paintings to sculpture, etc. to express the Gospel message visually throughout the space. We will also engage a contemporary digital and video ministry from wide screens TV's for video expressions of the Gospel message to wireless access, etc. We will also develop a library space and a place where quiet reading and contemplation may occur. In addition to the above ministries, we will have programmatic ministries available for the community to access such as, Seeker meetings, Bible studies, Book studies, Alpha type courses, addiction and recovery meetings, anger management meetings, health clinics, food distribution, etc. all available at this community space for the community.

The ministry of food and of sharing meals together is a significant means of building connections and relationships and thus opening up further opportunities for dialogue and for the sharing of the Gospel. We envision a dynamic food ministry integrated into the use of this space as we have a good sized commercial kitchen connected to the space.

Conclusion

We currently have a rather large space within our church facility that is closed off and inaccessible to our neighborhood community. This space is also being significantly under-utilized buy our church community. Through some creative attention to design we can open this space up for public use by our neighborhood community who are mostly non-Christians. We can then invite them in and actively and lovingly interact with them, meet them where they are on their spiritual journeys, and develop our relationships with them. We can dialogue with them, answer their questions in a non-threatening environment, meet their needs as best we can through some of our program ministries, provide them with a space for their own personal use, and over time share the Gospel of Jesus Christ with them in a loving, supporting, caring, open, and generous manner.

We believe that through the above ministry we will be available for opportunities for the Spirit to minister to others through us. John reminds us, "The Spirit alone gives eternal life. Human effort accomplishes nothing. And the very words I have spoken to you are spirit and life" (John 6:63; NLT). The Gospel message and the words of Jesus contain life and power and we are called to speak this life giving message and these life giving words into others as if we're planting seeds into them. We believe that this ministry for our neighborhood community will allow us gracious opportunities to lovingly speak these words of life into our neighbors as we're led by the Spirit to do so.

Bibliography

Crouch, Andy. Culture Making, Recovering Our Creative Calling. Downers Grove: IVP Books, 2008.

Jones, Scott J. The Evangelistic Love of God & Neighbor. Nashville, TN: Abingdon Press, 2003.

Lyons, David Kinnaman & Gabe. Unchristian. Grand Rapids: Baker Books, 2007.

McLaren, Brian D. Everything Must Change. Nashville: Thomas Nelson,

2007.

Peace, Richard. Holy Conversations. Downers Grove: IVP Connect, 2006.

Taylor, Craig Detweiler and Barry. A Matrix of Meanings, Finding God in Pop Culture. Grand Rapids: Baker Academic, 2003.

MP520-Book Review #1 By: Terrence Dwyer, May 7th, 2012
Lesslie Newbigin
The Gospel in a Pluralist Society
Grand Rapids, Michigan
William B. Eerdmans Publishing Company, 1989

Lesslie Newbigin was an ordained minister for the Presbyterian Church in Scotland where he served as a Church of Scotland Missionary to the Madras Mission in India. Newbigin served as a missionary there from 1936 until he retired in 1974. During this period he also served as Bishop to the Diocese of Madras for the Church of South India as well as the General Secretary of the International Missionary Council and as an Associate General Secretary of the World Council of Churches. After Newbigin retired he returned to England where he continued to preach, teach, and write extensively on theology and missiology until his death in 1998. Newbigin's lengthy missionary work of preaching the Gospel into an Indian culture filled with a plurality of religions and gods, eminently prepared him to return to the plurality of Western culture where he sought an authentic expression of the Gospel in the midst of Western pluralism.

Newbigin begins by defining pluralism as a characteristic of secular society in which there is no officially approved pattern of belief or conduct. Only those truths that can stand up under the critical examination of the modern scientific method can be taught as fact or truth and all the rest is just relative dogma. Newbigin's thesis is to examine how to preach the Gospel as truth in this situation without the Gospel being domesticated within the assumption of modern thought but challenges these assumptions and calls for their revision.

Newbigin challenges Descartes in his chapter on Knowing and Believing by describing a world of facts without value and a world of values which have no basis in facts which views the cosmos as having created itself without any purpose. Newbigin counters with the Christian story which gives us a set of lenses to look through to view the cosmos with meaning and purpose. In his chapter on Reason, Revelation, and Experience, Newbigin describes the differences between the two ways of understanding the world, one in which the self is sovereign and the other in which we only understand ourselves in relation to our community. Newbigin goes on in the next chapter on Revelation to defend the revelation of God throughout history and the particular revelation of God through Jesus Christ. In his great chapter on Election Newbigin describes the relational purposes of God in electing a select group of people who are responsible for relationally bringing the Gospel message to others. Newbigin defends the Bible as a universal history for humankind in that it gives a vision of cosmic history from beginning to end including all the nations and the one nation and the one man who is the bearer of the meaning of history for the sake of all. Newbigin describes history as having meaning in that history has a goal which is the fully revealed reign of the risen Christ. As faithful believers, our actions in the world now are signs which point to the reality of this coming Kingdom which gives hope to the world. In his chapter on the Logic of Mission, Newbigin states that the true meaning of the human story has been disclosed in Christ and that this truth must be universally shared. The heart of mission is simply the desire to be with him and to serve him and his mission with our lives. Newbigin argues that the Gospel message must be contextualized in a manner in which people can understand and receive the message. The faithful Christian community, including well trained and well led congregations living out the truth of the Gospel message, is that contextualization in the world representing the absolute truth of Jesus Christ.

I believe that Newbigin's book is an important work in the area of helping to establish an authentic expression of the Gospel message to a world filled with a plurality of religions and cultures. Newbigin's background of preaching the Gospel message into the plurality of religion and culture in India has trained him well on articulating the essential truths of the faith for mission to a pluralistic world. I believe that this book is eminently appropriate for our course here on transforming contemporary culture as Newbigin lays out in his work a sound missional theology for doing so.

Newbigin's thesis was to examine how to preach the Gospel as truth into a pluralistic society without the Gospel being domesticated within the assumption of modern thought but challenges these assumptions and calls for their revision. I believe the author succeeded in defending his thesis by challenging the fallen thought processes of the world and through affirming the revelation of God, Scripture, the reign of the risen Christ, and the mission of His Church in the world. What was a deeper revelation for me in this important work was the critical importance of believers living out the Gospel message in community with each other. This living out the Gospel message in community is the hermeneutic of the Gospel which is the contextualization seen by the world which transforms the culture and the world until Christ returns. In the same way, let your light shine before men, that they may see your good deeds and praise your Father in heaven (Matthew 5:16; NIV).

MP520-Book Review #2, By: Terrence Dwyer, May 7th, 2012
Wilbert R. Shenk
Write the Vision, the Church Renewed
Eugene, Oregon
Wipf and Stock Publishers 1995

Wilbert R. Shenk earned his Ph.D. from the University of Aberdeen in Scotland and he is the Senior Professor of Mission History and Contemporary Culture in the School of Intercultural Studies at Fuller Theological Seminary where he has taught since 1995. Prior to joining Fuller he served for 25 years as the director of and vice president of Overseas Missions for the Mennonite Board of Missions which included the oversight of mission ministry in some 20 countries. He is an ordained minister in the Mennonite Church and a founding member of the American Society of Missiology.

The thesis of this book may be stated as follows: The engagement of the church with modern Western culture has resulted in the marginalization of Christian faith. Simultaneously, the missionary movement has been the catalyst for extending the faith to other continents with the result that the majority of Christians are now found outside of the West. When the church in the West is truly renewed, it will be a church with integrity and clear sense of mission to its own culture. The author supports his thesis by assessing the integrity of the Church, the mission of the Church, evangelization, and the Church itself. Shenk argues that a "lack of integrity in the Church has undermined the credibility of the Church in modern Western culture. Wherever the Church is controlled by culture, it forfeits its prophetic word. To have credibility and command the loyalty of its members, the Church must have ecclesial integrity." (p.7) In this section Shenk reviews certain persons in history such as Wesley, Kierkegaard, Winnington-Ingram, Hobhouse, and Barth, all who in their own time assessed the Church as being compromised with current culture and called for the church to change course. "When the church has surrendered its independence, it can only echo the voice of society. And when the Church no longer speaks Truth to its culture – the Word alone can judge and transform- it becomes subject to culture. Cultural conformism ends in cultural captivity." (p. 28) The author goes on to state that the "true identity of the church will be (re)discovered in response to the presence of the kingdom of God in the lives of the people of God.

In his section on Mission, Shenk makes several important points as he articulately argues for the mission of the Church. He takes us through the history and theology of missions for the Church and concludes for the Western Church that what happened "out there" was mission and what happened "at home" was church. The crises in the church in the West was treated as a pastoral problem and not that the church in the West had lost its missional focus to its own culture. "A compromised church is a church that has surrendered its mission. The criterion by which we may judge the recovery of the church's identity is whether the church has a restored missional consciousness." (p. 32) Jesus is our model for a missionary encounter with our own culture as he met people where they were with compassion while speaking truth to them as he pointed them to a renewed life through God's loving redemptive power. "The faithful witnessing church will therefore, present a contrast to the surrounding culture and must expect to live in tension with the larger culture and possibly endure hostility. The church remains socially and salvifically relevant only so long as it is in redemptive tension with culture" (p. 48)

In his section on evangelism the author takes us through the history and theology of evangelism and ties evangelism with the integrity of the church. Shenk argues that a church that is busy with "activities" has been distracted from its primary task of announcing and demonstrating the reign of God and the way to integrity is to return to the task of evangelism which will require a break from captivity to culture and Christendom mentality. Shenk makes several additional key points in his section on the church where he reviews some history but then clarifies the true church and its mission. The vision for the church is one in which it is a worthy instrument for God's redemptive passion for the world, a holy nation who proclaims the mighty acts of God as ministers of reconciliation in the world.

I believe that Shenk's book is an important work in articulately establishing the groundwork for calling the church back toward a renewed vision of its mission for God. Shenk eloquently convicts the church without condemning her and offers a clear pathway for the church to return to her mission of preaching the Gospel and making disciples. I believe that this book is eminently appropriate for our course on transforming contemporary culture as Shenk lays out in his work a sound missional theology for transforming culture without acquiescing to it.

I believe the author succeeded in defending his thesis as he clearly demonstrated the loss of integrity within the church and he clearly offered the vision and the path for regaining it. He also clearly refocused both mission and evangelism back toward the mission of God for the church. This was an important and timely read for me as I have been seeking for unique ways to reach our current culture with the Gospel and this book has refocused me on the mission and the critical importance of building up disciples while not acquiescing to culture.

MP520-Book Review #3, By: Terrence Dwyer, May 25th, 2012
John Drane
After McDonaldization
Grand Rapids, Michigan
Baker Academic, 2008

Dr. John Drane is an adjunct professor at Fuller Theological Seminary and teaches at the University of Manchester in the MA in the Emerging Church Program. He is the former head of practical theology in the department of divinity at the University of Aberdeen. He wrote the acclaimed work, The McDonaldization of the Church which identified the catastrophic trend of Western churches offering uninventive worship to dwindling congregations. Drane is the author of many books including Introducing the Old Testament and Introducing the New Testament. Church attendance continues to decline throughout the West even though people are turning to spirituality in greater numbers. In After McDonaldization, Drane continues the conversation he began in The McDonaldization of the Church and reviews what it means to be Christian in a post-Christendom context as he studies the impact of globalization, consumerism, and the post 9/11 culture of fear and subsequent search for truth and their impacts upon the church.

Drane begins by stating his thesis that if the church continues on the same path, the decline in church attendance in the West will continue unabated and that this decline will be catastrophic. He asks instead how faithful discipleship might be imbedded into the culture and he encourages the church to take whatever steps are necessary to re-imagine church life. Drane exhorts the church to think outside the box and to imagine what the Christian future might look like and feel like if we allow ourselves to do so. He reminds us that our God's primary attributes are creativity and imagination and that now is the time to step out in faith into risky spaces for the sake of the church trusting that God is already there and that God is with us as we do so. The author examines the five key areas of culture, community, mission, ministry, and theology as he makes his argument supporting his thesis.

In his chapter on culture, Drane states that the reason churches are struggling is that the gap between the culture of the Church and the lived experiences of its members was widening on an almost daily basis. The Church simply is not speaking to the life experiences of its members and people are leaving in droves and not coming back. Their disillusionment was not directly connected to the Gospel as such, but they were rather unable to get beyond the institutional structures and systems in which the message had been embodied. Churches offer the same rigid structures that people find themselves trapped in and are trying to escape from. Drane argues that the post 9/11 culture of fearfulness is a bigger challenge than we realize and that one of the most important things the church can offer is hope and that re-imagining a relevant biblical eschatology of hope should be our top priority.

In his chapter on community, Drane argues that in the Conceptual Age that we are living in; everything is being questioned and redefined including our communities and even our families. Our inherited religious institutions have come to be regarded as not just irrelevant but implausible and unbelievable and secondary institutions are developing as a result such as on-line communities. Drane argues brilliantly here that rather than importing culture into the church to make it cool we need instead to become wombs of the divine and completely rebirth the church into the host culture. The inherited division between the sacred and the secular is to be dissipated if favor of a more organic unity of all things.

In his chapter on mission Drane argues that mission is better done ecumenically and that in today's post-modern world, mission is going to be more intuitive and relational rather than rational and logical presentations of Christian doctrine. He states that our concern to be relevant is destroying many churches when the call of the Gospel is to be incarnational. In his chapter on ministry he shares a study that revealed that people who left the church did not have problems with seating, music, sermons, or liturgy but that they left the church because of the acrimonious ways in which church people related to one another. He states that not only must we live out the Gospel message of loving one another but that we need to invite people to see things in light of the bigger story of what God is doing. In his chapter on theology, Drane argues that we have turned theology into an intellectual hair-splitting exercise that disregards the incarnational nature of the Gospel and which places ourselves at the control of the whole process which undermines the relational nature between God and ourselves.

In conclusion, Drane makes excellent arguments in support of his thesis and his call to re-imagine our ways of doing church is eloquently expressed in his work here. He challenges us to recycle what we have inherited from the past and to reshape them into something that will be more serviceable and more meaningful and lasting for those who follow.

MP520-Movie Review, By: Terrence Dwyer, May 26th, 2012
Amelie and Moulin Rouge

I chose to review Amelie and Moulin Rouge because I adore both of these films and because I greatly appreciate the extraordinary creativity in each of these films and in their own unique expressions of the search for love. There are multiple postmodern themes that run through each of these works but two that stand out to me are relational fragmentation and the meaning or purpose for existence. My thesis is that the main characters within each film search for love amidst the relational fragmentation of postmodern culture as the meaning and purpose of their existence.

Amelie is a young woman living in Paris and working in a café in 1997 when her life is awakened by the death of Princess Diana in a car wreck. She comes to the realization that life is fleeting and that she has yet to experience the love she desires so she begins by connecting with the people in her life in a deeper way in hopes of finding the love that she is yearning for. Amelie had a very difficult childhood in that her mother died tragically when Amelie was only eight years old. Her father was a physician who only touched her during examinations and who misdiagnosed a heart condition for Amelie whose heart raced whenever her father touched her as she was starving for human affection. She subsequently does not attend school with other children and is even further isolated from others where she does not receive the affection she so desires.

Despite her difficult childhood, Amelie grows into a lovely young woman who eventually begins her search for the love she desires by intentionally connecting with others once her life is awakened through the tragic death of Princess Diana. Her postmodern relationships are hopelessly fragmented but she whimsically perseveres and pursues making the connections that she hopes will give her life meaning and purpose and bring her the love that she so desires. Amelie begins he quest by eventually bringing together two regular but lonely customers in her café – Georgette and Joseph – who end up romantically together through Amelie's efforts. Through the amorous connection of Georgette and Joseph, Amelie vicariously experiences the romantic relationship she desires but cannot yet find. Amelie discovers an old box of toys in her apartment and she searches for the original owner and gives them back to him. He is thrilled to see his old toys and he relives his childhood through this gift from Amelie who is finally able to share and connect with another child which she was unable to do in her childhood. Amelie next becomes good friends with an aging artist who lives near her flat and whose bones are so brittle that everything in his flat must be padded. The advanced age and fragility of this old artist only serve to heighten Amelie's deep need for physical connection and deep bonding with another so her search continues. Finally, in an extraordinarily fragmented relationship, Amelie falls for Nino, a lonely adult video store clerk who enters her café but she has no idea how to approach and connect with him directly so she stalks him. Amelie identifies with and relates to the quirky and lonely Nino who has the odd hobby of collecting discarded photos from photo booths. In entering into relationships with others, Amelie finds meaning and purpose for her life through helping others and by being kind to them. Through her quixotic relationship with Nino, Amelie has found hope for the deep, romantic, and physical love that she has so longed for her entire life.

While Moulin Rouge also takes place in Paris, the setting is in the 1890's in the bohemian world of café's and music and theater of the Montmartre district of that time period. The late 19th century is the beginning of the heady times of postmodernism this film brings to light the postmodern themes of the search for the meaning and purpose of existence and of relational fragmentation. The main character, Christian, is a young man who leaves his wealthy family behind and searches for the meaning of existence in the decadence of the bohemian life of the theater where he seeks to become a playwright. Here he seeks to find and to write about truth, beauty, freedom, and love which he eventually experiences in Satine, the star of the Moulin Rouge, but who eventually betrays him due to her cruel circumstance. Knowing that she is dying of tuberculosis and that she cannot fulfill the life of love that Christian desires with her, she sacrifices her love for Christian in order to save the theater for her beloved owner Zidler. The postmodern theme of ethical and moral relativity appears here in Moulin Rouge as Satine is willing to sleep with the rich Duke of Worcester in order to save the theater. Betrayed by Satine, Christian storms away at the height of the premier of their show, but is reminded by his own words from his play that "the greatest thing he will ever learn is simply to love and to be loved in return." He returns to Satine only to have her die in his arms at the final curtain of their premier. Christian discovers and loses the deep love of his life all within minutes and while he has found the reason for existence and purpose in life, his existence is wretched as he has discovered and lost the very thing that gave his life meaning and purpose.

Both of these films deal with the postmodern theme of the search for meaning and purpose for existence. Once Amelie's life was awakened through the death of Princess Diana, Amelie found meaning and purpose for her life through making connections with others and by being kind to them and bringing happiness into their lives as best she could. Christian found meaning and purpose for existence through writing for the theater and ultimately through falling in love with Satine which he thought promised to give his life ultimate meaning and purpose but whose death shattered his dream. Satine's search for meaning and purpose for existence was satisfied in that she saved the theater for her beloved Zidler and she awakened the heart of Christian for love.

Both films also dealt with the postmodern theme of relational fragmentation with each film displaying extraordinary relational fragmentation throughout. Amelie's entire life is one of relational fragmentation as she was unable to connect with and have deep, meaningful, lasting relationships throughout most of her life. At the end of the movie we are left with the hope that the awakened Amelie who has found ways to connect with others through kindness will now be able to have the deep and meaningful relationships that she so desires. Relational fragmentation was also evident throughout the mercurial life of the theater in bohemian Paris as relationships were often bartered and transient at best. Christian found his love and the hope for the deep, meaningful, and lasting relationship he so desired in Satine but it was not meant to be.

Finally, the theme of ethical and moral relativity was vaguely expressed in Amelie through the immediate amorous relationship of Georgette and Joseph but which otherwise was not actively promoted. Moulin Rouge more openly and actively promoted ethical and moral relativity through the actions of Zidler, Satine, and the Duke of Worcester along with promoting the morally relative decadent bohemian lifestyle of those at the Moulin Rouge.

EV525: Contemporary Culture and Evangelism
Short Paper #1 – Response
By: Terrence Dwyer, November 12th, 2011

How would you describe the essence of faith/gospel to someone now?

I would describe the essence of my faith and the Gospel message with someone today from the perspective of the loving nature of God. God is love and God freely chose to share this love by calling forth creation into existence. This loving God gave human beings a certain autonomy or freedom to act and a freedom to choose to love God in return. We chose instead however to rebel against God and all of creation fell as a result and sin and death entered the world. In our broken and sinful humanness, we cannot repair our broken relationship with God. However, because God so loved the world, God sent his only Son Jesus into the world and he took all sin and death upon himself to the cross. Through his death on the cross and through his resurrection the power of sin and death in the world was defeated. Through our belief and faith in this free gift of love from God in Christ, our broken relationship with God is restored and sin no longer has power over us. We may still sin but the power of sin has been broken by Christ. We are also forgiven for all of our sin so we no longer need to carry the guilt for our sin. When we place our faith in Christ, God sends us the Holy Spirit who comforts us, teaches us, and guides us along the pathways back toward God. God has also revealed himself to us through Scripture which the Holy Spirit uses to teach and guide us along our path. Additionally, the power of death has been defeated by Christ and through our belief and faith in Christ we are freely given the gift of eternal life. We will still die in this life but the power of death has been broken and through Christ we will share in this gift of eternal life. Finally, God has also given us the community of faithful believers where we can be in fellowship with others who can mentor us and guide us along our path and where we can worship God together and participate with each other in works of mercy and justice for others.

-Do you think having this urgency is good for evangelism? Is it something we should encourage in others? How can we hold onto urgency and also patience and not being pushy?

I do believe that having a sense of urgency about sharing the Gospel is good for evangelism. My personal experience attests to this as I would have been lost if my uncle simply didn't feel like sharing the Good News he held that day. I believe that we should encourage others to have a sense of urgency about us when it comes to sharing the Gospel. The Apostle Paul certainly can be our inspiration here. I also believe though that being pushy about witnessing for the Gospel can have the opposite effect and drive people further away from Christ. I believe we should pray and be attentive to the Holy Spirit for those opportunities to share the Gospel and then to do so without hesitation when those opportunities arise.

Final Research and Missiological Application Paper
"So whether you eat or drink or whatever you do, do it all for the glory of God." 1st. Corinthians 10:31
By: Terrence Dwyer, June 5th, 2012
Fuller Theological Seminary
MP520 – Transforming Contemporary Culture
Professor: Dr. Wilbert R. Shenk

Introduction

I am continually beset by two nagging issues that I seek to address at least in part through this paper. The first is the significant decline in church attendance throughout North America and most certainly in our local community here in Oakland. The second is the glaring and complete absence of recognition of the reign and the presence of God in "secular" space. An example of traditional "secular" spaces that do not recognize the reign or presence of God are commercial businesses such as cafés and restaurants. My contention is that the Church must be more creative in taking its' mission into traditional secular spaces such as these and other "secular" enterprises. In this paper I will begin by reviewing the problem of declining church attendance that we are experiencing in North America as well here in our community of Oakland. I will then propose and analyze a potential response from the Church to this problem and included within this discussion will be our Missiological application. I will then critique this particular response from a biblical and theological perspective. Finally, I will offer an alternative approach to my proposal that is missiologically sound for comparison and then conclude.

Therefore, my thesis is that a Christian café is an appropriate Missiological space for the Church to engage the current culture in the missio Dei. To be clear, I am not arguing for cultural conformity here, but for the Church to occupy traditional cultural space as an alternative venue for the expression of its mission to the culture. Dr. Wilbert R. Shenk, Senior Professor of Mission History and Contemporary Culture at Fuller Theological Seminary states; "Mission should be conceived of as an inherently cross-cultural action, a movement mandated by the Triune God into territory that does not acknowledge the reign of God."

The Issue of Declining Church Attendance in the West

Eddie Gibbs, the Donald A. McGavran Professor of Church Growth at Fuller Theological Seminary and Ryan K. Bolger, Assistant Professor of Church in Contemporary Culture at the School of International Studies, have written extensively on the emergent church movement within the West. They have this to say about the decline of the Western Church; "Both in the U.K. and in the U.S., the decline of the major traditional denominations has been well documented. This decline began in the mid 1960's and continues unabated in most cases to the present time. This decline includes all traditions and it means that churches are now seeking to reestablish contact with people three and four generations removed." These authors also make the keen observation that "much of what we understand as historical church practices is simply cultural adaptations that occurred at other times and places in church history. The church must "de-absolutize" many of its sacred cows in order to communicate afresh the good news to a new world."

The Barna Group is one of the leading research organizations providing research data on the intersection of faith and culture. David Kinnaman, the President of the Barna Group, recently wrote this about the decline in church attendance in North America; "Millions of young outsiders are mentally and emotionally disengaging from Christianity. The nation's population is increasingly resistant to Christianity, especially to the theologically conservative expressions of that faith. A huge chunk of a new generation has concluded they want nothing to do with us. As Christians, we are widely mistrusted by a skeptical generation." These young outsiders are avid spiritual seekers and they hunger to have discussions, but they perceive Christians as unwilling to engage in dialogue and unwilling to listen. Christians are perceived as only interested in conversion and not at all interested in dialogue. Kinnaman uncovered six broad themes in his research about perceptions of Christians. We are perceived as hypocritical, too focused on getting converts, anti-homosexual, sheltered, too political, and judgmental.

Dr. Shenk offers a broader historical context for the decline of the Church in the West and argues that the engagement of the church with modern Western culture has resulted in the marginalization of Christian faith. Simultaneously, the missionary movement has been the catalyst for extending the faith to other continents with the result that the majority of Christians are now found outside of the West. "When the church in the West is truly renewed, it will be a church with integrity and clear sense of mission to its own culture." Shenk argues that a "lack of integrity in the

Church has undermined the credibility of the Church in modern Western culture. Wherever the Church is controlled by culture, it forfeits its prophetic word. To have credibility and command the loyalty of its members, the Church must have ecclesial integrity."

Dr. John Drane, Adjunct Professor of theology at Fuller Theological Seminary calls for the Church to think outside the box and to allow ourselves to imagine what the Church of the future might look like if we allow ourselves to imagine church differently than what we are doing now. He writes, "Many churches are now facing up to the reality of the decline that has been affecting all major denominations for 20 years and more, and we are realizing that to continue as we are may be comfortable, but could also be institutionally suicidal. Our options are simple. We either do nothing, and the decline continues, or we ask fundamental questions about how faithful discipleship might be incarnationally embedded in the culture, and take whatever steps may be necessary to re-imagine church life. If we truly believe in a God whose primary attribute is creativity and imagination, then we can step out in faith into even risky spaces, confident in the knowledge that we are not alone, and that God may well already be ahead of us."

A Proposed Response to the Problem and its Missiological Application

Mark Batterson is the Pastor of National Community Church which owns and operates one of the largest coffee houses in the Metro D.C. area. He says this about why they decided to build a coffee house instead of another church building, "Because Jesus didn't hang out in synagogues. He hung out at wells. Wells weren't just places to draw water. Wells were natural gathering places in ancient culture. Coffee houses are postmodern wells." My proposal here is a similar response toward engaging the culture in a "non-church" venue like Batterson's coffee house in Washington D. C. My proposal is to create a Christian café to engage the culture with the Gospel in a venue traditionally considered "secular" space. I propose that a Christian café is an appropriate Missiological space for the Church to engage the current culture in the missio Dei.

The essential use of the actual space will be as a café for a local Oakland neighborhood community and the café will be open and inviting and accessible for everyone within that community. It will be a space where believers and non-believers can mingle together in a venue traditionally considered to be "secular" space. The design of the space will be multi-functional and will incorporate a variety of areas for informal groups to gather and discussions to take place. From comfortable seating around a fire pit, to a large table for large group gatherings, to an outdoor patio seating area, along with traditional café seating arrangements. It is in these settings where believers in Jesus Christ who are deeply committed and connected to the Church may engage and participate in one on one and in group dialogue where the Gospel can be discussed in an open, whimsical, and non-threatening manner.

In addition to places for engaging in dialogue where the Gospel message can be shared, we envision a digital and a live music ministry integrated into the space expressing the Gospel message in a variety of engaging and contemporary music styles. In addition to the music ministry, we will engage a variety of contemporary art expressions from drawings to paintings to sculpture to express the Gospel message visually throughout the space in addition to embedding the Word of God visibly into certain physical structures of the space. We also envision engaging a vibrant film and video ministry showing a wide variety of film and video expressions of the Gospel message. We also envision a "digital free" area within an area of the space much like a "smoke free" area where quiet reading, contemplation, and where digital free conversation may take place. In addition to the above ministries, we envision additional ministries available for the community to engage with such as guest speakers, guest preachers, and guest musicians, along with Bible studies, book studies, and seeker type classes. In addition, various community groups may want to include addiction and recovery meetings, anger management meetings, health awareness, and free food distribution, among others, all available at this Christian café for use by the entire community.

Missionary and Theologian Lesslie Newbigin's lengthy missionary work of preaching the Gospel into an Indian culture filled with a plurality of religions and gods eminently prepared him to return to the plurality of Western culture where he sought an authentic expression of the Gospel in the midst of Western pluralism. Newbigin defines pluralism as a characteristic of secular society in which there is no officially approved pattern of belief or conduct. Only those truths that can stand up under the critical examination of the modern scientific method can be taught as fact or truth and all the rest is just relative dogma. Newbigin's argument is to examine how to preach the Gospel as truth in this situation without the Gospel being domesticated within the assumption of modern thought but challenges these assumptions and calls for their revision.

The Missiological purpose of these café type spaces is to create open and inviting spaces where these conversations can take place daily between pluralist culture and the Church. Our Triune God is relational and has relational purposes in electing a select group of people who are responsible for relationally bringing the Gospel message to others. In a pluralist society where millions of young outsiders are mentally and emotionally disengaging from Christianity the Church needs to create new and imaginative spaces where opportunities to share the hope of the Gospel can take place in dialogue. These conversations are far less likely to take place in traditional church venues in our pluralist society and the Church must seek more creative ways to reach this culture with the Gospel.

Newbigin argues that the Gospel message must be contextualized in a manner in which people can understand and receive the message of the Gospel and I argue here that these café spaces are one possible way to contextualize the Gospel message into today's pluralist culture. Brothers and sisters in Christ living out the hope of the message of the Gospel in community with each other and in front of and side by side of non-believers in creative and imaginative spaces is the hermeneutic of the Gospel. This is one way of contextualizing the Gospel which will be seen by the world and which will be transformative to the culture and the world until our Lord Jesus Christ returns.

A Critique of this Response from a Biblical and Theological Perspective

"When they landed, they saw a fire of burning coals there with fish on it, and some bread. Jesus said to them, "Bring some of the fish you have just caught." So Simon Peter climbed back into the boat and dragged the net ashore. It was full of large fish, 153, but even with so many the net was not torn. Jesus said to them, "Come and have breakfast." None of the disciples dared ask him, "Who are you?" They knew it was the Lord. Jesus came, took the bread and gave it to them, and did the same with the fish. This was now the third time Jesus appeared to his disciples after he was raised from the dead." (John 21:9-14; NIV)

This description of Jesus humbly displaying hospitality toward his disciples during his third revelation to the disciples after being raised from the dead is an extraordinarily moving picture of our Lord. Jesus prepared well in advance for the arrival of his guests as he had the fire burning with fish cooking on it and with bread already prepared. He asked for and received some of the disciple's fish to use in their meal together which he cooked for them and then he served them their breakfast. This is extraordinary humility and hospitality from our Lord and through this experience the disciples came to know and commune with the risen Christ. Eating and drinking together, fellowshipping around a meal together, in dialogue with each other and getting to know one another are characteristic of the ministry of Jesus Christ and are ministry characteristics embedded within the ethos of these café's.

"A new command I give you: Love one another. As I have loved you, so you must love one another. By this everyone will know that you are my disciples, if you love one another." (John 13:34-35; NIV) Brothers and sisters in Christ living out the hope of the message of the Gospel in community with each other is the hermeneutic of the Gospel. These café experiences is the Gospel of peace being lived out and contextualized within community with seekers and non-believers who will witness the presence of the Holy Spirit in the love and joy that believers will openly show for one another.

In the same way, let your light shine before men, that they may see your good deeds and praise your Father in heaven (Matthew 5:16; NIV). In a society where millions of young outsiders are mentally and emotionally disengaging from Christianity these café spaces are places where the light of Christ may shine before others and a place where the good deeds of brothers and sisters in Christ may be seen and observed and ultimately with all glory given to God. These community spaces will be places where peaceful works of mercy and justice emanate from within the community and are for the community. These works of mercy and justice will be opportunities for believers and non-believers to walk and work side by side where the light of Christ may shine before others and where glory may be given to God and where the hope of the Gospel message can be shared.

Dr. Richard J. Mouw, the President of Fuller Theological Seminary, author, and professor of Christian philosophy argues that everything ultimately belongs to God and will be redeemed by God. He writes, "We do not have to abandon the works of human culture to the Devil. All of the commercial and technological and military "stuff" that we see around us still belongs to the world that God has made and will someday redeem. We must train ourselves to look at the worlds of commerce and art and recreation and education and technology, and confess that all this "filling" belongs to God. And then we must engage in the difficult business of finding patterns of cultural involvement that are consistent with this confession. If, in a fundamental and profound sense, God has not given up on human culture, than neither must we." "The earth is the LORD's, and everything in it, the world, and all who live in it." (Psalm 24:1; NIV)

A Missiologically Sound Alternative Proposal

What I am proposing above will be challenging to accomplish on a variety of different levels, one of which will be the expense involved in acquiring and creating spaces such as the ones I've described above. Another alternative is to look at the traditional church structures that the Church has accumulated over the years some of which now stand empty or are nearly vacant. Many of these structures hearken back to the era of Christendom and many appear as uninviting, fearfully imposing fortresses within their communities. A Missiologically sound alternative proposal; is to rehabilitate certain church structures that could be readily transformed from their current traditional usage into these cafe' spaces. Certain people may balk at setting foot into traditional church space but these kinds of objections may be overcome through creative rehabilitation of the space. Thus our Missiological goals may still be achieved through the rehabilitation of existing space as an alternative to acquiring and creating new space.

Conclusion

We began this brief review by assessing the problem of declining church attendance that we are experiencing in North America. We proposed and analyzed a potential response from the Church to this problem through the creation of unique and imaginative café spaces where believers and non-believers can meet and where the hope of the Gospel can be lived out, observed, and experienced by believers and non-believers alike as the light of Christ shines through brothers and sisters in Christ in community with each other. We included within our discussion the Missiological application of these café spaces and we critiqued our modest proposal to the problem of the decline of the Western church from a biblical and theological perspective and we considered a Missiological sound alternative approach to our proposal.

These café spaces are not seeking to conform to the culture but are places for the Church to occupy as an alternative venue for the expression of its mission to culture. These spaces are appropriate spaces for the Church to engage the current culture in the missio Dei. "So whether you eat or drink or whatever you do, do it all for the glory of God."(1st. Corinthians 10:31; NIV)

Bibliography

Bolger, Eddie Gibbs and Ryan K. Emerging Churches. Grand Rapids, Michigan: Baker Academic, 2005.

Drane, John. After Mcdonaldization. Grand Rapids: Baker Academic, 2008.

Lyons, David Kinnaman & Gabe. Unchristian. Grand Rapids: Baker Books,

2007.

Mouw, Dr. Richard J. When the Kings Come Marching In. Grand Rapids: Wm. B. Eerdmans Publishing Co., 2002.

Newbigin, Lesslie. The Gospel in a Pluralist Society. Grand Rapids, MI: William B. Eerdmans Publishing Company, 1989.

Shenk, Wilbert R. Write the Vision: The Church Renewed. Eugene, OR: Wipf and Stock Publishers, 1989.

CHAPTER 8: APOLOGETICS

PH 510 Christian Apologetics   Professor: Dr. Kimberly Thacker
Final Exam, By: Terrence Dwyer, March 10th, 2010

Section 1: Short-answer

Toulmin focuses on Isaac Newton as one of the key architects of the modern worldview in the 17th century. Newton followed upon Descartes who had initially asserted that human reason was the foundation for truth which he summed up in "I think therefore I am". Newton built upon Descartes' modern worldview beginning by mathematically showing that reality has an absolute existence beyond the human mind and that the human mind can come to know this reality through scientific reasoning. Newton showed how matter in the universe is governed by fixed laws which were established at the creation of the universe. Newton asserted that matter is in itself inert and required a higher agency to set it into motion. Newton thus believed in a creator God who is the highest, most powerful, self-moving agent in nature. Newton also believed that God has a very logical divine mind that set all of creation into place and got it up and running according to certain permanent physical laws which Newton uncovered, described, and proved in his seminal work "The Principia". The affect that Newton had upon the modern worldview mind was that God came to be understood as the grand architect of the universe who got things going according to eternal and unchanging laws but who didn't intervene. According to Newtonian thinking there was no need for God to intervene as it might upset the perfect mathematical balance of God's own creation.

Zacharias puts forth an excellent apologetic for the existence of God to those who don't believe in the existence of God due to the existence of evil in the world in his chapter 5 entitled, "Is God the source of my suffering?" Zacharias states that if evil exists, then one must conclude that good exists in order to perceive the difference between good and evil. If good exists, one must conclude that a moral law exists by which to measure good and evil and if a moral law exists then it would follow that there is an ultimate source of moral law or at least an objective basis for moral law. As Christians we believe that God is necessary for us to even conceive of the notions of good and evil. A non-Christian may argue that through the process of natural selection that things like evil may appear to exist but they are just the permutations or random "outliers" within a universe of blind physical forces and genetic replications. The DNA neither knows nor cares as it replicates onward. There is no good, no evil, no justice and no God. Some DNA is lucky and other DNA gets hurt in its' process of marching onward.

Richard Dawkins argues that people act in a moral way toward each other for essentially four reasons related to the process of natural selection and gene replication. The first reason is that people will care for, defend, share resources with, warn of danger, and generally show altruism towards close kin because of the statistical likelihood that kin will share copies of the same gene pool which is seeking to replicate itself. Secondly, people act morally toward each other for reciprocity such as the repayment of favors given, and the giving of favors in anticipation of payback which is the basic principle for all trade and barter between humans enhancing survival. Thirdly, people act morally toward each other for purposes of acquiring a good reputation for generosity and kindness which enhances gene replication. Finally, people act extravagantly generous toward others in a manner of way of advertising and demonstrating superiority as a way of attracting mates and thus further ensuring gene replication.

I believe that it is important for Christians in our contemporary postmodern context to know that the Bible is a historically accurate and reliable text. The Biblical text that we have today is reliable because there are far more and far older copies of the Bible than of any other ancient text. Using criteria for the reliability of ancient manuscripts, the Bible we have today has a very high probability of being an accurate copy of the original texts. We have 24,000 ancient manuscripts of the Bible, some from as early as the 2nd century A.D., while there are just 650 ancient manuscripts for Homer's Illiad. We have many copies of the Bible from different locations which are in agreement with each other as well as attestations from third party texts quoting passages from the Bible. There are some variants in the text which can be accounted for due to scribal error but none of these variants affect any major ideas, theological themes, or historical events. We also know that the Bible is historically accurate in that third party external sources attest to the historical accuracy of the Biblical text. Examples of these external source documents are the historical writings of Josephus,

Tacitus, Pliny the Younger, and ancient Jewish literature. Additionally, the fulfilled prophecy within the Biblical text is also evidence for the texts' historical reliability. The Bible accurately foretells specific events in detail many years before they occur. There are approximately 2,500 prophecies in the Bible of which around 2,000 have already occurred and fulfilled to the letter without error. The probability of this is unusually extraordinary and is further attestation to the historical accuracy and reliability of the Biblical text.

I believe in Jesus Christ when he says, "I am the way, and the truth, and the life. No one comes to the Father except through me" (John 14:6 ESV). I am not pluralistic in that I believe in Jesus when he says that no one comes to the Father except through him. Jesus claimed to be the Christ, the son of God, and he claimed that he and the Father are one. He also performed many well documented miracles and extraordinary healings that attest to his claim. I therefore believe that Jesus is the way, the truth, and the life and that pluralism does not satisfy my need for knowing the way to God. I am also not relativistic in that I believe in what Jesus says when he says that he is the truth. I believe his claim to the truth for the same reasons I mentioned above about his claim to the way. I therefore believe Jesus is the truth which satisfies my need to know the truth. My life experience has taught me that there is absolute, objective truth in this universe and Jesus satisfies my need for an answer to the existence of this truth. This is good news for any non-Christian in our contemporary society because belief and faith in Jesus Christ and in his claims gives one eternal salvation, forgiveness of sins, acceptance and a relationship with God and with others, self-worth, identity and a life purpose in addition to many other blessings in this world.

Section 2: Essay

In my discussion with Susan about Jesus I would begin with simply affirming the historical existence of Jesus for her as she didn't seem to know very much about Jesus. I would confirm for her that scholars from all backgrounds agree that the historical evidence confirms without a doubt that Jesus was an actual historical figure who lived on the earth in the early 1st century. There is also agreement among scholars from all backgrounds that Jesus was a Jewish rabbi, a religious leader and teacher and a known miracle worker. These facts are attested by Christian, Jewish, Muslim and other scholars and historians both religious and secular.

Secondly, I would affirm for Susan in our discussion of the divinity of Jesus as she was unsure of what that means and whether or not people actually believed that to be true anymore. I would tell Susan that I absolutely believed in the divinity of Jesus and that millions of Christians believe today and have believed throughout the ages in his divinity. I would point out for Susan that Jesus was a singularly unique religious leader and teacher in that he made extraordinary claims to be the divine Son of God and demonstrated his divinity through his extraordinary actions here on earth. Some of these actions were spiritual acts which only God could perform such as; forgiving sins, bringing the kingdom of God, judging humanity in the future, and granting eternal life through himself. Jesus also either calls himself or is called by others certain titles which point to his divinity such as the Christ, the Messiah, or the Son of God. Jesus also performed extraordinary miracles signifying that he is the Son of God by casting out demons, healing people, raising the dead and exercising control over nature. People were astounded by these miracles at the time and thousands of people followed him around seeking healing from him. Jesus also taught with an authority never seen before by challenging and changing interpretations of Jewish law and claiming to be teaching God's original intent regarding these laws.

Jesus also made several other unique statements revealing his divinity such as calling God his Father and teaching us that we can do the same if we follow him. He also claimed to be divine by saying that he was one with the Father, and that he was the way the truth and the life and that he was the way to God. Jesus also referred to himself as the bread of life and the light of the world. Finally, Jesus was arrested and condemned to death for blasphemy specifically because he claimed to be equal to God. Jesus discusses his death and resurrection for the salvation of sins with his disciples well before these events happen.

Thirdly, I would confirm the evidence for Susan in our discussion that Jesus did in fact raise himself from the dead for our salvation from sins as Susan had no idea that people still believed in that. I would initially affirm for Susan that the Scriptural evidence that we have describing the events of the resurrection is more reliable than any other ancient document we have because of the many very early manuscripts we have from texts originally written during the 1st. century. I would follow that affirmation with the empty tomb description in the Gospel texts along with how Roman crucifixions worked by expediently killing their victims. Jesus was no doubt dead, buried, and sealed in a guarded tomb by Roman guards who would be executed if they failed in their duty to guard the tomb. However, the tomb was found to be empty.

Susan would most likely be interested to know that the text asserts that Jesus first appeared to women after his resurrection. This is unusual within that ancient cultural context as women's testimony at that time didn't count so anyone making up this story would not have the first witnesses in the text be women. If the resurrection text were fabricated they most certainly would have had Jesus first seen by the most credible male witnesses such as Jesus' closest male followers such as disciples like Peter, James, and John.

Jesus also was seen by many groups of witnesses after the resurrection including his disciples and many of his followers including an appearance to 500 people at one particular appearance. Jesus did not live to an old age but ascended into heaven after these resurrection appearances. Finally, the followers of Jesus were radically transformed after his resurrection. During the arrest and execution of Jesus and prior to his resurrection, the disciples and followers of Jesus were fearful, scattered and in hiding from the authorities. Upon seeing Jesus after the resurrection, his disciples and followers came out of hiding and became emboldened and were publicly proclaiming Jesus with the consequences of losing their homes and livelihoods, being arrested, tortured, and executed. Subsequently many of Jesus' followers were martyred for their unwavering belief in his death and resurrection for the salvation from our sins. It is highly unlikely that these followers of Jesus would suffer and die so terribly for something they knew was a lie. It is very plausible that they genuinely believed that Jesus had indeed risen from the grave.

If Mr. Triplett came to me several years after this happened still wrestling with these theological questions I would be deeply concerned for him and his emotional well-being as his pastor. The central issue that Mr. Triplett was wrestling with was his understandable but misguided belief that his sinfulness had somehow caused the death of his son. He was consumed with the theological question of whether or not God had taken his son's life as a payment for his own sinfulness or to teach him a lesson. Additionally, Mr. Triplett was suffering from severe guilt from his own sin against God on the day of his son's death which he has yet to resolve. As his pastor, I would seek to speak into Mr. Triplett's life in an attempt to move him from his misguided theological belief and in an attempt to offer him a pathway toward relief from his guilt. I would use Scripture to speak into Mr. Triplett's life in each of these areas.

I would seek to resolve the theological question first as much of his guilt stems from his misguided belief that God took his son's life as payment for his sins on the day of his son's death. It is critical here for Mr. Triplett to dissect himself theologically from the death of his son. He needs to clearly understand that the life of his son is separate and apart from his own life. Here the tragic story of Job may help Mr. Triplett. Upon hearing that his seven sons and three daughters had been killed Job says, "Naked I came from my mother's womb, and naked shall I return. The Lord gave, and the Lord has taken away; blessed be the name of the Lord. In all this Job did not sin or charge God with wrong" (Job 1:21-22 ESV). Job understood that God gave his children to him at birth and God has taken them in their deaths. Mr. Triplett needs to come to a similar humble understanding that his son's life belonged wholly to God. The psalmist also speaks eloquently to our allotted time here on this earth, "Your eyes saw my unformed substance; in your book were written, every one of them, the days that were formed for me, when as yet there was none of them" (Psalm 139:16). The book of Ecclesiastes also speaks to this even more succinctly, "a time to be born, and a time to die; a time to plant, and a time to pluck up what is planted" (Ecclesiastes 3:2). Mr. Triplett would need to see from these texts and understand that the length of the life of his son was written by God before his son was even born. Nothing Mr. Triplett could do or not do could alter the number of days his son was to live on this earth. Mr. Triplett would need to see and fully accept that his actions on that day had absolutely nothing to do with his son's death. Coming to this theological understanding would begin the process of freeing Mr. Triplett from believing that he caused his son's death.

Connected to the above misguided theological belief, Mr. Triplett also erroneously believed that his son's death was God making him pay for going against his wishes that day. Mr. Triplett's theology was again misguided and needed correcting here. Mr. Triplett would need to clearly understand that the entire payment for all sin has already been paid for through the death and resurrection of God's own son Jesus Christ. God did not need to take Mr. Triplett's son to make him pay for his sins that day as God had already paid for all sin through the death of his own son. I would again speak Scripture into Mr. Triplett's life here to help him see this truth more clearly. "But God shows his love for us in that while we were still sinners, Christ died for us" (Romans 5:8, ESV). From 1st. Corinthians, "That Christ died for our sins in accordance with the Scriptures, that he was buried, that he was raised on the third day" (1 Corinthians 15:3-4, ESV). From these scriptures Mr. Triplett would need to see and understand that the payment for his sins and for the sins of all humankind has already been paid through the death of Christ.

As his pastor, I would also like to take a moment through the use of Scripture to reassure Mr. Triplett regarding the well-being of his son whom he described as a dedicated Christian man. "For God so loved the world, that he gave his only Son, that whoever believes in him should not perish but have eternal life" (John 3:16, ESV). I would reassure him that his son is alive and well and with Christ as Paul says in 2nd. Corinthians, "We are confident, I say, and would prefer to be away from the body and at home with the Lord" (2 Corinthians 5:8, ESV).

Finally, I would attempt to offer Mr. Triplett a pathway toward relief from his guilt by speaking into his life the assurances that we find in Scripture regarding the forgiveness of our sins. In Romans we hear the assurance that, "There is therefore now no condemnation for those who are in Christ Jesus" (Romans 8:1, ESV). "For he has rescued us from the dominion of darkness and brought us into the kingdom of the Son he loves, in whom we have redemption, the forgiveness of sins" (Colossians 1:13-14, NIV). "If we confess our sins; He is faithful and just and will forgive us our sins and purify us from all unrighteousness" (1 John 1:9, NIV). As difficult as it must be for Mr. Triplett to forgive himself for his sins against God on that particular day he must eventually do so in order to be free from the burden of guilt that he is carrying. Perhaps God spoke so directly to him on the day of his son's death because of God's love for him. God knew that his son's earthly life was ending that day and God knew the personal anguish that his sinful behavior would bring so God spoke to Mr. Triplett that day out of God's deep love for him.

My longtime friend Dan fits the description of the nominal Christian outlined in this question including having the overall feeling of depression about life in general as well as a lack of self-worth and significance. I am genuinely concerned about Dan's well-being and would like to make the following points in sharing with him during an upcoming lunch meeting.

I would make the point with Dan that I believe his overall feeling of depression and lack of self-worth and significance is directly tied to his lack of clarity about who he is in Christ and the purpose Christ has for his life. I would encourage Dan by reminding him of his identity in Christ Jesus through the use of Scripture. Jesus says, "I am the light of the world. Whoever follows me will never walk in darkness but will have the light of life" (John 8:12, ESV). When we remain in darkness we live inauthentic lives with ourselves and with others. We live with inner guilt, shame and low self-worth. We need to come into the light of Christ by being honest about the negative parts of our lives and to experience the loving acceptance and forgiveness of Jesus who restores us to a right relationship with God and with others. By allowing Jesus to transform our lives in this manner he gives our lives worth and a purpose. I would remind Dan that he is loved (1 John 3:3), accepted (Ephesians 1:6), and a child of God (John

1:12).

I would continue to encourage Dan to seek after God as we are made for relationship with God and to be willing to change as God asks him to change. I would remind Dan that we all need to own up to the brokenness in our own lives and to accept God's plan of forgiveness and commit to follow him. We cannot overcome the sin that is in our lives through our own power but only through Jesus Christ may we overcome sin. "Who will rescue me from this body of death? Thanks be to God through Jesus Christ our Lord!" (Romans 7:24-25, ESV). It is the sin in our lives that negatively influences our attitudes and our self-worth. We need to be healed, cleansed, and transformed to be restored to our relationship with God and with others. Paul says in Corinthians, "Therefore, if anyone is in Christ, he is a new creation. The old has passed away; behold, the new has come. All this is from God, who through Christ reconciled us to himself and gave us the ministry of reconciliation" (2 Corinthians 5:17-18). I would also greatly encourage Dan to enter into a church community where he can learn the ways of love, acceptance, forgiveness, encouragement, growth, and service toward others. I would remind Dan that we also become transformed by entering into community with each other. Paul says in Philippians, "Do nothing from rivalry or conceit, but in humility count others more significant than yourselves. Let each of you look not only to his own interests, but also to the interests of others. Have this mind among yourselves, which is yours in Christ Jesus" (Philippians 2:3-5).

I would conclude with Dan by encouraging him that God has a purpose for his life. That he was created in the image of God to worship and glorify God and to love and serve others. Jesus asks us to accept our purpose and he invites us into his kingdom by our surrendering all our worldly pursuits for purpose and to follow him. Paul says in Ephesians, "For by grace you have been saved through faith. And this is not your own doing; it is the gift of God, not a result of works, so that no one may boast. For we are his workmanship, created in Christ Jesus for good works, which God prepared beforehand, that we should walk in them" (Ephesians 2:8-10). I would also tell Dan about one of the great early church philosophers, Augustine of Hippo and of his great work, Confessions. In this work Augustine explains that our lives are given true meaning and special significance by doing the good works which God has prepared beforehand for us to do because it brings us closer to the very source of our life and of all reality. We love and do unto others as we would like to be loved and have done unto us.

Bibliography

Cottingham, John. Western Philosophy, an Anthology. Malden, MA: Blackwell Publishing, 2008.

Dawkins, Richard. The God Delusion. New York: Houghton Mifflin Company, 2008.

Hugh Ross, Ph.D. Fulfilled Prophecy: Evidence for the Reliability of the Bible. Menlo Park 2011.

Thacker, Dr. Kimberly. The Bible. Menlo Park: Fuller Seminary, 2011.

Thacker, Dr. Kimberly. Human Identity and Purpose, Part 2. Menlo Park: Fuller Seminary, 2011.

Thacker, Dr. Kimberly. Jesus Historical Existence, Divinity, and Resurrection Menlo Park: Fuller Seminary, 2011.

Toulmin, Stephen. Cosmopolis. Chicago: The University of Chicago Press, 1990.

Zacharias, Ravi. Jesus among Other Gods. Nashville, TN: Thomas Nelson, 2000.

PH 510 Christian Apologetics
Session #4 – Core Human Identity
By: Terrence Dwyer, January 27th, 2011

My core human identity is wrapped up within my identity in Christ.

Galatians 3:26-29;
26 So in Christ Jesus you are all children of God through faith, 27 for all of you who were baptized into Christ have clothed yourselves with Christ. 28 There is neither Jew nor Gentile, neither slave nor free, nor is there male and female, for you are all one in Christ Jesus. 29 If you belong to Christ, then you are Abraham's seed, and heirs according to the promise.

Therefore, my core human identity is consumed by my identity in Christ. At my core, I no longer exist but it is Christ who lives in me. In addition to my core identity I also can lay claim to the following promises of God which impact my identity. All of these on this list in addition to my

core human identity in Christ are radically different from what my surrounding cultural context tells me who I am which is independent, self-reliant, competitive, strong, of this world, godless.
- I am loved – 1st John 3:3
- I am accepted - Ephesians 1:6
- I am a child of God - John 1:12
- I am Jesus' friend - John 15:14
- I am a joint heir with Jesus, sharing His inheritance with Him - Romans 8:17
- I am united with God and one spirit with Him – 1st Corinthians 6:17
- I am a temple of God. His spirit and his life live in me – 1st Corinthians 6:19
- I am a member of Christ's body – 1st Corinthians 12:27
- I am a Saint - Ephesians 1:1
- I am redeemed and forgiven - Colossians 1:14
- I am complete in Jesus Christ - Colossians 2:10
- I am free from condemnation - Romans 8:1
- I am a new creation because I am in Christ – 2nd Corinthians 5:17
- I am chosen of God, holy and dearly loved - Colossians 3:12
- I am established, anointed, and sealed by God – 2nd Corinthians 1:21
- I do not have a spirit of fear, but of love, power, and a sound mind- 2nd Timothy 1:7
- I am God's co-worker – 2nd Corinthians 6:1
- I am seated in heavenly places with Christ - Ephesians 2:6
- I have direct access to God- Ephesians 2:18
- I am chosen to bear fruit - John 15:16
- I am one of God's living stones, being built up in Christ as a spiritual house – 1st Peter 2:5
- I have been given exceedingly great and precious promises by God by which I share His nature – 2nd Peter 1:4
- I can always know the presence of God because He never leaves me - Hebrews 13:5
- God works in me to help me do the things He wants me to do - Philippians 2:13
- I can ask God for wisdom and He will give me what I need - James 1:5

Main Points of Cottingham chapters 2.3 and 5.4

2.3 – Supreme Being and Created Things: Rene Descartes, Principles of Philosophy
Descartes' ontology gives us three categories of substance:
1) Substance in the strict sense, the independent, self-sufficient creator – God

2) Extended substance or matter – our bodies, nature, etc.
3) Thinking substance – our created minds

To each substance there belongs one principal attribute; in the case of the mind – this is thought. In the case of the body – this is extension. The extension of the world is indefinite, earth and matter are composed of one and the same matter, all the variety in matter, all the diversity of its forms, depends upon motion. God is the primary cause of motion and God always preserves the same quantity of motion in the universe. Geometry and mathematics can explain all of these principles.

5.4 – The Partly Hidden Self: Sigmund Freud, Introductory Lectures on Psychoanalysis

Freud proposed a revolutionary new concept of the mind challenging the long standing identification of the self with the conscious thinking subject. Freud argued that a large part of what makes up the mind is often hidden from our consciousness – "a divided self".
Freud argues that the desires, attitudes, and actions that make up our conscious selves, are strongly influenced by unconscious mental processes – wishes, beliefs, fears, and anxieties of which we are often unaware.
Psychological symptoms are formed as a substitute for something else which remains submerged. Perhaps something like an early childhood trauma may surface later in life as a psychological symptom. These symptoms vanish when their unconscious antecedents have been made conscious.

PH 510 Christian Apologetics
Session #5 – Salvation Passage, Cottingham 12.11, Zacharias 1
By: Terrence Dwyer, February 3rd, 2011

Salvation Passages:
Romans 5:8
8 But God demonstrates his own love for us in this: While we were still sinners, Christ died for us.
John 3:16-17
16 For God so loved the world that he gave his one and only Son, that whoever believes in him shall not perish but have eternal life. 17 For God did not send his Son into the world to condemn the world, but to save the world through him.

The above two passages are meaningful to me in reflecting upon my own life experience and how the gift of salvation entered into my life and saved my life such as it was. God convicted me of my own deep sinfulness yet freely and graciously gave to me the gift of salvation through His Son Jesus and through the power of the Holy Spirit. These passages remind me of both the conviction of my sinfulness in Romans 5:8 and the love of God in freely giving me salvation in John 3:16.

I would use these passages to explain salvation to others who are not Christian by sharing my own story of both sinfulness and salvation. I would use the Romans 5:8 passage (perhaps also along with Romans 3:9-12 and 3:23) to express how we are lost and sinful creatures yet deeply loved by God. So much so that God initiates His love for us while we are still deeply into our own sinfulness and rebelliousness. I would use the John 3:16-17 passage to further express God's deep love for us through the gift of eternal salvation that has been given to us through His Son Jesus Christ. I would advise that a decision needed to be made because God calls for belief in His Son in the giving of the gift. The gift is given by God but the gift must be accepted for the gift to be received.

Cottingham 12.11:
Religious Beliefs as Necessary for Meaning: by, William Lane Craig "The Absurdity of Life without God"

Craig argues that man is the cosmic orphan who is burning to answer the fundamental questions of his origin and his destiny. Without God, man and the universe are doomed. Our life and that of the entire universe is plunging toward extinction thus the life we live is without ultimate significance, value, or purpose. If mankind ends in nothing than he is nothing and his existence in the final analysis is utterly meaningless.

There is no ultimate meaning without immortality and God.
Immortality alone does not make things any better – it actually makes things worse as now your meaningless life lasts eternally. For ultimate significance in life, man needs God and immortality.

There is no ultimate value without immortality and God.
Without God, there is no ultimate value. Reason on its own gives us no basis for acting morally. Without God there are no objective standards of right and wrong. For in a world without God, good and evil do not exist, there is only the bare valueless fact of existence, and there is no one to say you are right and I am wrong.

No ultimate purpose without immortality and God.
If God does not exist then your life is not qualitatively different from

that of a dog. You are just a miscarriage of nature thrust into a purposeless universe to live a purposeless life. The adoption of a religious perspective is not just a matter of abstract theology but connects vitally with one's conception of the value and significance of human life. If God exists then, there is hope for man.

Identity: A creature created by God
Purpose: To enact God's will in life in relationship to Him
Morality: Given to us by God

Ravi Zacharias - Chapter One

In chapter one Ravi tells the story of how he came to believe in Jesus Christ. He was a poor student in a family and a culture that worshipped the intellect. His relationship with his father was especially difficult due to these high expectations which Ravi couldn't fulfill. He felt that his life was meaningless and he felt trapped.

He was invited by his sister to hear a Christian speaker one night who talked about the love of God in John 3:16. Ravi was the only one in the whole meeting who went down to the front for an altar call at the end of the meeting. He said he didn't understand the vocabulary but that he knew that his life was wrong and that he needed somebody to make it right. He knew God had to matter but he didn't know how to find Him.

He decided to save both he and his family any more embarrassment from his failures so he attempted suicide. At the hospital a person read to him from John 14, "Because I live you shall live also" which gave him a purpose to live in this life. Ravi said, "Piecing together God's love in Christ, the way that was provided because of Christ, and the promise of life through Him, on that hospital bed I made my commitment to give my life and my pursuits into His hands". He goes on to say, "My commitment stands now as the most wonderful transaction I ever made".

PH 510 Christian Apologetics
Session #6 – Cottingham 6.6; the Argument from Design: David Hume, "Dialogues Concerning Natural Religion"
By: Terrence Dwyer, February 10th, 2011

One of the most enduring and popular arguments for the existence of God is the "argument from design". David Hume critiques this argument through his dialogue between Cleanthes, a proponent of design, and Philo an opponent of design. Cleanthes proposes that we may conceive something of the nature of the Author of Nature by observing the apparent intelligent designs within nature. Through analogy we may infer that the mind of man must be similar to the mind of the Creator but on a much smaller scale. We conclude upon seeing a house that there must have been a builder or an architect for that house. Similarly, through our experience of the universe we conclude that there must be an architect or builder of the universe.

Philo responds by arguing that arguments based on analogy are of limited use and are basically weak arguments. He argues that any similarities between the universe and a product of human design such as a house are very thin. He states that the dissimilitude between the two is so striking and the resemblance so slight that you cannot really accept the viability of the analogy. Secondly, he notes that the apparent order and directedness of natural phenomena are not in itself proof of design. Matter itself, for all we know, may contain the source of order within itself. Why fasten on rational design as the only possible cause of the order we find? Philo makes an interesting point here when he says that a very small part of this great system, during a very short time, is very imperfectly discovered to us; and do we thence pronounce decisively concerning the origin of the whole? He goes on to say what peculiar privilege this little agitation of the brain which we call thought, that we must make it the model of the whole universe.

Finally, Philo concludes his argument by pointing out that all reasoning concerning cause and effect must be based on past instances, yet in the case of the universe we are by definition dealing with something unique, singular, without parallel or specific resemblance.

Bibliography

Cottingham, John. Western Philosophy, an Anthology. Malden, MA: Blackwell Publishing, 2008.

PH 510 Christian Apologetics
Session #7 –Description of an experience of suffering resulting in questioning God's existence
By: Terrence Dwyer, February 17th, 2011

When I was eleven years old my father committed suicide leaving me orphaned and having to rely upon my extended family for my care and upbringing. The earlier tragic death of my mother when I was not quite three years old had deeply impacted me. However, the abandonment by my father via suicide was more than my eleven-year-old mind or emotions could process and I instantly turned my back on God and no longer believed in God. In my state of mind at the time I thought that there was no way a loving God would allow my beloved father to do such a thing. So, I simply stopped believing in God. I certainly did not feel God's love during this time of my life. On the contrary, I not only felt abandoned by my mother and my father but I also felt abandoned by God. I did not feel God's involvement at all in my life during this period.

PH 510 Christian Apologetics
Session #8 –An apologetic argument from Lindsley
By: Terrence Dwyer, February 24th, 2011

One of Lindsley's apologetic arguments in his book entitled "Love, The Ultimate Apologetic" is that love is never sure apart from commitment. He argues that loving relationships cannot be continued, sustained or nurtured without commitment. The text he uses to base his argument is Mark 8:34-38; 'The way of the Cross'

34 Then he called the crowd to him along with his disciples and said: "Whoever wants to be my disciple must deny themselves and take up their cross and follow me. 35 For whoever wants to save their life[a] will lose it, but whoever loses their life for me and for the gospel will save it. 36 What good is it for someone to gain the whole world, yet forfeit their soul? 37 Or what can anyone give in exchange for their soul? 38 If anyone is ashamed of me and my words in this adulterous and sinful generation, the Son of Man will be ashamed of them when he comes in his Father's glory with the holy angels."

Jesus calls us to the radical commitment of following his example by laying down our lives, denying ourselves, taking up our cross, and following Him. This kind of radical commitment is the kind of commitment that sustains and nurtures loving relationships. Many people take commitment for granted and they are not aware that other worldviews fail to motivate or sustain commitment and that commitment and love are inseparable.

Atheists can be very committed to their atheism or even very passionate about their political causes, but a big part of atheism is autonomy. Atheists are by definition not accountable to anyone or to any moral values outside of whatever personal code they decide for themselves. Nothing in atheism requires them to commit themselves to anything.

Pantheism on the other hand holds that all is one; everything is divine and all a part of God. Pantheists can be very committed to causes such as the environment, holistic health, peace and justice. However, if that is the case that all is one and all is divine, then why would you want to be committed to change anything at all? If all matter is somehow illusory, how can you judge anything more worthy than another thing except by personal choice or corporate preference?

Atheism or pantheism have no adequate basis to judge meaning, purpose, or moral values that would show us where we ought to commit our lives or what we ought to love. Unless we are committed, love cannot be sustained. Jesus calls us to just such a radical commitment which shows us the pathways of love and enables us to sustain our love. Jesus says in Matthew 22:37-40;

37 Jesus replied: "Love the Lord your God with all your heart and with all your soul and with all your mind.' 38 This is the first and greatest commandment. 39 And the second is like it: 'Love your neighbor as yourself.' 40 All the Law and the Prophets hang on these two commandments."

I shared the above apologetic argument from Lindsley's book with one of my non-Christian friends and he disagreed with the premise of the argument. He felt that atheists, pantheists, and Christians all share a certain common understanding of what love is. He felt that two atheists could commit to a lifelong loving relationship as well as two pantheists could commit to a lifelong loving relationship. He didn't believe that you had to be a Christian in order to behave in a committed manner in a loving relationship. He understood the core of the author's argument but didn't agree with the premise that only Christians can have the necessary type of commitment needed to sustain a long term loving relationship.

PH510 Christian Apologetics: Dr. Kimberly Thacker, Fuller Theological Seminary
Paper #2: A Christian interaction and response to John Locke's, Essay Concerning Human Understanding
By: Terrence Dwyer, February 10th, 2011

John Locke was an influential Enlightenment thinker of the 17th century. He was an English philosopher and physician and is generally regarded as the Father of Liberalism. Locke's theory of the mind is often cited as the origin of modern conceptions of identity and the self. Locke was the first to define the self through a continuity of consciousness. He argued that the mind was a blank slate or a Tabula Rosa which was contrary to pre-existing Cartesian philosophy. Descartes argued, "I noticed certain laws which God has so ordained in nature, and of which He has implanted such notions in our minds." Locke took issue with this innate principle and argued that the mind begins as a blank slate and then asks, "Whence has it all the materials of reason and knowledge?" To which he famously replied, "In one word, from experience".

PH510 Christian Apologetics: Dr. Kimberly Thacker, Fuller Theological Seminary
Paper #2: A Christian interaction and response to John Locke's, Essay Concerning Human Understanding
By: Terrence Dwyer, February 10th, 2011

John Locke was an influential Enlightenment thinker of the 17th century. He was an English philosopher and physician and is generally regarded as the father of liberalism. Locke's theory of the mind is often cited as the origin of modern conceptions of identity and the self. Locke was the first to define the self through a continuity of consciousness. He argued that the mind was a blank slate or a Tabula Rosa which was contrary to pre-existing Cartesian philosophy. Descartes argued, "I noticed certain laws which God has so ordained in nature, and of which He has implanted such notions in our minds." Locke took issue with this innate principle and argued that the mind begins as a blank slate and then asks, "Whence has it all the materials of reason and knowledge?" To which he famously replied, "In one word, from experience".

Locke was instrumental in the development of the philosophy of empiricism which is a theory of knowledge, or epistemology, that asserts that all knowledge comes through experience via one's senses plus the mind's subsequent reflection on the data acquired. Empiricism emphasizes the role of experience and evidence, especially sensory perception, in the formation of ideas, over the notion of innate ideas or tradition. Empiricism in the study of science emphasizes those aspects of scientific knowledge that are closely related to evidence, especially as discovered in experiments. It is a fundamental part of the scientific method that all hypotheses and theories are to be tested against observations of the natural world, rather than resting solely on a priori reasoning, intuition, or revelation.

Locke takes issue with the philosophy of innate principles which argues that there are certain fundamental truths which the soul receives in its very first being and brings these truths into the world with it. Locke argues that these "Innatists" typically appeal to "universal assent" which are these fundamental truths that the Innatists claim are accepted by everyone. Locke argues that even if universal assent were established it would not prove innateness. Locke goes on to say that these supposed innate principles are "so far from having a universal assent that there are a great part of mankind to whom they are not so much as even known". He cites the cases of idiots and children as being prime examples of having no awareness of such universal truths. Locke states that to imprint anything on the mind without the mind's perceiving it seems hardly intelligible.

Locke does not deny that human beings have innate capacities, but he argues that a capacity to come to know a truth is not at all the same as innate knowledge of the truth. He concludes that the human mind does not have the least glimmering of any ideas which it does not receive either from sensation or subsequent reflection. Locke's training, education, and experience in the science and study of medicine appears to have shaped his thinking toward the philosophy of empiricism. Locke was also most likely influenced in his thinking by his close association with noted medical scientists of his day such as Robert Boyle, Thomas Willis, and Thomas Sydenham. The development of the science of medicine during this period was especially focused upon gaining new knowledge and understanding through scientific experimentation and observation. The rigorous discipline of the application of medical science may have ultimately influenced Locke's philosophy of empiricism.

A Christian response to Locke's main argument that all knowledge comes from experience can be developed through a review of what Scripture teaches about knowledge. In Exodus 31:2-4 we read that God fills Bezalel with wisdom, understanding, and knowledge so that Bezalel can perform all kinds of crafts for the building of the Tabernacle.

2 "See, I have chosen Bezalel son of Uri, the son of Hur, of the tribe of Judah, 3 and I have filled him with the Spirit of God, with wisdom, with understanding, with knowledge and with all kinds of skills— 4 to make artistic designs for work in gold, silver and bronze,

In Numbers 24:26 we see knowledge coming into the oracle Balaam from God.
16 the prophecy of one who hears the words of God,
who has knowledge from the Most High,
who sees a vision from the Almighty,
who falls prostrate, and whose eyes are opened:

In 2 Chronicles 1:10-12 we see the story of Solomon requesting wisdom and knowledge from God and God promising to give both wisdom and knowledge to Solomon.

10 Give me wisdom and knowledge, that I may lead this people, for who is able to govern this great people of yours?" 11 God said to Solomon, "Since this is your heart's desire and you have not asked for wealth, possessions or honor, nor for the death of your enemies, and since you have not asked for a long life but for wisdom and knowledge to govern my people over whom I have made you king, 12 therefore wisdom and knowledge will be given you. And I will also give you wealth, possessions and honor, such as no king who was before you ever had and none after you will have."

In the New Testament we also see that knowledge is something that is in part at least given by God. We certainly learn and gather data through our senses and we continue to learn as we reflect upon the data gathered, but Scripture seems to clearly say that God also imparts knowledge directly into humans. In Matthew 13:11 Jesus says,

11 He replied, "Because the knowledge of the secrets of the kingdom of heaven has been given to you, but not to them.

Colossians 1:9 is quite concise on the source of our knowledge as coming from the Spirit.

9 For this reason, since the day we heard about you, we have not stopped praying for you. We continually ask God to fill you with the knowledge of his will through all the wisdom and understanding that the Spirit gives,

Finally, in Ecclesiastes 2:26 we see again God directly distributing wisdom and knowledge into a person during the course of a person's life.
26 To the person who pleases him, God gives wisdom, knowledge and happiness, but to the sinner he gives the task of gathering and storing up wealth to hand it over to the one who pleases God. This too is meaningless, a chasing after the wind.

While I don't disagree with Locke's assertion that knowledge is obtained through the senses and that we also gain additional knowledge through reflection upon the data gathered; I do disagree with Locke that this is the source of all knowledge. Scripture clearly expresses in both the Old and New Testaments that God infuses knowledge and wisdom into living humans according to God's will.

Also, Locke's argument that there are no innate principles stamped upon the mind of man which the soul receives in its very first being and brings into the world with it; seems to also be contradicted by Scripture. Psalm 139 appears to be speaking of a soul that has innate knowledge of the complexities of its' creation.

14I praise you, for I am fearfully and wonderfully made. Wonderful are your works; my soul knows it very well.
Finally, in Genesis 1:27 we see the creation of mankind.
27 So God created mankind in his own image,
in the image of God he created them;
male and female he created them.

To borrow a phrase from Locke, it seems hardly intelligible for the Creator to create mankind in His own image without including "in his own image" an innate knowledge of the Creator.

In conclusion, Locke makes some excellent points regarding our obtaining knowledge through our senses and then we gain additional knowledge as we reflect upon the data that we have gathered. However, Locke seems to have been unduly influenced by the rigors of the discipline of his studies in medical science and he neglects entirely the interests of the Creator in His creation. Scripture clearly shows that God imparts wisdom and knowledge directly into whomever God chooses during the course of a person's life for God's own will and purposes. Scripture also seems to show that God imprints knowledge of at least Himself into His creation and Scripture seems to reveal that the soul is aware of this.

Bibliography

Bibles, Crossway. The ESV Study Bible. Wheaton, Illinois Good News Publishers, 2008.

Cottingham, John. Western Philosophy, an Anthology. Malden, MA: Blackwell Publishing, 2008.

IEP, Internet Encyclopedia of Philosophy. 2001.

Markie, Peter, Stanford Encyclopedia of Philosophy
Palo Alto, CA, 2008.

PH510 Christian Apologetics: Dr. Kimberly Thacker, Fuller Theological Seminary
Paper #3: Love, the Ultimate Apologetic
By: Terrence Dwyer, March 3rd, 2011

Some of my extended family members are non-believers and when we get together during the holidays we sometimes get into discussions regarding our belief systems and I would like to explore in this paper a possible conversation that we might have. Some of these family members practice the teachings of Buddhism, and some practice New Age Universalism, and others Pantheism.

My mother-in-law recently passed away but just a few weeks before passing she professed her faith and belief in Jesus Christ. We had several conversations about our faith over the years and I had shared the Gospel with her on more than one occasion. A few weeks prior to her death she approached me about Jesus and we discussed the good news of the Gospel again in detail and we read the Bible together and prayed together and she began reading the Bible on her own. After her death, one of my wife's sisters approached a "spiritual medium" to contact the spirit of her mother as she was feeling "troubled" over her mother's death. The "medium" apparently became startled during the session and asked if she knew that her mother was a "Christian". Shortly thereafter, my mother-in-law's older sister, a devout, lifelong, practicing Buddhist became a Christian and will be baptized this coming Easter. These recent events have no doubt deeply impacted my wife's family and I would like to use this paper to in part prepare for our next conversation which will no doubt be about the Christian faith at some point during our time together.

In presenting the core of our Christian witness as love; Lindsley argues that love is never sure apart from commitment. Love is never sane apart from conscience. Love is never safe apart from character. Love is never stimulated apart from community and that love is never seized apart from courage. In this paper and in my discussions with my sisters-in-law I would like to focus on just two of Lindsley's apologetic arguments for Christianity with those two arguments being love and commitment and love and conscience.

People today often have a number of relationships with various partners which often end abruptly or not well at all. People in these relationships often claim the lack of spiritual maturity of their partners and that they needed to move on as their pathways toward love were being hindered, disrupted, or blocked by their partners. They felt that they had spiritually grown as far as they could in their relationship and that they had to move on to continue to grow in love. My contention has been that the deeper pathways of love are learned in a relationship over time. As one walks through life together with another person they encounter a whole gamut of obstacles to their love that they have to learn to overcome together which inevitably deepens their love if they remain committed to each other. Committed lovers also experience with each other an ever expanding array of ways to express and receive love to each other over time.

Lindsley argues that love is never motivated or sustained or fulfilled without a conscious commitment to do so. Love will not continue without commitment. Lindsley argues from Mark 8:34-35 where Christ explains the commitment required of a disciple:

34 Then he called the crowd to him along with his disciples and said: "Whoever wants to be my disciple must deny themselves and take up their cross and follow me. 35 For whoever wants to save their life will lose it, but whoever loses their life for me and for the gospel will save it.

Lindsley goes on to say that to deny oneself in this way means to obliterate self as the dominant principle of life and to make God the ruling principle in your life. Jesus said, "I have come that they may have life, and have it to the full" (John 10:10). Following Christ is the way to fullness in life. By denying self and by living for and in Christ I am free to fully love unconditionally in my relationships. I can remain in a committed relationship and experience the richer and deeper pathways of love because my total commitment to Christ enables me to forgive another as Christ has forgiven me and to unconditionally love another as Christ unconditionally loves me. My hope then is that my argument and my conversation with my family members would reveal that it is ones commitment to Christ that truly enables one to achieve the highest pathway of love and that we experience the deepest and richest love through a long term committed relationship with another.

A second conversation that I would like to have with my family members would involve love and conscience. I have heard certain family members say that they don't believe in sin or evil or hell and that these are Christian manifestations. There is no such thing as sin so there is no need to have feelings of guilt. We are one with God and are therefore perfect just as we are. However, there had been times over the years where certain family members had begun intimate relationships with others while still in a seemingly committed long term relationship with another person. These incidents caused a great deal of hurt and anguish for the people in these seemingly long term committed relationships and to a certain extent to members of the extended family who cared for them. My family members probably experienced some guilty feelings in their consciences after these occurrences had happened and the subsequent pain inflicted. I would like to have the conversation that our conscience is our guide toward moral behavior and that the guilt we may feel at times is healthy in that it is guiding us away from morally undesirable behavior and toward morally desirable behavior.

Lindsley argues from Paul who said, *"I do my best always to have a clear conscience toward God and all people" (Acts 24:16)*. The Biblical view places front and center the reasons why we are guilty and how we can be acquitted from it. We need to have our consciences cleansed by confessing our sin and receiving forgiveness and then strive to maintain a clear conscience through resolving to avoid sin. How well we live our spiritual lives and maintain our moral and emotional health depends greatly upon whether we get and keep a clear conscience. We are able to do this because God took our sin and put it on Christ and He took Christ's perfection and put it on us. *"God made him who had no sin to be sin for us, so that we might become the righteousness of God" (2 Corinthians 5:21)*.

I would enjoy having this conversation with my beloved family as the perfection they seek and have been unable to attain is already there for them through Jesus Christ. The imperfections and guilt that they may feel may be given to Christ who stands ready to accept them just as they are. I believe that this conversation would be an opportunity to share the good news of the Gospel with each of them just as I had the opportunity to share the good news of the Gospel with my mother-in-law before she passed.

Bibliography

Bibles, Crossway. The ESV Study Bible. Wheaton, Illinois Good News Publishers, 2008.

Lindsley, Art. Love, the Ultimate Apologetic. Downers Grove, IL: Intervarsity Press, 2008.

PH510 Christian Apologetics: Dr. Kimberly Thacker, Fuller Theological Seminary
Paper #1: Personal Apology for why I follow Jesus Christ
By: Terrence Dwyer, January 18th, 2011

As far back as I can remember I have had a belief in God. My Roman Catholic family upbringing included regularly participating in the Catholic liturgy and personally receiving the administration of the Sacraments. Our family also practiced prayer at meal times and we seemed to have a general recognition and acceptance that God existed and that Jesus was the Son of God. Thus at a fairly young age through the introduction and accepted practices of my family and extended family I came to acknowledge, worship, and submit to God as best I could as a young child and I didn't question my inherited belief system.

Unfortunately, my family suffered from an unusual amount of misfortune early in my life. Prior to my birth, an older sister died tragically from a sudden illness which severely impacted my parent's faith. Less than three years after my birth my mother also died tragically from a sudden illness. My father lost his faith and hope in the midst of these heartbreaking events and he spiraled downward into depression and severe alcoholism and eventually committed suicide when I was eleven years old. All of my inherited faith in God immediately ceased on the day of my father's death as I intentionally turned my back on God and went my own way in life. I wanted nothing to do with a God that would allow my best friend, my beloved father, to be taken from me in such a way.

The emotional trauma of these events was far too much to bear and I too turned to alcohol and drugs at a very young age to anesthetize the acute emotional pain that I was experiencing in life. Unfortunately, these choices exacted a significant toll on my developmental abilities at a critical formative period of my young life. I too eventually spiraled downward into severe alcoholism and was very near suicide myself at half my father's age when he died.

During this time, I had the good fortune of working for an uncle whom I deeply respected and who also happened to be a born-again Christian. He richly exhibited the fruits of the Spirit in his personality as he was joyful, peaceful, confident, loving, and generous and I was very attracted to these qualities in him. He quite intentionally told me about Jesus and salvation and hell and heaven and told me I had a choice to make in the matter and he planted the seed of the Gospel into my soul. A few years later, when I was very near suicide myself, I reached out at the last moment for that hope of the Gospel and expressed a deep yearning toward God to receive whatever it was that my uncle seemed to have. God answered this tiny, seemingly insignificant yearning with a sudden infusion of the Holy Spirit into my being. This Spirit began to immediately clean up my depraved way of life and also introduced me to the Bible and began to teach me about who Jesus is. I was thrilled at this new found lease on life and I immediately began believing in God again and in Jesus and in the Holy Spirit and I began seeking and following the ways of the Lord.

Shortly after this intense time of spiritual rebirth I began praying and communicating to God and I noticed that God seemed to be communicating back to me through the Spirit, through the Bible and through nature and the world around me and through others. My prayers were being quickly answered which spurred me onto further communication and prayer to God. I experienced an instantaneous, miraculous healing of my addiction to alcohol and drugs and God answered my prayers for a mate and blessed me with my wife among many other blessings. My faith in God and in Jesus and in the Holy Spirit continued to grow.

Over the ensuing years my faith was tested through significant testing and trials but these occurrences only seemed to deepen my trust and faith in God. I also was blessed to have encountered appearances of the living Jesus at sporadic moments in my life which significantly strengthened my belief in Him. These occurrences also greatly enhanced my understanding and belief that Jesus is very much alive and He seems to be quite active in this world. I also personally experienced another significant instantaneous miraculous healing as well as encounters with beings that I can only best describe as angels. These deeply spiritual experiences further encouraged my faith and revealed to me a spiritual world beyond this one which assures me and gives me peace and hope. I also encountered Jesus at a moment of deep anguish and despair in my marriage when He taught me deeply about the way of forgiveness and of unconditional love. Me dependence upon Jesus to forgive and to love unconditionally grew exponentially.

The community of believers in Jesus has welcomed me into their midst and they have been wonderfully loving, nurturing, and challenging to me and my family to grow in our faith in Jesus. Their witness and their encouragement and support of my various calls to go deeper with Christ have been a terrific blessing to me. Certainly, there have been disappointments with some and I have certainly been a disappointment to others but through it all we seem to be growing in our faith in Jesus.

This call into ministry and into seminary at this late stage in my life has been deeply humbling and challenging to me. After all of these years my trust in the Lord is such that when He calls I follow even though I don't always agree with where we are going. He has cared for me and provided for me and my family and abundantly blessed me beyond my wildest expectations so I have no reason to doubt Him but I still do at times due to my own weaknesses. Sure there have been some very hard times but He didn't abandon me in them, on the contrary I felt His presence both in the blessings and in the hard times. I look forward to seeing Him in the next life along with all of my friends and family who are already there with Him. However, until then, because of all of the many occurrences and interactions mentioned above, I chose to continue to follow Jesus Christ wherever He may continue to lead me in this life.

PH 522: Perspectives on Christ and Culture; Professor Dr. Kimberly Thacker
Fuller Theological Seminary – Final Paper – week#10 assignment
By: Terrence Dwyer, August 25th, 2012

I will focus my discussion in this paper on four specific areas from this course which have helped to shape my theology concerning humanity and the way in which I interact with others and with culture. There were several aspects of this course which helped to guide and shape my theology for ministry but I will address only four within the confines of this assignment. These four areas are the image of God in dialogue with Barth and Brunner, Calvinism as a life system in dialogue with Abraham Kuyper, Christ transforming culture in dialogue with Richard Niebuhr, Richard Mouw, and Andy Crouch, and finally, Multiculturalism in dialogue with Charles Taylor.

Beginning with Barth and Brunner and their discussion on the image of God in humanity, I discovered that how I held my view of the image of God in humanity impacted my sense of urgency in preaching the Gospel of Jesus Christ. This class helped me to achieve further clarity on this view for my ministry. Barth would view the image of God in humanity as being totally obliterated by the fall. Man has sinned and is a sinner who can only be saved through the grace of God in Jesus Christ. The image of God in which man was created has been completely wiped out without any remnant left remaining. Barth argues that man is a being that is utterly dependent upon God and must be wholly saved by God. God alone must reconcile, justify, and sanctify his fallen creatures. Thus my sense of urgency in preaching the Gospel is quite high while holding to Barth's view of the image of God in humanity.

Brunner on the other hand would argue that yes the original image of God within man has been destroyed by sin but there remains yet a remnant of the image of God within man. Brunner approaches his argument for the existence of this remnant within man from different angles. Brunner first argues from the functional point of view stating that as humans our function in creation is to rule over the earth as the pinnacle of the created order. As such our dominion over the earth is an expression of the image of God within. Brunner also argues from the substantive viewpoint that the world and all of God's creatures including mankind are the creation of God and thus are imprinted with the stamp of the creator God within them. As evidence of this stamp man has a conscience of responsibility of which they are conscious of and are able to come to an awareness of the will of God. Brunner also states that man is capable of recognizing the preserving grace of God both evidently at work in nature unconsciously and evident consciously through the reason of man. Brunner also argues that the very point of contact for the reception of the divine grace of redemption is the very remnant of the image of God within man. Holding more toward Brunner's view of the image of God within man doesn't carry with it the same sense of urgency in preaching the Gospel.

Brunner's view carries with it some sense of man's responsibility of conscience in knowing the will of God and of knowing the preserving grace of God through creation. Barth's view carries with it our utter dependence upon the grace of God for our salvation. We are utterly hopeless and helpless without the intervention of the grace of God in Jesus Christ. I hold more to Barth's view of the image of God within man thus I believe I have more of a sense of urgency toward preaching the Gospel of Jesus Christ in my interactions with others and with culture and in my ministry. This was an important clarification for me from this class.

I have to say here that I am deeply grateful for your introducing me to Abraham Kuyper whom I had not read or even heard of prior to your assigning his Lectures on Calvinism which I found to be brilliant. I am looking forward to reading everything I can find of Kuyper's in the months ahead – thank you.

Kuyper has put into words what I have experienced in my personal relationship with God, in my relationships with my fellow human beings, and in my relationship to the world in which we live. Kuyper has given me the framework upon which to hang my world view and my theology through his adept articulation of Calvinism. Kuyper clarifies Calvinism as follows; "It does not seek God in the creature as Paganism; it does not isolate God from the creature as Islamism; it posits no mediate communion between God and the creature as does Romanism; but proclaims the exalted thought that although standing in high majesty above the creature, God enters into immediate fellowship with the creature, as God the Holy Spirit." (Kuyper, p. 21) Kuyper sums up how Calvinism addresses the three fundamental relations of all human existence: our relation to God, our relation to man, and our relation to the world. "For our relation to God: an immediate fellowship of man with the eternal, independently of priest or church. For the relation of man to man: the recognition in each person of human worth, which is his by virtue of his creation after the Divine likeness, and therefore of the equality of all men before God and his magistrate. And for the relation to the world: the recognition that in the whole world the curse is restrained by grace, that the life of the world is to be honored in its independence, and that we must, in every domain, discover the treasures and develop the potencies hidden by God in nature and in human life." (Kuyper, p. 31) This articulation of Calvinism rings true to my personal experience of my relation to God, my relation to my fellow man, and my relation to the world and this gives me the framework from which to minister in the world until Christ calls me home or returns in glory.

Thirdly, coming to an understanding of Richard Niebuhr's fifth typology of Christ the transformer of culture brought further clarity to me toward the critical importance of preaching the Gospel for the transformation of culture. Niebuhr states; "Christ is the transformer of culture in the sense that he redirects, reinvigorates, and regenerates that life of man, expressed in all human works, which in present actuality is the perverted and corrupted exercise of a fundamentally good nature; which, moreover, in its depravity lies under the curse of transiency and death, not because an external punishment has been visited upon it, but because it is intrinsically self-contradictory." (Carson, p. 27)

Accordingly, my ministry and my interactions with others and with culture will integrate this understanding of the interaction between Christ and culture as one in which Christ is risen and is currently present within the world through the power of the Holy Spirit and through His Church. Christ is actively engaged in the conversion and the transformation of the hearts of individuals toward loving God and loving one another. Jesus Christ is thus actively engaged in the transformation of culture as these individuals with transformed hearts move to transform their surrounding culture toward the ways of Christ. Jesus commands his disciples in the Gospel of Mark, "Go into all the world and proclaim the gospel to the whole creation." (Mark 16:15; ESV)

One of the better revelations for me from this course was from Richard Mouw in When the Kings Come Marching In. Although I wanted to believe that all of human culture belonged to God I found myself still holding back from putting all my weight into this belief as I felt that some of human culture was just too far gone and beyond even God's reach. Mouw gave me the permission to truly believe that yes all of human culture belongs to the Lord and thus all are truly meant to hear the Gospel message. Mouw opened up all of culture to me and allowed me to accept all of human culture without judgment. Mouw states, "But we must first of all allow this knowledge to shape the basic attitudes and expectations that we bring to our wrestling with the practical questions. We must train ourselves to look at the worlds of commerce and art and recreation and education and technology, and confess that all of this "filling" belongs to God. And then we must engage in the difficult business of finding patterns of cultural involvement that are consistent with this confession. If, in a fundamental and profound sense, God has not given up on human culture, then neither must we give up. "The earth is the Lord's and everything in it" – even the ships of Tarshish." (Mouw, p. 42) Thus Mouw has helped me to fully accept that all belongs to God and that as a people of God we are to engage within culture all to the glory of God.

Crouch also helped me to see more clearly in his work, Culture Making, that culture is not only how we make sense of the world in that it is the lens through which we view and interpret the world, but that culture is all that humans have added to the world from the beginning of our creation up until today. Culture is what we inherit from the previous generations and culture is what we bequeath to the generations to follow us. Crouch argues that culture is continually remaking the world and that culture continues to shape the horizons of the possible. Culture has the effect of making things that were once impossible now possible and culture can also have the reverse effect of making things impossible that were once possible. If we as humans desire to change culture than the only way to change culture is to create more of it within the milieu of a continually changing culture.

Crouch however said this about culture making, "The resurrection shows us the pattern for culture making in the image of God. Not power, but trust. Not independence, but dependence. The second Adam's influence on culture comes through his greatest act of dependence; the fulfillment of Israel's calling to demonstrate faith in the face of the great powers that threatened its existence comes in the willing submission of Jesus to a Roman cross, broken by but also breaking forever its power. So, just as we can say that culture is what we make of the world, in both senses, we can say that the Gospel is the proclamation of Jesus, in both senses. The Gospel is the arrival of God's realm of possibility in the midst of human structures of possibility." (Crouch, p. 145-146) Thus Jesus creates new culture and Christ and the church are actively engaged in the conversion and the transformation of the hearts of individuals toward loving God and loving one another and thus are actively engaged in the transformation of culture as these individuals with transformed hearts move to transform their surrounding culture toward the ways of Christ.

To sum up this section, Niebuhr clarified for me that Christ is the transformer of culture through the transformation of the hearts of individuals. Mouw opened up all of culture to me by helping me to see that everything in culture ultimately belongs to the Lord which he will ultimately transform. And finally, Crouch helped me to see that culture is never static but that it is ever changing and Christ is at work transforming culture through transforming hearts. The importance of preaching the Gospel of Jesus Christ within my interactions with others and within my ministry has now been even further emphasized and clarified for me as a result of this course.

Finally, I want to briefly touch on the importance of multiculturalism as a credible witness to the culture of what God is doing in the world through the Gospel of Jesus Christ. I believe that the multicultural church living, loving, and worshipping together is a light to the world that points toward the Kingdom of God and it is integral toward how I seek to engage in ministry in the church and in the world. Charles Taylor writes in Multiculturalism, "Our identity is partly shaped by recognition or its absence, often by the misrecognition of others, and so a person or group of people can suffer real damage, real distortion, if the people or society around them mirror back to them a confining or demeaning or contemptible picture of themselves. Nonrecognition or misrecognition can inflict harm; can be a form of oppression, imprisoning someone in a false, distorted, and reduces mode of being." (Taylor, p. 25)

For the church to be the church as the light shining toward the Kingdom of God, we must fully embrace multiculturalism in all its aspects within our organizational structure as the Church – the Body of Christ here on earth. I believe anything less than that misrepresents the Kingdom of God to the world and this misrepresentation can cause great harm and drive people further from the Lord instead of drawing people closer to the Lord. For the remainder of my ministry to the Lord and to his church I will strive to encourage and further embrace multiculturalism in my ministry and within the church. This course helped me to gain even further clarity on the importance of multiculturalism in the church and in ministry.

In conclusion, there were several aspects of this course which helped to guide and shape my theology for ministry but the four areas that most shaped my study were the image of God in dialogue with Barth and Brunner, Calvinism as a life system in dialogue with Abraham Kuyper, Christ transforming culture in dialogue with Richard Niebuhr, Richard Mouw, and Andy Crouch, and finally, Multiculturalism in dialogue with

Charles Taylor.

PH522-Mid-Term Exam
By: Terrence Dwyer, July 30th, 2012

1. Define in your own words a substantive understanding of the word 'Culture'

In Genesis 1:28 God tells Adam and Eve to "fill the earth and subdue it." This filling of the earth is more than just filling the earth with their off spring. This filling of the earth is also all of the things that we as humans have added to the earth in all our interactions with each other and with nature. This filling up of the earth with all of these things is our cultural filling that we as humans have added to the earth. Originally, our cultural infilling was intended to be obedient and faithful to God and to glorify God. However, our cultural in-filling that was originally intended to glorify God has become distorted as a result of the Fall and our cultural in-filling has become perverse and idolatrous bringing offense to God. However, "the earth is the Lord's and the fullness thereof "and God is redeeming our in-filling through the work of Jesus Christ. This is essentially my understanding of culture.

2. What does Andy Crouch mean by the statement, "culture is what we make of the world, in both senses"?

In the first sense of the word culture is the way in which human beings make sense of the world. Culture is the lens through which we view the world and try to interpret and make sense of the world. Culture is what we make of the world in the deeper sense of deriving meaning from culture. We come into this world as essentially blank slates as babies and we absorb our culture like sponges in order to interpret the amazing world into which we are born and to derive our meaning.

On the other hand, culture in the second sense of the word is what we actually add to the world by making something of the world which we was handed over to us by previous generations. We inherit their culture and we create culture and add to it and hand it on to the next generation. What we make and add to culture is what we make of the world in the second sense.

from 3. How does Mouw's understanding of both Creation and the Fall differ Niebuhr's description of the Christ Against Culture position?

Mouw argues in "When the Kings Come Marching In" from the

viewpoint that "the earth is the Lord's and everything in it" meaning that everything that man has added to the earth since creation including everything after the Fall ultimately belongs to the creator God and that God has not given up on his creation. Through the work of Christ God has redeemed and is redeeming his creation through the Holy Spirit and the Church until Christ returns again. Niebuhr's description of Christ against culture is at odds with Mouw's theology here as Christ against Culture proposes a separation from culture for the Church. This typology proposes that the sole authority over the Christian is Christ and the Christian is to reject all other loyalties inherent within the claims of culture. There is a clear line drawn under this typology between the people of God and the people of the world whereas with Mouw's understanding all belongs to God and the people of God are to engage within culture all to the glory of God.

4. Describe one of the Carson's critiques or expansions on Niebuhr's typologies and why you agree or disagree.

Carson critiques Niebuhr's fifth typology of "Christ the Transformer of Culture" by stating that this fifth typology is supported only in restricted forms within the New Testament and not in the strong form that Niebuhr would like to see adopted. Carson claims that Niebuhr wants this conversionist paradigm to prevail as it is the only paradigm for which Niebuhr offers no criticism. Carson goes on to state that in its pure form this paradigm cannot be found in any New Testament document nor in any great figure of church history until F. D. Maurice justifies it not upon Scripture but upon absolutizing one motif. I tend to agree with Niebuhr here in that this is the typology that I too want to see prevail and put into practice in my ministry. However, I reluctantly have to agree with Carson in that I too do not see substantive Scriptural evidence or substantive historical examples from the Church for this paradigm.

5. What do Anabaptists mean by Constantianism?

What the Anabaptists mean by the term Constantianism is in reference to the relationship between Church and state. Prior to the Roman Emperor Constantine legalizing Christianity and aligning the Christian faith with the state, the Church was a minority religion in an environment that was hostile toward it. During the reign of Constantine however, Christianity became legalized and the Church eventually became aligned with the state and a patron of the state. Constantianism then is where Christianity is advanced in allegiance with the state and the interests of the state are protected by the Church. Thus the Church lost its separateness and distinctness from the state as a result of this Constantianism. The Church surrendered its prophetic voice toward the state and in that sense ceased being the Church.

Anabaptists believe that the Church and the state are to remain separate and distinct while both being under the reign of God where the Church is a source of renewal for society and where the state protects society.

6. What do Hauerwas and Willimon mean by the phrase "the church is an alternative polis?"

What Hauerwas and Willimon mean by the phrase "the church is an alternative polis" is that the church is an alternative colony or alternative community in the world. They refer to the church as resident aliens existing as an adventurous colony of a people of faith living within a hostile world of unbelief. This colony of believers is God's means of a major offensive upon the world beginning with Jesus Christ who is the supreme act of divine intrusion upon the world. The colony is God's means for saving the whole world. The colony is God's alternative community than that which exists in the world and this community is God's purpose for the whole world. I like Hauerwas and Willomon's comment that "the church does not need to feel caught between the false Niebuhrian dilemma of whether to be in or out of the world – the church is not out of the world – there is no other place for the church to be than here" (RA, P.43).

7. In your own words, define the term "revolutionary subordination."

Revolutionary Subordination to me is the voluntary subordination to the authority of the governing powers in place currently in this world knowing that it is Jesus Christ who truly reigns and his reign will one day be revealed to all. Through the Gospel of Jesus Christ I have been liberated and set free from all the powers of sinful domination which previously ruled over me and I accordingly reject sinful governmental domination over me. However, I may voluntarily submit to such domination knowing that it is Christ who truly reigns. This is my act of Revolutionary Subordination as I endure a toleration of the existence of worldly government and I refuse to engage in revolution or insubordination against these governments. I chose instead to serve God in subordination to the governing powers with patience as I await the return of Jesus who will rule in righteousness. This does not mean that I morally approve of or even obey all of my government's dictates.

8. Describe three ways Brunner discusses the presence of grace in the world outside of the cross.

Brunner describes the presence of grace in the world outside of the cross in his discussion of creation in that God's grace exists in creation itself. Wherever God does anything he leaves the imprint of his nature upon what he does therefore creation is at the same time a revelation and a self-communication by God. God's image is also imprinted in mankind as we are created in the image of God and even though that image has been destroyed in the fall there still remains a remnant of the divine image within. Also there is Brunner's concept of God's preserving grace where God preserves his creation even though it has fallen and that all of human activity comes within the purview of this preserving grace. Brunner also argues for ordinances of preservation from which we could recognize the will of God as normative for our own actions. Brunner also describes a point of contact for the reception of the divine grace of redemption and that this point of contact is the remnant of the image of God residing within mankind.

9. Why does Barth react so strongly to Brunner? Describe the central theological point he is seeking to protect.

Barth reacts quite strongly to Brunner's theology and states that the original image of God that man was created with has been obliterated by sin and no longer resides within. Barth also argues that Scripture alone is our sole source of knowledge of God and therefore rejects any general revelation of God in nature. Bath also rejects the idea of any preserving grace active from the moment of creation until now preserving God's creation that would be apparent to us. Accordingly, Barth argues that there are no ordinances of preservation from which we could recognize the will of God as normative for our own actions. Finally, Barth states that there can be no point of contact remnant of the image of God within man for the saving action of God due to the fall. The theological point that Barth is keen to protect here is that through sin man is utterly and hopelessly lost and incapable acknowledging any revelation. Salvation is only through the grace of God in the revelation of God in Jesus Christ. Barth says it best, "Man is a being that has to be overcome by the Word and the Spirit of God, that has to be reconciled to God, justified and sanctified, comforted and ruled and finally saved y God." (NT, p.126)

Essay questions:
1. With reference to the Biblical Drama (Creation, Fall, Redemption, New Creation), discuss in detail ONE of Niebuhr's typologies.

In reference to Niebuhr's first typology of "Christ against Culture" and the biblical drama we have the Trinitarian Creator God creating and establishing all things. Sin subsequently entered into God's creation through the Fall which corrupted all aspects of life on earth. All the people of creation are accountable to their Creator God. God is not redeeming the culture of this fallen world but is preserving the culture through God's covenantal promise to Noah of Gen. 8:20 -9:17. God has however entered into this world beginning with Jesus Christ who is the supreme act of divine intrusion upon the world. God is thus simultaneously redeeming a people for himself through the covenant he made with Abraham and brought to fulfillment in Jesus Christ. Beginning with the work of Jesus Christ, God has established a new colony of redeemed people who are the people of God which he is gathering in his church. God will welcome his church into the new heaven and the new earth when Jesus Christ returns again. Until then, Christians living in the church on earth are serving God as if exiles living in Babylon. Christians are living in a land that is not their own and their environment can be hostile toward them.

Niebuhr describes life under this paradigm as uncompromisingly affirming the sole authority of Jesus Christ over the Christian and resolutely rejecting the culture's claims to loyalty. "Loyalty to Christ encompasses all doctrinal, moral, and social realms and the counterpart to this loyalty to Christ and brethren is the clear rejection of cultural society where a clear line of separation is drawn between the children of God and the world." (Carson, p. 13) Typical of life in the colony under this paradigm is withdrawn from society and exclusionary such as monks living in monasteries or like the Amish of North America living in their own separate communities. These colonies strive to live highly principled, moral, and often uncompromising lives as they seek to submit solely to the authority of Jesus Christ. In practice however, this paradigm is unsustainable because we inevitably make use of culture in some manner as we live out our lives on the earth. Even the very words we use are words which are embedded within our culture so we cannot fully escape our culture. Examples of other groups who seem to strive to live out this paradigm on earth are the Mennonites, and Quakers, and Jean Vanier and his L'Arche communities among others.

2. Explain this statement by Andy Crouch, "the only way to change culture is to create more culture." What does he mean by this and why does he argue that this is true? Include some specific practical examples to illustrate his point and whether or not you agree.

Crouch argues in Culture Making that culture is not only how we make sense of the world in that it is the lens through which we view and interpret the world, but that culture is all that humans have added to the world from the beginning of our creation up until today. Culture is what we inherit from the previous generations and culture is what we bequeath to the generations to follow us. Crouch argues that culture is continually remaking the world and that culture continues to shape the horizons of the possible. Culture has the effect of making things that were once impossible now possible and culture can also have the reverse effect of making things impossible that were once possible. Crouch gives the example of traveling by horse between Boston and Philadelphia where automobiles and interstate freeways have made what was once impossible now possible. However, at the same time it is now impossible to make that same journey by horse so what was once possible is now impossible. If we as humans desire to change culture than the only way to change culture is to create more of it within the milieu of a continually changing culture. Crouch rightly argues that it is an inappropriate response to critique or condemn our culture and that if we desire to change culture than we must simply create more culture.

Crouch also argues that Jesus was a creator and cultivator of new culture and was thus a culture maker in his radically different teaching, radical social interactions and acceptance of those in society who were considered social outcasts, radical confrontations with the established religious order, radical dependence upon God, the way of the Cross, and the resurrection. Through it all Jesus created new culture and Christ and the church are actively engaged in the conversion and the transformation of the hearts of individuals toward loving God and loving one another and thus are actively engaged in the transformation of culture as these individuals with transformed hearts move to transform their surrounding culture toward the way of Christ.

I agree with Crouch and am greatly encouraged by his work as I have for some time felt compelled to work toward creating new culture for Christ by honoring Christ in such things as coffee shops and cafés. It disturbs me that God is devoid in such places and not honored within these unique public spaces within God's creation. However, I am cognizant that we may only point toward Christ and until he returns we are not physically creating the Kingdom of God but are pointing toward it through the culture we create.

3. Compare and contrast Barth and Brunner's views of the image of God in humanity. Include an explanation of how each would define the characteristics of the imageo dei and at least one difference in the practical application of their two views.

Barth would view the image of God in humanity as being totally obliterated by the fall. Man has sinned and is a sinner who can only be saved through the grace of God. The image of God in which man was created has been completely wiped out without any remnant left remaining. Brunner on the other hand would argue that yes the original image of God within man has been destroyed by sin but there remains yet a remnant of the image of God within man. Brunner approaches his argument for the existence of this remnant within man from different angles. Brunner first argues from the functional point of view stating that as humans our function in creation is to rule over the earth as the pinnacle of the created order. As such our dominion over the earth is an expression of the image of God within. Brunner also argues from the substantive viewpoint that the world and all of God's creatures including mankind are the creation of God and thus are imprinted with the stamp of the creator God within them. As evidence of this stamp man has a conscience of responsibility of which they are conscious of and are able to come to an awareness of the will of God. Brunner also states that man is capable of recognizing the preserving grace of God both evidently at work in nature unconsciously and evident consciously through the reason of man. Brunner also argues that the very point of contact for the reception of the divine grace of redemption is the very remnant of the image of God within man.

Barth's answer to Brunner's arguments for the existence of a remnant of the image of God within man are essentially that man is utterly and totally lost due to sin and any trace of any remnant of the image of God within man has been destroyed by sin. Barth argues that man is a being that is utterly dependent upon God and must be wholly saved by God. God alone must reconcile, justify, and sanctify his fallen creatures.

One difference in the practical application of their views is in preaching the Gospel. Brunner's view carries with it some sense of man's responsibility of conscience in knowing the will of God and of knowing the preserving grace of God through creation. Barth's view carries with it our utter dependence upon the grace of God for our salvation. We are utterly hopeless and helpless without the intervention of the grace of God in Jesus Christ which makes the Gospel message that much more absolute and urgent under Barth.

PH 522: Perspective on Christ and Culture; Professor Dr. Kimberly Thacker
Kuyper Paper
By: Terrence Dwyer, August 8th, 2012

I chose to review Abraham Kuyper's fourth lecture on Calvinism and Science. Kuyper submits four points for our consideration in this chapter regarding Calvinism and science which are; (1) that Calvinism fostered a love for science, (2) Calvinism restored to science its domain, (3) Calvinism delivered science from unnatural bonds and finally, (4) Calvinism found a solution for the unavoidable scientific conflict. Kuyper begins his thesis by offering a brief historical demonstration of his argument in the history of the defense of Holland from the attack of Spain where the town of Leyden stood fast in their defense against insurmountable odds. Having saved Holland from Spain the states of Holland gave the people of Leyden the gift of the University of Leyden which is world renowned for its scientific discoveries. The Calvinistic Netherlands loved and fostered the sciences and Leyden's University is the convincing proof. (Kuyper, p. 110-112)

Kuyper emphasizes his first point by connecting his argument to the Calvinistic view of pre-destination by claiming that fore-ordination means the certainty and the existence of all things including the entire cosmos which is governed by one principle which is the one Supreme will of God that directs all things toward a pre-established plan. Faith in the unity, stability, and order of all things cosmically as the counsel of God's decree awakens within us a deep love for science as we investigate, discover, and learn of the phenomena of God that governs the cosmos. (Kuyper, p. 112-117)

Kuyper eloquently argues his second point by stating that Calvinism put an end once and for all the dualistic contempt for the world and the resulting neglect of the temporal and the under-valuation of cosmic things. Under Calvinism he argues that cosmic life regained its worth by virtue of its capacity as God's handiwork and as a revelation of God's attributes. Calvinism thus ended any thoughts that he who occupied himself with nature was wasting his pursuit of vain things. Instead, for God's sake our attentions must not be withdrawn from the study of nature and creation but that this study must retain its place of honor beside the study of the soul. (Kuyper, p. 118-121)

Before defending his third point, Kuyper takes a brief interlude here to introduce the doctrine of common grace for us. Kuyper explains that God by his common grace restrains the operation of sin in man partly by breaking its power, partly by taming his evil spirit, and partly by domesticating him. Thus where evil does not manifest itself fully we owe it not to our uncorrupted nature but to God alone who holds evil in check through his common grace. Thus it is not only the church that belongs to God but the entire world belongs to God and both must be investigated as it is our task to know God in all his works both terrestrial and celestial. (Kuyper. P. 122-126)

In defending his third point that Calvinism set science free from bondage Kuyper explains that for ages there were two dominant systems of church and state along with the dominant world view of the dichotomy of body and soul. Science initially established itself as a separate third system but eventually surrendered its independence to the Pope in order to secure special privileges. Calvinism, through its discovery of common grace and belief that all things belong to God to be investigates, enabled science to once again break free from under the domain of the church and to thrive as its own system independent of both church and state. (Kuyper, p. 127-130)

Kuyper's last point stems from his third in that the emancipation of science will undoubtedly lead to a conflict of principles for which Calvinism offers the solution. The chief conflict in question is the conflict between those who confess their belief in the Triune God and His Word and those who seek their solutions to the world's problems in Deism, Pantheism, or Naturalism. Kuyper labels the former Normalists and the latter Abnormalists and goes on to say, "He who is not born again, cannot have a substantial knowledge of sin, and he who is not converted, cannot possess certainty of faith; he who lacks the Testimonium Spiritus Sancti, cannot believe the Holy Scriptures, and all this according to the thrilling saying of Christ himself: "Except that a man be born again, he cannot see the Kingdom of God." (Kuyper, P. 137) Kuyper quotes the Apostle Paul saying that the natural man receives not the things of the Spirit of God and goes on to say that with regard to the present condition of things we have to acknowledge that there are two kinds of human consciousness: that of the regenerate and that of the unregenerate and these two cannot be identical. Calvinism's solution then is to charge those who are regenerate to fully investigate and fully record as a fact of phenomena of God in your entire scientific endeavor. (Kuyper, p. 131-141)

I would counsel Melissa by initially affirming her gifts and skills as a scientist and to encourage her toward fulfilling these gifts within her chosen vocation as a scientist and to prayerfully consider this change of vocation as a calling from God. I would also affirm her gifts and skills as a counselor and how these gifts can also be utilized within her scientific vocation as she lives out her faith in God within the scientific community. I would explain that she is not working outside of the church but that she is the church and wherever she goes her work has eternal significance and meaning for the Kingdom of God.

I would also counsel Melissa that her choice of vocation is a legitimate calling for any Christian with her skills and that it is a theologically sound decision for her chosen vocation. I would explain that all of creation belongs to God and that this truth should awaken within all of us a deep love for science as we investigate, discover, and learn of the phenomena of God that governs all of creation. God calls us to be scientists in Genesis where God commands us to have dominion over the earth and within the essence of that command is our call as humans to investigate, discover, and learn all that we can about God's wonderful creation. I would also urge Melissa to take seriously her faith as she enters this vocational calling as she is entering a vocation that historically does not honor or recognize God as the creator of the cosmos. Her calling into this vocation as a believer is a high calling to investigate, to record, and to honor God in all that she uncovers as a scientist that points to the God of all creation. Finally, I would counsel Melissa in the importance of staying connected to a community of faith and if her current community does not accept her vocational calling as a scientist then she should either seek out those within her community that do accept this calling and connect with them or she should seek out another community of faithful believers that would accept and support her in her vocational calling.

PH522-Perspectives on Christ and Culture: Professor Dr. Kimberly Thacker
Book Review: "When the Kings Go Marching In" by Dr. Richard J. Mouw
By: Terrence Dwyer, July 9th, 2012

The Ships of Tarshish —Mouw argues here that what we refer to as "heaven" as described by the Holy City of Revelation 21 should be central to our understanding of the heavenly condition. Mouw explains that our bodiless presence with the Lord after death is not our final state but we are to be resurrected to a new life in Jesus Christ and as such our new life is directed toward this Holy City where God's redemptive purposes for his creation will be realized. (Mouw; p. 19) We do not build this city here and now but this city comes "down out of heaven from God" (Rev. 21:2) as the Lord is its builder and maker. The prophet Isaiah pictures this Holy City as a center of commerce with vessels and commercial goods and much commercial activity. (Mouw; p. 20) However, the Shalom of the Lord and the fullness of the knowledge of the Lord will be present throughout all of creation and the curse of sin will be lifted from the earth and God's righteousness will heal and transform all of creation. (Mouw; p. 22) All the commercial vessels and goods throughout the city will have their purposes transformed from serving pagan culture to serving God in his redeemed creation. All the nations who took great pride in their military and technological strength will be brought low and in that day the Lord alone will be exalted. (Mouw; p. 26) The judgment of Lord on these idolatrous nations is not meant to destroy them but to tame and transform them for service in the Holy City here they become vessel for ministry in the New City – their function has thus been transformed and it is their former idolatrous function that has been destroyed. (Mouw; p. 29)

Mouw goes in to argue that God commanded his creatures to fill the earth and to subdue it that in our rebellion against God we have distorted this process of filling and subduing but yet the earth is the Lord's and everything in it and God will work to transform and redeem all that we have filled the earth with. We will be transformed beings and everything that we have created and filled the earth with will also be transformed in their function for God's use. (Mouw; p. 35-36)

The Kings of the Earth – Mouw argues in this chapter that just as the vessels and goods of commercial activity will be transformed from an idolatrous function to a ministerial function; the sinful patterns of power and domination in political rule will also be healed and restored to their proper function of servanthood in the governance of human affairs. (Mouw; p. 63) Government in a fallen world must be a coercive government wielding the power of the sword in response to sin but they are also affected by sin and governments can become beastly and idolatrous. (Mouw; p. 64) God will call all of these governments to judgment in the Holy City where there will be a reckoning of accounts. (Mouw; p. 59) Mouw argues here that the Holy City will be inhabited only by those who confess Jesus Christ as their Lord and Savior but there will be an episode where non-believing people and their kings will be allowed to enter into the Holy City as participants in a political reckoning process. (Mouw; p. 59) The kings of the earth representing all of the nations and the cultures of the earth are to be brought into the Holy City before God where there will be a political reckoning for those who misused their power which comes from God alone. Jesus has "disarmed the principalities and powers and made a public example of them." (Col. 2:15) Good governments stripped of their rebellious and idolatrous ways by God will instead serve and nurture the people of God and will become a force for giving life. Thus, the reference in Isaiah 60:16 to "sucking the breast of kings." (Mouw; p. 63)

The Milk of Many Nations – Mouw explains in this chapter that Isaiah 60 depicts the Holy City as a meeting place for all the nations of the earth where both Jew and Gentile will live in the redeemed City enjoying the benefits of "the milk of nations." (Mouw; p. 75) This new eternal Holy City will be represented by "every tribe and tongue and people and nation." (Revelation 5:9) Mouw makes the interesting point here that there is no one human individual or group which can fully manifest the image of God and that the image of God is collectively possessed among all the peoples of the earth. (Mouw; p. 84) Thus all the diverse cultural riches throughout all the earth are to be brought into the Holy City and that which has been parceled out must now be gathered in for the glory of the Creator. (Mouw; p. 86)

Therefore Mouw argues that at the very least we the Church should be actively working today toward abolishing ethnic and racial discrimination within the Christian community as a model of what life will be like in the Holy City where peoples of all the earth will be gathered. (Mouw; p. 89&93)

The Light of the City – In this chapter Mouw focuses on Jesus Christ as the only light that fully illumines the Holy City as described by both Isaiah and John. As the Lamb of God Jesus draws all kings and all cultures to himself who will return their authority and power to the Lamb who sits upon the throne. Jesus came to redeem all of creation that was infected by sin and the cleansing of Christ must not only reach our hearts but also into every aspect of creation. (Mouw; p. 109-110) The authority of Jesus will be known by all and Jesus will rule with peace and righteousness. Practically, this truth deeply impacts how we live out our lives in this age as the Church as we seek to bring glimpses of the Holy City to our current culture but our ultimate response is no other than to give the Lamb of God all our worship, honor, praise, and glory. (Mouw; p. 117)

CHAPTER 9: SYSTEMATIC THEOLOGY

ST501 – Systematic Theology
Book Reading Response #1: "The Beauty of the Earth" by Steven Bouma-Prediger
By: Terrence Dwyer, November 7th, 2011

The author of this text seeks to provide an Evangelical Christian vision for the creation care of the planet earth. He begins by describing the web of the inter-connectedness between earth's many ecosystems such as forests, mountains, and lakes. He then paints a fairly bleak and foreboding picture of several of the significant ecological issues we are currently experiencing on the earth. Some of these significant issues are the exponential population growth, increase in hunger and food production shortages, species extinction, deforestation, and lack of water, lack of arable land, mounting waste, inequitable energy consumption, air quality, and significant climate change. While the author's message of hope from Isaiah 54 in his concluding chapter was somewhat comforting, one cannot come away from his second chapter on "What's wrong with the world" without feeling particularly alarmed and wondering if the call toward radical change may have come too late.

The third chapter asking whether or not Christianity was to blame for our bleak ecological situation touched on some very key criticisms of the Christian faith which the author owned up to. Among these arguments is the charge in Genesis 1:28 to have dominion over the earth have led to the exploitation of creation. The Christian traditions of the dualism of the body and soul and of matter and spirit have led to the denigration of the earth. I believe the above two charges against the faith have some merit and that the author might have lightly dismissed these charges. However, the author nicely dismissed the charge against Christianity that it played a leading role in the rise of Western science and technology and thus in the despoliation of the earth. I also believe that the eschatology charge against the church has merit and that the author here too dismissed this charge too lightly. I appreciate the difficulty the author faced in defending the faith on the one hand while owning up to our transgressions on the other but I think on some of these charges the author let the church off way too easily in light of our overwhelming complicity in the crime. That being said, the author's counter arguments against secular materialism and denial of creation were convincing.

The author makes a convincing and beautiful case from Scripture for creation care drawing principally from Genesis, Job, Colossians, and Revelation. In Genesis God makes a covenant with all of his creatures, in Job God is the at the center of creation man is not, in Colossians all things are held together through Christ the Creator and the Redeemer and in Revelation we see a renewed earth with God dwelling with us in a world of shalom. While his arguments are convincing and encouraging it is also a bit disheartening to the degree that these same texts have been in the church for quite some time while we willingly participated in the despoliation of the earth without any apparent outcry from within the church. The author's arguments for how we should think of the earth are excellent foundational statements for our evangelical theology of ecology. His appeal to what kind of people we should be was quite eloquent but perhaps a bit quixotic.

In reading this text I could not help but consider the comparisons of the issues surrounding ecological theology and those of feminist theology and even those of liberation theology. The earth has been dominated, oppressed, despoiled, and marginalized much like the tribulations of women and similar to the tribulations of the poor. The earth has been powerless and without a voice for far too long and ecological theology has to give earth and all of her inhabitants a voice. Our historical patriarchal language for God has too long been tied to domination and imperialism which has played a significant role in the desecration of our planet's finite resources. Our very language for God needs to be changed toward a more holistic and ecological view of God if we're to implement the significant changes the author is calling for in this text. Our anthropocentric viewpoint is contributing to the ecological destruction of the planet and we need to alter this viewpoint by perhaps first altering our language for God. The Latin call for a new hermeneutic can perhaps start with a new more holistic language for our Creator. The underlying values of society need to be reshaped and perhaps the feminist call for holistic God language can also be tied to ecological theology's need for the same.

Perhaps the North American church can pause and listen to the holistic wisdom and language of our Native American theologians in their respect for creation and for their belief in the vital connection between God, human beings, and all of the earth. They generally refuse to refer to God in an anthropomorphic term which is perhaps where we need to start. I believe that there is much that ecological theology can draw from feminist theology, Latin American theology, and Native American theology in that their struggles of being marginalized are similar to creation's own experience of being marginalized by her caretakers.

ST501 – Systematic Theology
Book Reading Response #2: "Can Evangelicals Learn from World Religions?" by Gerald R. McDermott
By: Terrence Dwyer, November 26th, 2011

The author of this text claims that the Christian understanding of its' own revelation is less than it could be and that Christians may gain a broader understanding of its' own revelation through the study of other religions. The author is quick to point out that the question of salvation through Christ is not under review here but only truth and revelation as held by other traditions and how the normative claims of these other traditions may lead us to a deeper understanding of the revelation of Christ.

The author begins by defining the term evangelical and then looks briefly at how evangelicals have viewed other religions throughout history. Here the author reviews and critiques the existing framework for our understanding of salvation as restrictivist, inclusivist, or pluralist. Restrictivists argue that all unevangelized are doomed. Inclusivists argue that no one is saved apart from Jesus but that one does not need to know Jesus during this lifetime to be saved by Him. Pluralists argue that there are many ways to God of which Jesus is only one of the ways to God. He concludes that most all religions are essentially restrictive and therefore seeking a wider understanding of revelation from other religions gives us a deeper understanding of our own.

The author reviews the various means through which we experience the revelation of God through nature, reason, Scripture, and ultimately God's revelation of Himself in Jesus Christ. He argues here that revelation from one perspective can often be distorted and by looking at God's revelation from multiple perspectives we will gain a deeper understanding of revelation itself. McDermott next builds a convincing Biblical case that God has given knowledge of Himself to people and traditions outside of the Hebrew and Christian traditions and that indeed a recurring theme in the Old Testament is Yahweh's desire for all the world to know that He is Lord. McDermott also shows here that both Jesus and Paul believed that Christians could learn about God from individuals who knew little or nothing about Jesus.

The author argues convincingly for revelation in other religions from Scripture and from the work of Jonathan Edwards and other theologians. He affirms that there is a revelation in other religions and that God reveals these truths at different levels and degrees depending upon the spiritual receptivity and maturity of the person receiving the revelation. Through general revelation the heavens are telling the glory of God and the law of God is written upon every human heart. The author concludes that among the world religions are promises of God in Christ and that these promises are revealed types planted there by the triune God. Seeing these truths in other religions can help Christians sharpen their thinking about these truths. McDermott then shows how Thomas Aquinas learned to better understand Scripture from Aristotle and how Calvin learned from Renaissance humanism.

After building his case for revelation the author finally reviews a few religions in depth for their own unique revelations. I found the review on Buddhism to be the most insightful and helpful in understanding and representing his argument for revelation. The Buddhist insight that transcendent truth lies beyond sense perception and intellectual conception admonishes us to recognize that God is qualitatively and infinitely different from us. This insight can teach us a higher reverence and respect before our mysterious and ineffable God. Buddhism can also teach us that nothing exists on its own but that every substance in creation is dependent upon God and related to every other substance. Thus, the mystery of God can be found in all of creation which isn't necessarily pantheistic and can teach us to respect and care for creation. Finally, Buddhist spiritual practices can teach us to better live in the spirit and meditate on the mystery of God all of which gives us a new perspective toward understanding our own revelation of God in Christ.

Daoism reminds us that God works in mysterious ways and that reality is not always what it seems and the wisdom of God is often opposite of human wisdom. These teachings and insights can again give us another perspective on the Biblical teachings that God if often paradoxical producing strength through human weaknesses. Confucianism teaches that true joy comes from wholehearted commitment to the good and the beautiful and from this we can learn a deeper understanding of what it means to be radically committed to Jesus Christ and forgoing some of the amenities of life for the sake of the Gospel. From the Muslim faith we can learn much regarding humble submission to God, all of creation as God's glory, regular and disciplined prayer life, charity, and public faith.

McDermott has given me much to reflect upon toward learning a deeper understanding of my own faith from the revelations found here in these other faith traditions. I agree with the Buddhist insight that transcendent truth lies beyond our abilities to grasp which also gives me a much deeper appreciation of the loving heart of God in the giving of Himself in Jesus Christ. I believe that there is more than enough Scripture to warrant creation care but I also find helpful the alternative perspectives of reverence for God and for all of His creation found in the other traditions.

Finally, the spiritual disciplines and practices of some of the other traditions found here challenge me to dig deeper into my own spiritual practices and disciplines. I find myself wanting to learn more about the spiritual practices and disciplines of the early church. I agree with the author's premise that evangelicals can learn from other world religions and I believe this author proved his argument that there appears to be certain general revelations of truth found in these other traditions.

ST501 – Systematic Theology
Reading Response #1: Key Concepts in Revelation
By: Terrence Dwyer, October 17th, 2011

Define the following issues: the meaning of general revelation and the means to the knowledge of God, inspiration, illumination, and the authority of Scripture. Be sure to critically engage Grenz's understanding of inspiration, illumination, and the authority of Scripture; assess the strengths and weaknesses of his approach and compare it to your traditions' beliefs about these issues.

General revelation is the theological concept that God's existence can be known by everyone as God reveals himself through creation. General revelation is available through nature to all humans who have been made in the image of God and equipped by God to access at least some knowledge of the divine. Psalm 19:1 states that the heavens declare the glory of God and Romans 1:20 states that God's invisible attributes have been clearly seen through what has been made. General revelation may be contrasted with special revelation where in special revelation God has chosen to reveal himself through miraculous means such as appearances, visions, dreams, Scripture, and most importantly – Jesus Christ.

Thomas Aquinas was a strong proponent of general revelation while Karl Barth was a strong opponent of general revelation as a humanist theology from classical liberalism. Barth argued instead that revelation is grounded in God alone and that divine revelation is redemptive and salvific only and only in and through Jesus Christ. Aquinas argued that humans have the means to the knowledge of God through God given reason. Aquinas argued that humans can, through their sensory experiences of nature, come to a genuine knowledge of God through intellectual and philosophical reflection and the reasoning out of propositional truths. Others argued that we come to the knowledge of God through religious experiences. Schleiermacher argued from immanence that finite humans have an intuition of the infinite which gives rise to our utter dependence upon God while Otto argued from transcendence that humans have an intuition of the "the holy other". Others argue for personal encounters with the living Christ such as Paul's encounter with Christ on the road to Damascus. Another means to the knowledge of God is through God's self-revelation. An example of such a self-revelation by God is the creation of the Scriptures through the work of the Holy Spirit. Barth argued that God's self-disclosure is found exclusively in Jesus Christ.

Grenz states that inspiration is the work of the Holy Spirit in influencing the writers of Scripture to produce writings which adequately reflect what God desired to communicate to us. Grenz goes on to say that illumination is the ongoing work of the Holy Spirit of continually speaking to humans through Scripture through the process of enlightening the minds of humans toward a deeper understanding of Scripture. Grenz then states that Scripture is authoritative in the life of the believer and in the church as it is the Holy Spirit who utilizes the instrument of Scripture to infallibly speak through Scripture to us.

Grenz however argues for an emphasis on the illumination of Scripture as the Holy Spirit continues to speak through the Scriptures to the church which must use both Christian tradition and the contemporary cultural context to influence how we are to understand the Biblical text. This approach has its benefits in that it speaks more toward the eschatological nature of the church as the Holy Spirit works toward creating a world centered on Christ as God ultimately intends for creation.

However, his approach also has its' drawbacks in that it runs the risk of subjectivism whereby we make the inspiration of the text dependent upon our hearing the voice of the Holy Spirit. Grenz avoids this by affirming that we objectively declare the Word of God to be divine Scripture whether we subjectively acknowledge this. My own Presbyterian tradition is in accordance with the Reformed tradition of the Westminster Confession of Faith, which Grenz affirms, where all of Scripture is declared authoritative as it is the vehicle through which the Holy Spirit speaks and is to be the Supreme Judge by which all controversies of religion are to be determined.

ST501 – Systematic Theology
Reading Response #2: Liberationist Approach to Revelation
By: Terrence Dwyer, October 17th, 2011

What are the unique features of Liberationist and intercultural approaches to revelation? How does a Liberationist approach help critique mainstream theologies of revelation? What are some potential weaknesses of such an approach?

Liberation theology affirms the problem of sin and alienation that has disrupted the relationship between humans and the divine. This fallen state affects the human reception and perception of divine revelation. Divine revelation occurs then in situations of great oppression and suffering which may offer a different perspective than situations where oppression and suffering are apparently absent. According to the experience of Noel Leo Erskine; in situations where there is great suffering, poverty, oppression, and sin; Liberation theology inextricably links divine revelation and salvation together. Sin is the root cause of poverty, crime, social, and economic injustices and people need to be free from this sin. Sin is not only individual but it is also endemic and systemic and holds entire classes of people in bondage. The God who is revealed in Jesus Christ is the God of salvation from the condemnation of sin and also the God of freedom from the bondage and injustices of sin. Jesus Christ is the emancipator, the justifier, and the reconciler from this bondage to sin.

Those living under oppression and suffering also feel cursed and condemned by God and carry within them a pervading sense of worthlessness. Liberation theology connecting revelation and salvation offers the Good News of Jesus Christ who takes all sin and condemnation upon himself and offers justification and complete forgiveness and freedom from condemnation. Those who feel cursed and condemned may love and accept themselves as God readily accepts and loves them through Jesus Christ. Through God's grace, this new relationship with self and with God also enables new relationships with others. Through Jesus Christ the reconciler, the walls of separation and alienation between the classes that fostered systemic sin are eventually broken down as eyes are opened toward liberation versus oppression. Revelation is thus a new way of being in the world as it is a new way of identifying self.

According to Brunner, revelation is an encounter with the divine who offers the divine self to humanity. This revelation of the divine self utterly transforms humanity as this new knowledge of the divine gives new light and life, salvation and freedom to the person receiving the revelation. Revelation and salvation are again inextricably linked together through Jesus Christ.

An additional feature of Liberation theology is from the work of Elizabeth Johnson who reminds that God is essentially inscrutable and that no name can capture the meaning of God. The source of authority concerning the revelation for women's liberation theology is therefore not Scripture or Jesus Christ but the revelation received in their experience as women and they do not need to go outside their experience to encounter revelation. As sources of authority for revelation, both Scripture and Jesus Christ may actually increase the oppression of women. Revelation of the divine is found within their experience of the divine in their situation.

The liberation approach helps critique our mainstream theologies of revelation in that the liberationist gives us a different and broader perspective of divine revelation. The reality of systemic sin and oppression appears lacking from mainstream theologies. Although salvation appears to be appropriately emphasized in mainstream theologies; liberation and reconciliation appear to be under emphasized in comparison to liberation theologies. However, a potential weakness of such an approach may be an over emphasis on liberation and reconciliation versus the utter sufficiency of salvation through the revelation of Jesus Christ.

ST501 – Systematic Theology
Reading Response #3: Objections of Pluralistic Theologies to Christian Theology
By: Terrence Dwyer, October 31st, 2011

State the main objections of pluralistic theologies to traditional Christian theology. In your opinion, what are the main Evangelical rebuttals?

One of the main objections of pluralistic theology to traditional Christian theology is the pluralist's view that no one single religion can lay claim to the ultimate total truth of the divine. Pluralists believe that ultimate total truth is inaccessible to humans. Pluralists view all religions as human interpretations and expressions of their human experiences, images, concepts, and responses to the divine. Pluralist John Hick refers to this divine being as the Ultimate Truth or the Ultimate Reality and he argues that each of the world's religions is like a planet orbiting around this Ultimate Truth. Christianity, pluralists contend, must move from its' dogmatic center to a more pluralistic view of the Ultimate Truth at the center as all of the world's religions are complimentary ways of interpreting this Ultimate Truth.

Pluralists argue that Christianity's claim that Christ is the exclusive mediator and salvific event between God and mankind cannot be a valid claim. Pluralists state that all religions have similar phenomenological themes of love, hope, and salvation, etc. God is love for example is a common phenomenological theme among the world's religions. If this same Ultimate Truth is present in all religions, then one particular religion like Christianity cannot make a valid absolute and exclusive claim regarding this Ultimate Truth. Pluralists also argue that religion is a function of locality as there are strong ties between religion, ethnicity, and culture. People in China tend to be Buddhists while people in India tend to be Hindu for example.

Pluralists also argue that there is a common metaphorical and mythical nature in the language used to describe and interpret the human experience of the Ultimate Truth and that these metaphors cannot be taken at face value. Pluralists contend that the divinity of Jesus for example must be viewed metaphorically and complimentary to that of the divinity revealed in Buddha for example. Pluralists go on to state that the many historical and suprahistorical claims of various religions are either lacking in evidence or improvable. Pluralists contend that the evidence supporting the historical death and resurrection of Jesus is lacking and that his incarnation is a myth.

Some of the main Evangelical rebuttals to the arguments of Pluralism are that there are indeed truths inherent in various religions but that these truths do not invalidate the exclusive claims of Christianity. The Pluralist claim that all religions share certain similarities does not imply that all religions are therefore the same. The Pluralist view that all religions are wrong in their exclusiveness and in their claims to the truth has in effect simply created just another more imperialistic religion. In my opinion, I believe that our main evangelical rebuttal is the revelation of the Ultimate Truth himself in Jesus Christ as revealed in Scripture. No other text in history has been scrutinized as closely as Scripture. Within this text we find statements from Jesus Christ who claimed to be the Messiah of God and who said such things as, "I am the way, and the truth, and the life, no one comes to the Father but through me."(John 14:6)

ST501 – Systematic Theology
Reading Response #4:
By: Terrence Dwyer, November 7th, 2011

Native American theology is faced with a unique set of circumstances in that they are a deeply spiritual people but they are also a tribal people with hundreds of separate and distinct tribes. They are also an indigenous people whose land has been occupied and they have been conquered and oppressed by their occupiers. Their challenge is to find ways to express their Native American Christian theology in language that is not of the language of their dominant occupiers. The specific term God is often missing in Indian languages as their spirituality embraces every aspect of their life and God is not separated out. In this regard Native American theology can be considered somewhat Panentheistic. Native American's traditionally believe that all living beings are connected to each other and they receive their life and their energy from the Creator or from the Great Mystery.

I was struck by the similarities between Native American theology and feminist theology in that they both struggled with developing language for God that they could accept and identify with verses adopting the language of their occupiers or oppressors. I was also struck by the similarities between the two in their language chosen for God as Creator, Sustainer, Redeemer, Lover, and Friend. There also is some commonality in their understanding that God is a God of liberation who acts on behalf of the oppressed. Additionally, there is commonality in their ecological theology in that their common language for God is not patriarchal but is holistic and nonhierarchical.

When I think of Latin American theology I think of Liberation theology and the great work done by Latin theologians such as Gustavo Gutierrez of Peru, Leonardo Boff of Brazil, and Robert Munoz of Chile. Much of Latin American history has been written by their conquerors and their indigenous peoples have become marginalized and poor much like the Native Americans in North America. However, Latin American theology reminds us that God has revealed himself to the poor and the oppressed and God is their very source of strength and hope. This theological reality leads to criticism of the prevailing ideological theologies of the powerful that marginalize the poor and powerless. A new hermeneutic for understanding and interpreting Scripture is required and this new hermeneutic gives us a new practice toward the care and liberation of the poor, the oppressed, and the marginalized.

Gutierrez affirms that to love God is to love one's neighbor and that we are to take concrete actions on our neighbor's behalf and especially for the poor and powerless neighbor's among us. As a Catholic priest, Boff argued courageously against the hierarchies found in human society, including the church, and he argued for more equitable social models based upon the model found in the Trinity. It is interesting to note the comparison between the historical issue of achieving a new hermeneutic apart from the prevailing dominant theologies of both the Native American experience and the Latin American experience and that which is occurring today here in our North American urban environments with the Occupy Wall Street movement. Will the North American church achieve a similar liberationist theology for the North American poor and marginalized who have been cast aside in today's dominant consumerist culture whose constituents are in large part members of the North American church?

ST501 – Systematic Theology
Reading Response #5:
By: Terrence Dwyer, November 13th, 2011

Discuss Grenz's idea of the "Structures of Existence" and how it may relate to Walter Wink's idea of "powers." Be sure to include your own understanding of how to best speak of evil and the demonic in contemporary Evangelical theology.

Grenz's idea of structures of existence is a much broader

understanding of the role and function of cosmic spiritual forces than that of the spiritual activity of individual angels and demons. Grenz states that there are large inescapable structures for human existence within which the context for human existence takes place. These structures penetrate our daily lives and are so common to us that they often go unnoticed. Examples of these structures are things like political, economic, religious, moral, and intellectual systems. These systems are designed by humans and they give structure and context for our human lives but the systems themselves exist independently of us and ultimately lie beyond our abilities to control them. Grenz argues that these large structures of human existence are intended by God for good for our governance and for fostering community. These structures are separate and distinct from the angelic beings who serve God in governing the world. These angelic beings work with and through these large structures of human existence by guiding the structures toward our benefit and for advancing the cause of good. However, evil spiritual beings may also work through these large structures of human existence for evil purposes and for our detriment. By doing so, these evil spiritual forces may bring us into bondage to these systems themselves which then become vehicles for idolatry and for advancing the cause of evil. The Apostle Paul speaks about these evil spiritual forces in Ephesians 6:12; "for our struggle is not against flesh and blood, but against the rulers, against the authorities, against the powers of this dark world and against the spiritual forces of evil in the heavenly realms". God however is reconciling these structures of human existence back to good and to their original intent and purpose through the work and reign of Jesus Christ.

Similarly, theologian Walter Wink also speaks of human structures and systems that are real and collective entities that have a spiritual component to them. This spiritual component informs the character of the human structure or system and thus can influence the structures or systems for good or evil. Wink explains that these principalities and powers that were intended for good have fallen and are being used for evil and for domination of humans. These principalities and powers must be redeemed and they are redeemed through the saving and redemptive work of Jesus Christ who inaugurates the domination free Kingdom of God. Wink's theology however is Panentheistic in that God is within the world. Wink's theology is also contradictory to Scripture in that he doesn't affirm the transcendent role of angels nor does he recognize Satan as a personal being. He groups these spiritual forces together and describes them as powers and makes them more immanent than transcendent.

In my own understanding of evil and the demonic in contemporary evangelic theology I would speak of these as being realities of our fallen nature which Christ has come to defeat and to redeem. While these forces may appear to still have power, they have been defeated by the work of Christ who holds all power and authority. Through faith in Christ these powers no longer have power and authority over us and in Christ we are under the loving, forgiving, and redeeming power and authority of Jesus Christ who is redeeming these powers and authorities to himself and his kingdom.

ST501 – Systematic Theology
Theological Reflection #1
By: Terrence Dwyer, October 13th, 2011

Explain briefly the nature and task(s) of systematic theology in the theological curriculum, the relationship between systematic theology and other theological disciplines, and the practical implications of systematic theology to faith, ministry, and mission.

Systematic Theology encompasses the intellectual reflection upon our faith and the subsequent ordering and articulation of our religious belief system. We do the task of Systematic Theology to define our belief system in the context of competing religious and non-religious belief systems. We also do the task of Systematic Theology to summarize the major biblical themes, to bring them into summary form, and to instruct and edify the faithful from generation to generation.

"Systematic Theology is an integrated discipline which searches for a coherent, balanced understanding of Christian truth and faith in light of God's revelation and in the context of the history of Theology and contemporary world and cultures" (VMK-lecture 1).

In relation to other theological disciplines, Systematic Theology differs from Biblical Theology in that Biblical Theology is concerned with Biblical interpretation and exposition, while Systematic Theology is concerned with giving clear statements about certain topics of Christian faith from the Bible. Systematic Theology also differs from Historical Theology in that Historical Theology is concerned with the historical development of truth for the church over the ages, Systematic Theology is concerned with formulating statements of faith that are applicable to the current age in light of historical developments. Systematic Theology also differs from Philosophical Theology in that Systematic Theology bases its discussion on revelation whereas Philosophical Theology does not commit itself to any particular kind of revelation or religious commitment.

We are an integral part of the eschatological Body of Christ. Systematic Theology gives us the training and the tools that we need as members of the Body to carry on the work of our forebears and to pass on our work to the next generation with thoughtful consistency.

ST501 – Systematic Theology
Theological Reflection #2
By: Terrence Dwyer, October 17th, 2011

What can Karl Barth's neo-orthodox theology of revelation contribute to an Evangelical theology of revelation? What are its potential weaknesses?

Barth's theology of divine revelation in his main theological work, Church Dogmatics, significantly contributes to an Evangelical theology of revelation. Barth's theology of divine revelation was a result of his strong reaction to classical liberalism and its' emphasis on natural revelation. Barth denied natural revelation as an anthropocentric and humanist theology of revelation. Barth insisted instead that divine revelation is grounded in God himself, not in nature, in history, or in human words. Divine revelation is redemptive in nature for Barth. For Barth, to know God is to have a genuine salvific experience of God. Divine revelation for Barth is thus only redemptive or salvific in nature and is grounded in God himself as an act of divine grace and is found only in and through Jesus Christ who is the only mediator between God and humanity. For Barth, divine revelation is a personal encounter with God through Jesus Christ.

Barth's complete rejection of natural revelation seems to run up against the Genesis account of creation where "traces" of God can be found in the Creators' own creation and where humans made in the image of God are thus capable of some kind of knowledge of the creator God. Natural theology should however be rightly placed under and made dependent upon God's self-revelation.

Barth also describes the Bible as the testimony of the primary witnesses of God's self-revelation and is not itself a primary form of revelation. For Barth, the Bible is a human and fallible witness which becomes the Word of God through the illuminating work of the Holy Spirit. However, for Scripture to be a trustworthy witness it needs to be more than just a witness.

ST501 – Systematic Theology
Theological Reflection #3
By: Terrence Dwyer, October 20th, 2011

Select three theologians, each from a different historical period. Compare their views of God, and highlight the distinctive features of their traditions.

The three theologians I've selected to briefly review are Origen (184-254A.D.) from the Patristic era, Thomas Aquinas (1225-1274A.D.) from the Medieval era, and Rene Descartes (1596-1650 A.D.) from the Modern era. The Patristic fathers of the early church period developed their theologies amid the syncretism and polytheism of the Roman Empire. The Patristic fathers also developed their theologies under the influence of a prevailing Platonic philosophy in addition to the philosophies of Stoicism and Gnosticism. Origen held that God could not be comprehended by human intelligence and that knowledge of God is fully known only as revealed by God through Scripture and especially through Jesus Christ. Origen defended the principle of unity in opposition to the multiplicity of Platonism and he foundationally affirmed the Trinity and the eternally begetting of the Son.

The mystical orientation from the Eastern tradition at the beginning of the medieval period held that God is a mystery who was incomprehensible and indefinable. Intellectualism and the study of theology grew prominent in this era and the simple idea of God was not sufficient to satisfy the minds of the time of the existence of God. Thomas Aquinas thus set out to prove that the existence of God could be determined from the creation of God. Aquinas proposed five arguments to prove the existence of God; God is the first mover, the first cause, the necessary being, the highest good, and the one who shapes the universe. Aquinas also proposed five attributes of God; God is simple, God is perfect, God is infinite, God is immutable, and God is one.

Descartes comes after the Reformation and is considered the father of modern philosophy. Descartes sought to determine where the origin of the idea of God comes from within the human mind. He finds that within his finite human mind he has the idea of an infinite and perfect being which he attempts to doubt away but finds that he cannot. He concludes that the only way his finite mind could conceive of such an idea is that the idea itself had to have been placed there by the infinite being. Here the image of God implanted in God's creation of Genesis 1:26-27 comes to mind. God plants the idea of God within His creation.

ST501 – Systematic Theology
Theological Reflection #4
By: Terrence Dwyer, October 24th, 2011

Present briefly the main arguments and affirmations of open theism, as well as your own critical (as well as affirmative) views. What do you see as some of the pastoral implications of open theism, either positive or negative?

Open Theism is an attempt to revise Classical Theism from within orthodox Christianity. Some of the main arguments are Open Theists do not accept the unchanging, sovereign God of Classical Theism and therefore support a more open, loving, and relational God. Open Theists argue that Classical Theism depicts God as the final cause of all that happens, denying human freedom, and unmoved by what happens in the world. Open Theists argue that God is love and is more like that of a loving parent who desires to be in relationship with creation. This loving, communal, and relational God allows humans limited freedoms to make choices and this personal and flexible God responds and interacts. Although God is still omniscient, the future is partially open depending upon the choices that humans make.

Some of the affirmations for Open Theism are that Open Theists make their arguments from within Scripture and they do offer a more contemporary context then Classical Theism. Open Theism also brings up the significance of Greek metaphysical philosophy upon the origins of Classical Theism which bears consideration. I find the arguments of Open Theism to be appealing, practical (such as God answering prayer), and in agreement with the loving, flexible, and interactive God that I find depicted in Scripture. My concern is the emphasis on the significance of the human being within Open Theism. Are we simply attempting to dethrone God? Pastorally, I find the God of Open Theism to be much more loving, approachable, and compassionate toward those that I may be ministering to.

ST501 – Systematic Theology
Theological Reflection #5
By: Terrence Dwyer, November 3rd, 2011

Explain briefly the main heresies combated and corrected in the evolving patristic doctrine of the Trinity.

Many of the early church Christians were Jews who believed that what God was doing through Christ was foretold by the prophets and was a continuation of what God had begun throughout the Old Testament period. These Jews also held that God was one as they strongly rejected multiple gods. These early church Christians held that God is one but they also understood that God had uniquely revealed himself in Jesus Christ whom they asserted and believed to be divine. They also experienced the divine presence of the Holy Spirit as God among them but who they experienced as neither the Father nor the Son. The challenge for the early church was to theologically combine their belief in the one God with their experiences of the divine Jesus and the divine Holy Spirit.

An early attempt to explain the divinity of Christ, called dynamic Monarchianism, sought to preserve the Father as the divine monarch with divine power descending upon Jesus. Jesus was not God but was a carrier of the divine power of God. Another explanation, called modalistic Monarchianism, stated that the Father, Son, and Spirit are three modes through which the divine expresses himself. However, this expression of three is not part of the eternal essence of God but is the manner in which God chooses to reveal himself to humans in time.

Early church proponents of the heretical view that Christ was "made" by the Father were known as Arians and the early church combated and corrected this heresy at the Council of Nicaea in 325. Based upon the theological arguments of Origen and Athanasius, the council successfully argued that the Son was eternally begotten not made and is of one substance with the Father.

Finally, the deity of the Spirit was also similarly challenged by Macedonius who followed the heretical Arian position but this argument was finally put down during the 2nd Ecumenical Council at Constantinople in 381. Athanasius successfully asserted the full deity of the Spirit as equal to the Son and the Father as necessary for our faith and salvation. The council agreed and affirmed the full deity of the Spirit.

ST501 – Systematic Theology
Theological Reflection #6
By: Terrence Dwyer, November 4th, 2011

What are some key contributions of women to our understanding of God and Trinity? What are some of the ways evangelical theology may find feminist views problematic?

One of the key contributions of women theologians to our understanding of God is their opening up of the discussion on the traditional language historically used to describe God. Much of the traditional language historically used to describe God may be deemed to be sexist and hierarchic. This patriarchal language used to describe God has been interpreted at times to legitimize the dominance and the oppression of women by men. Women theologians such as Elizabeth Johnson and Sally McFague among others have called for a reexamination of the language used to describe God. Their argument is that any words or phrases used to describe God can only be metaphorical as we cannot truly know God. Our words therefore do not describe God but merely point to God. The male metaphorical language that has been traditionally used is patriarchal and exclusionary toward women.

The work of women theologians has been the identifying and the deconstruction of the patriarchal language and how it has been used historically against women. These theologians have also offered forth alternative language options as substitutes for and compliments to the traditional patriarchal language for God. This discussion has opened up the debate on the very nature of God as McFague for example offers alternative metaphorical language describing God as mother, lover, and friend.

Perhaps the greatest contribution by feminist theologians is their work in ecological theology where their revision of the God language from the patriarchal to a more holistic and sensitive language. Their work here has brought greater attention to the perils of patristic God language in the area of ecological theology. Problematic in their approach here for certain evangelical theologians will be the feminist theologian's elevation of the status of creatures and the creation. Their elevation of creation could possibly be considered pantheistic which evangelical theologians will rightly denounce. However, McFague argues that creation is not to be confused as God but that creation is the place where God meets us.

ST501 – Systematic Theology
Theological Reflection #7
By: Terrence Dwyer, November 11th, 2011

Option 1 - Attempt a personal statement entitled "My understanding of the doctrine of creation" in critical dialogue with views studied this week and last. Be sure to address the question of whether evolutionism and the Christian theology of creation can be reconciled with each other.

My Understanding of the Doctrine of Creation

My understanding of the Doctrine of Creation is that the existence of the universe and of our world is a free, non-necessary act of God, and creation is a loving act of God. God's loving nature is revealed in the Triune God as God is love within himself. God calls the universe into existence as an act within God's own freedom and does so as an act of love to share his own existence. Creation flows from the loving relationship within the nature of the Triune God. The Father is the primary role in creation with the Son being the principle of creation and the Holy Spirit is the divine power in the act of creation. God is sovereign in his creation and acts in accordance with his loving character in fulfilling the purposes of his creation. My understanding of the Doctrine of Creation follows more closely with the classical view of creation and with Pannenberg's classical and Trinitarian view of creation.

While the other more Panentheistic views of creation, such as Moltmann's and McFague's, are more appealing at times and less divisive with my non-Christian friends, I do not find the biblical support that I need for these views in order to put my full weight behind them. It is very appealing to think that the world is in God and that God is in the world or in McFague's case that the world is God's body. However, I find that these views tend to elevate the creature and lessen the Creator and I therefore hold to Pannenberg's more classical view of creation which works within both Scripture and Tradition.

I believe that God can quite easily handle all that science can uncover and reveal about the universe as I believe that all knowledge will eventually point to and glorify the Creator God. Darwin himself believed that there was a Creator God who initiated and breathed life into the early life forms of his evolution theory. The theory of evolution and the Bible are not necessarily mutually exclusive as evolution may reveal to us how creation evolved over long periods of time while the Bible and the story of Adam

Rev. Terrence S. Dwyer

reveal to us our origin in God and our relationship with God and with each other.

ST501 – Systematic Theology
Theological Reflection #8
By: Terrence Dwyer, November 11th, 2011

Produce a personal statement about your current understanding of the doctrine of providence; be sure to dialogue with both Grenz' and Schwarz' views.

I believe that God's act of creation of calling the universe into existence is ultimately an eschatological event which leads to the doctrine of the providence of God as God fulfills the purpose of creation. I agree that the doctrine of providence is the ordering of creation toward God's ultimate purpose which can be best understood through the concepts of preservation, concurrence, and governance. Preservation refers to the continuous agency of God in maintaining the existence of creation. I appreciate Grenz's expansion upon the meaning of preservation for us by asserting that we derive meaning for our lives by knowing that through Christ we are participating in the eschatological purposes of creation. Concurrence refers to the cooperation of God with his creation in allowing his creation to act as it does within the powers assigned to it by God. Grenz reminds us here that God extends his goodness toward all of his creation, even the rebellious, and that God calls us to work and to pray. Governance refers to God's teleological care and control over creation and Grenz argues here that the eschatology of creation is moving toward the establishment of community of fellowship with God and with all of creation.

In contrast to Grenz briefly; Schwartz argues that the doctrine of providence can best be understood through the concepts of General and Special providence with Special providence encompassing miracles and prayer. General providence on the other hand is best understood through the concepts of preservation within nature which acknowledges that God has established natural processes within creation. General providence may also be understood through the second concept of preservation through moral conduct where God preserves his creation through natural laws and a conscience given to humans. Finally, General providence may also be understood through the third concept of the historical process where God honors the limited freedom given to humans yet where God's ultimate purpose for creation is still fulfilled.

ST501 – Systematic Theology
Theological Reflection #9
By: Terrence Dwyer, November 25th, 2011

As best you can, and in critical dialogue with the historical and traditional views studied this week, state your understanding of the image of God.

My understanding of the image of God is derived from Scripture which teaches us that we are created in the image and likeness of God (Genesis 1:26-27, Genesis 5:1-3, Genesis 9:5-6, 1 Cor. 11:7, and James 3:9). The first Scriptural reference is prior to the fall and the remaining references are after the fall. Being created in the image and likeness of God we are unique creatures of God in that as human beings we can reason and we have free will. God also put us in charge of His creation giving us dominion over it and giving us certain powers to carry out our responsibility. We also are uniquely created by God to have the capacity to have a relationship with God and with each other. My understanding of the image of God is also derived from our church history and church tradition where three basic positions have developed throughout our history regarding our being created in the image of God.

The first position is called the structural view, the substantive view, or the classical view in that this was the view held by the early and medieval church. This view holds that our being created in the image of God means that we have certain characteristics or capacities that are inherent within our human structural makeup that resemble the corresponding qualities of God. Some of the key elements of these characteristics are our ability to reason and our free will.

The second position is called the relational view which came out of the reformation period and was advocated by Luther and Calvin among others. This view holds that the fall perverted and deformed our image and that we are utterly depraved. This view holds that the divine image is more of an act than a human possession and that through the work of Christ our image has been restored and Christ is our image bearer before God. Through Christ and the Holy Spirit we are enabled to be in relationship with God.

The final view is the dynamic view which is an eschatological view in that the image of God is seen as a future goal or a future destiny which we are moving toward. Through the Holy Spirit and through Scripture, the divine image is progressively restored over time with our final image being born as resurrected humans in the new creation.

ST501 – Systematic Theology
Theological Reflection #10
By: Terrence Dwyer, November 26th, 2011

Learning from and in critical dialogue with relevant materials studied this week attempt a personal statement about the nature and implications of sin and the fall.

I believe that Adam was the historical first human being with whom God covenanted with in the Garden of Eden to not eat from the forbidden tree. Adam was the head of all of humankind and therefore represented all of humanity in this covenant with God. When Adam failed and disobeyed God by breaking the covenant of obedience, both sin and death entered into the creation and to all of Adam's descendants. As a result of this sin, fellowship with the Creator was broken, community with each other was broken, harmony with creation was broken, and the ground became cursed. As descendant of Adam I am born into this sinful and depraved state of being as Paul says "we are children of wrath" (Ephesians 2:3).

By being born into this lost state of being, the implication for my life is that I am alienated from my Creator and from my human community, I stand condemned by God through my inheritance, I find that sin has a power to enslave me, and that I am utterly powerless to do anything of my own accord to remedy this situation. I am utterly dependent upon the grace and mercy of God to remedy this predicament for me which He does through the free gift of Himself in Jesus Christ.

A Brief Examination of the Arguments
For and Against Open Theism
By: Terrence Dwyer
December 1st, 2011
Fuller Theological Seminary
ST501 Systematic Theology 1: Theology and Anthropology
Professor: Dr. Veli-Matti Kärkkäinen

Introduction

My purpose in writing this paper is to personally gain a deeper understanding of Open Theism by examining the arguments for and against this relatively recent theological approach toward understanding the nature of God. I first learned of Open Theism in this class and found myself initially attracted to this theological understanding of God as it spoke to my personal experience of God as a loving and personal God who allows me to have my own free will. I also initially believed that Open Theism would assist me in my pastoral role. I thought that a solid understanding of Open Theism might assist me toward pastorally sharing with others the nature of our loving and personal God and also to better explain such things as the existence of evil or the importance of prayer among other pastoral issues that inevitably come up. However, upon closer examination I now have some reservations regarding Open Theism which I will address in the conclusion of this paper.

My plan is to briefly review Classical Theism and the impact of Hellenization upon Classical Theism to set up the arguments for Open Theism. I will then review some of the arguments for Open Theism from theologians Clark Pinnock and John Sanders among others. I will next review some of the arguments against Open Theism from theologian Millard Erickson among others. Open Theology has often been referred to by its' critics as just another form of Process Theology so I will briefly contrast the differences between Open Theology and Process Theology. I am therefore not seeking to defend a thesis in this paper but to simply briefly examine the arguments for and against Open Theology to gain a better understanding of this theology.

My own thoughts and comments will be interspersed throughout the paper as I wrestle with this theology and I will finally conclude and summarize my examination with my own set of conclusions drawn from this brief review.

Classical Theism and Hellenistic Influence

Much of our view on the nature of God comes from Classical Theism which was developed by the patristic theologians of the early church period. Some of these early church fathers were Justin Martyr, Tertullian, Origin, and Augustine to name a few. Their views of Classical Theism were further developed by the scholastics of the medieval period such as Anselm of Canterbury and most notably Thomas Aquinas in his great work Summa Theologica. Classical Theism thus developed over time certain attributes of God. These are:

-Pure Actuality: God is absolute actuality in pure form with no matter to actualize his potentiality.

-Immutability and Impassability: God does not change, cannot be moved, and cannot be acted upon.

-Timelessness: God is eternal and timeless.

-Simplicity: God has no parts and is changeless.

-Necessity: God's existence is necessary and God cannot be other than who he is.

-Omnipotence and omniscience: God knows all and God possesses the capacity to do all.

Open Theists argue however that these early Classical Theist views of God were formed within and influenced by the Greek cultural framework within which they lived. These early church fathers lived within an intellectual atmosphere that was dominated by Greek philosophy and Open Theists argue that Classical Theism was thus tainted by this influence. Open Theists argue that the early church fathers and the scholastics imported their views of God from Greek philosophy by in part linking the God of the Bible to Plato's philosophies of the Form of the Good. Open Theists go on to argue that the scholastics of the medieval period adopted Aristotle's philosophy of God as the static unmoved mover. Thus these early Christian thinkers developed and built their doctrines of God by borrowing from these Greek philosophical traditions instead of exclusively building their views from the divine revelations of Scripture. These static, unchanging, impassible views of God imported from Greek philosophy seem to be at odds with the God found in Scripture who is actively involved in his creation and in the events of the world.

I cannot argue much here against the Open Theist's charge that the Patristics' and the Scholastics were influenced by Greek philosophy as it does seem to be the case. This has been an ongoing debate within the church for centuries as even Tertullian asked his famous question, "What has Athens to do with Jerusalem?" However, I cannot help but have sympathy for the dilemma that these early church fathers faced in living within a dominant Hellenized culture and working with the Greek Septuagint (LXX) text. I don't think that you can easily separate Biblical thought from the influence of Hellenization as the Septuagint and the New Testament texts are so influenced by the Greek language. How else were these early church fathers supposed to communicate their doctrines of God to the world around them other than with what they had access to within their known world? In defense of these early theologians they wrote extensively against Greek and other pagan philosophies of their time and they extensively quoted Scripture in doing so which is quite contrary to the charge of the Open Theists that these early church fathers adopted pagan philosophies. However, that being said, the God of the Bible does seem to be quite actively involved in his creation and there does appear to be a give and take in the relationship between God and humans. This revelation of God in Scripture does not reconcile well with the Classical view of God and thus Open Theology seeks to address this lack of harmony to which we will now turn.

Arguments for Open Theism

The basic premise of Open Theism is that God is love and that love is God's most important attribute. A God of love is caring, sensitive, and responsive which means that a God of love is dynamic rather than static and unmoving. It also means that a God of love interacts with his creation and his creatures and that a God of love allows human free will which in part plays a role in the course of history. A loving God is open and inviting to his creation to participate with him toward bringing the future into being.

Open Theists revisit and redefine certain attributes of God that are held by the Classical view. Some of these redefinitions of God's attributes by the Open Theists are as follows:

-Pure Actuality: Classic Theism teaches that God is completely independent of his creation but Open Theism teaches that God is dependent upon the world in certain respects.

-Immutability and Impassability: Classic Theism teaches that God is unchangeable and unmovable but Open Theism teaches that God is open to the world and responsive to developments in human history.

-Timelessness: Classical Theism teaches that God is timeless and eternal and exists outside of time and sequence. Open Theism teaches that God is temporally everlasting in that the God who created time and space enters into the experience of time.

-Simplicity: Classical Theism teaches that God has no parts and is changeless. Open Theism teaches that God takes on forms to facilitate his self-revelation. Hasker states, "The doctrine of divine simplicity, so crucial to the classical understanding of God, has been abandoned by a strong majority of Christian philosophers, though it still has a small band of defenders."

-Omnipotence and omniscience: Classical Theism teaches that God knows all and has the capacity to do all. Open Theism teaches that God willingly surrenders power to his creation and that God does not foreknow every future choice or every human decision.

Open Theism delivers us from the unmovable and unchangeable God of the Greek philosophers to the relational, dynamic, and loving God that we find in the divine revelation of Scripture. Open Theism views the triune God as relational and whose perfect love seeks loving relationships with human beings. Humans have been given free will for this very purpose to freely choose to participate in this loving communion to share in this love.

Practically speaking Open Theism makes a positive difference in our lives and in our discipleship. Our lives matter as God is not an alien and disinterested being but a God who is interested in our lives. Our relationship with God is transformative as we interrelate with him. Our freedom also brings with it responsibility for us to move and to act and make decisions versus not acting at all if we believe God has ordained everything. God's gifts of grace and salvation to us are open for us to accept and are not forced upon us as we are free to choose to accept them. The process of sanctification under Open Theism also makes sense in that we are free to choose to participate and cooperate with the Holy Spirit in the process of sanctification. Our response to God's call to discipleship also makes sense as God depends upon us to take responsibility and to persevere as his covenant partner. The interactive nature of prayer also makes sense under Open Theism as we petition God in prayer and God hears and responds and guides us in our relationship with him.

Open Theism however has not been met with open arms in evangelical theological circles. On the contrary, Open Theism has been strongly attacked. So much so that Clark Pinnock remarks in the conclusion of his seminal work; "On a personal level, I wonder why I have been so savagely attacked when I thought what I was doing was taking the Bible more seriously, encouraging us all to think more profoundly, and addressing some important questions surrounding our cherished relationship with God." Charges against Open Theism include such things as, related to Process Theology, polarization between sovereignty and freedom, denial of God's ultimate power, and diminishing of God's glory among others. It is to these criticisms of Open Theism to which we will now turn.

Arguments Against Open Theism

One of the arguments against Open Theism is their selective utilization of Scripture. Opponents argue that the totality of Scripture does not support their argument and that Open Theists simply carefully selected only those Scriptures that support their own argument. Open Theists neglect to address Scripture that in addition to God's love also speak of God's holiness, his wrath and vengeance, his judgment, that he is to be feared, and that he is jealous. Opponents argue that all of God's attributes deserve equal weight along with love in the descriptions of God.

Opponents of Open Theism also argue that Classical Theology has not followed the Thomistic model in all respects with Luther's references to the suffering God for example. Also, critics say that there is less of a Greek view on such things as God's impassability in Classical Theism than Open Theists will allow and that Open Theists overstate the limitations of Classical Theism. Opponents also state that Open Theists' rejection of divine foreknowledge on the basis of its conflict with human freedom assumes an incompatibility. Additionally, opponents argue that Open Theists charge the original Classical Theologians with being influenced by their surrounding culture but that the Open Theologians themselves make no recognition for the effects of being influenced by their own current culture. Finally, critics also charge that Open Theism is simply a thinly disguised version of Process Theology which we will now briefly address.

Comparison to Process Theology

There are many similarities to between Open Theology and Process Theology and some of these similarities are: they both speak about the love of God; they both emphasize human freedom, they both criticize conventional theism, they both espouse a dynamic understanding of God, and they both focus on the relationship between God and his world. However, there are also many clear differences between Open Theology and Process Theology and it is not a fair assessment to charge Open Theology as a thinly disguised version of Process Theology.

Process Theology is a natural theology based upon metaphysics whereas Open Theology is based upon Biblical and historical Christianity. Process Theology denies creation ex nihilo while Open Theology affirms it. Process Theologists deny the final victory of God over evil while Open Theologists affirm it. Open Theology also affirms God's omnipotence, miracles, and the supernatural while Process Theology denies them. Open Theology also states that God limits himself but Process Theology represents God as limited and finite. Finally, Open Theology represents that God's relationship to the world is asymmetrical and that God is ontologically independent of it.

While there are certain similarities between Open Theology and Process Theology; there are also significant theological and philosophical differences between the two and I don't believe that it is a fair or an appropriate academic charge to state that Open Theology is a thinly disguised form of Process Theology. After briefly reviewing some of the arguments for and against Open Theology I will now conclude my examination by reviewing some of the conclusions that I've drawn from this study.

Conclusion
I believe the opponents charges that Open Theology is heretical is an overstatement of their case and I believe that Open Theism warrants time in the evangelical academic arena for further review, discussion, and debate. I believe that there is some merit to the Open Theists claims that the Patristics' and the Scholastics were influenced by Greek Philosophy as some of the Patristics' themselves were concerned about this influence. I believe that some of the criticisms raised by the open Theists on this particular issue alone warrant a long hearing and much further study. On the other side of that argument however, I believe that Open Theists and others need to take a closer look at Open Theism and how this relatively new theology is emanating from Western Culture at this particular point in time. What are the implications of the influence of Western Culture upon the current views of the nature of God in Open Theology? I believe that this may warrant some further study as well.

Unfortunately, academic debate is stymied from polemics and I believe there is much to be learned from academic criticisms when taken with maturity. I believe that there is room for both Classical Theism and Open Theism at the evangelical table at least for purposes of inquiry, discussion, and debate. Open theists for their part could do more toward being less one sided in their criticisms and in their caricatures of Classical Theology. Classical Theists for their part could do more toward listening to the criticisms of the Open Theists and work more toward a constructive dialogue between them.

Personally, I am wary of anything that seems attractive at the outset and then upon further review seems to dethrone the Creator while simultaneously elevating the creature. This is essentially what I have found through my examination here of Open Theology. While this may not be a fair assessment it is what I have to go with at this stage of my theological development. I do believe I now have a better understanding of both Open and Classical Theology after this review and I am grateful for that. I discovered a plethora of excellent material on both Classical and Open Theology in doing the research for this review and I am looking forward to doing much more study in this area. I am however at this juncture reluctant to cast aside two thousand years of Classical Theism to wholly embrace Open Theology. I will however listen to their criticisms of Classical Theism and seek to grow and learn from them.

Bibliography

Erickson, Millard J. The Evangelical Left, Encountering Post conservative Evangelical Theology. Grand Rapids, Michigan: Baker Books, 1997.

Grenz, Stanley J. Theology for the Community of God. Grand Rapids, Michigan: William B. Eerdmans Publishing Co., 2000.

House, Norman L. Geisler and H. Wayne. The Battle for God. Grand Rapids, Michigan: Kregel Publications, 2001.

John B. Cobb, Jr. and Clark H. Pinnock. Searching for an Adequate God, a Dialogue between Process and Free Will Theists. Grand Rapids, Michigan: William B. Eerdmans Publishing Co., 2000.

Kärkkäinen, Veli-Matti. The Doctrine of God, a Global Introduction. Grand Rapids, Michigan: Baker Academic, 2004.

Pinnock, Clark H. Most Moved Mover, a Theology of God's Openness. Grand Rapids, Michigan: Baker Academic, 2001.

Pinnock, Rice, Sanders, Hasker, & Basinger The Openness of God, a Biblical Challenge to the Traditional Understanding of God. Downers Grove, Illinois: InterVarsity Press, 1994.

Sanders, John. The God Who Risks, a Theology of Providence. Downers Grove, Illinois: InterVarsity Press, 1998.

Sinkinson, Tony Gray & Christopher. Reconstructing Theology, a Critical Assessment of the Theology of Clark Pinnock. Waynesboro, GA: Paternoster Press, 2000.

Personal Theological Statement
On God and the God World Relationship
By: Terrence Dwyer
December 3rd, 2011
Fuller Theological Seminary
ST501 Systematic Theology 1: Theology and Anthropology
Professor: Dr. Veli-Matti Kärkkäinen

My personal theological statement begins with my belief in the one holy and eternal God who exists in three persons as God the Father, God the Son, and God the Holy Spirit, but who share the same divine essence and divine being. I believe that there is one and only one true God who is the perfect God and is absolute actuality in pure form. I believe that God is sovereign, unchanging, and immutable. I believe that God is timeless and eternal, and that God is omnipotent and omnipresent. I adhere to Classical Theisms' views concerning the attributes of God while at the same time respecting and listening to the criticisms of these views held by Open Theists' among others. I am aware that these Classical views originated from the early church fathers and that they may have been influenced in their thought by Greek philosophy.

My understanding of the Doctrine of Creation is that the existence of the universe and of our world is a free, non-necessary act of God, and creation is a loving act of God. God's perfect loving nature is revealed in the Triune God relationship of God the Father, God the Son, and God the Holy Spirit. God calls the universe into existence as an act within God's own freedom and does so as an act of love to share his own existence. Creation flows from the loving relationship within the nature of the Triune God. The Father is the primary role in creation with the Son being the principle of creation and the Holy Spirit is the divine power in the act of creation. God is sovereign in his creation and acts in accordance with his loving character in fulfilling the purposes of his creation. My understanding of the Doctrine of Creation follows more closely with the classical view of creation.

God has revealed his character and his deep love for humanity through the general revelation of creation, through the special revelation and witness of Scripture, through the special revelation and sacrificial gift of himself in Jesus Christ, and the indwelling presence of the Holy Spirit. All of God's creation retains the handprint of his goodness, including human beings who are made in his image, although the disobedience of the first humans brought death and depravity into God's creation.

"Then God said, 'Let us make mankind in our image, after our likeness. And let them have dominion over the fish of the sea and over the birds of the heavens and over the livestock and over all the earth and over every creeping thing that creeps on the earth.' So God created mankind in his own image, in the image of God he created them; male and female he created them." Genesis 1:26-27 (ESV)

Human beings are creatures made by God in the image of God, which requires an understanding of how we who are created can be in the image of God who was not created. We are not identical, but we have certain characteristics that mark us as created in the image of God. Being made in the image of God is demonstrated by our ability to reason and have free will and by humankind's God given responsibility to have dominion over the world. These attributes describe some of the outcomes of being made in God's image, rather than the source.

I believe that one important way that we were made in the image of God is that we were created for relationship. The Triune God is our model for loving relationship and as such we are created to be in loving relationship with God and with each other. Our capacity for relationship with God and each other defines our humanity and is an important aspect of how we are created in God's image.

Secondly, I believe that we are created by God to work concurrently with God to preserve and to care for this beautiful world that God created. God gave human beings dominion over all things that God created on earth and I understand creation to be an eschatological event. I understand this to mean that human beings are to exercise responsibility in the same manner in which God rules with deep respect, great care, and extraordinary wisdom in concurrently caring for the creation of God. I believe that God preserves creation by continually sustaining the physical existence of the universe. I also believe that God provides for his creation through his teleological care and control over creation.

Finally, I understand that part of being made in God's image is that this includes and transcends gender. Genesis 1:26-27 affirms that "in the image of God he created them; male and female he created them." The fullness of our identity of being made in God's image is not limited or defined by gender. The unique elements of our gender are part of our human identity in ways that do not conflict with the understanding that all people are made equally in God's image. As such, I respect and listen to feminist and liberationist theologians in their criticisms of some of the patriarchal language found in Scripture and how this language has been used at times throughout history for domination and oppression. I listen to and respect the strides being made by these theologians not only in liberation theology but also in the area of ecological theology.

I believe that Adam was the historical first human being and therefore represented all of humanity in a covenant of obedience with God. When Adam failed and disobeyed God by breaking the covenant of obedience, both sin and death entered into the creation and to all of Adam's descendants. As a result of this sin, fellowship with the Creator was broken, community with each other was broken, harmony with creation was broken, and the ground became cursed.

As a descendant of Adam I am born into this lost state of being and the implication for my life is that I am alienated from my Creator and from my human community. I stand condemned by God through my inheritance, I find that sin has a power to enslave me, and that I am utterly powerless to do anything of my own accord to remedy this situation. I am utterly dependent upon the grace and mercy of God to remedy this predicament for me and for all of humankind which he does through the free gift of himself in Jesus Christ.

Jesus Christ is God and is the only Son of God, fully human and fully divine. Jesus Christ fulfilled Scripture's promises to Abraham and his descendants and to all of mankind for a redeemer who would proclaim the reign of God and his victory over sin and death. Jesus accomplished this victory through his sacrificial death on a cross for the sins of humanity. Jesus' sacrificial death reconciled us to God and restored God's good creation from the power of sin and death. The ultimate realization of this victory over the power of death will be experienced when Jesus returns at the end of the age. We have a choice to accept this gift by accepting the grace extended to us through Jesus Christ, so that we can receive forgiveness and reconciliation and eternal salvation.

The Holy Spirit dwells within all believers who have accepted God's forgiveness through the gift of faith in Jesus Christ. I believe that the Holy Spirit is God and is our powerful and tangible guide in life, our comforter in times of trouble, and the protector of our soul, and our teacher and revealer of truth. I believe that the Holy Spirit is constantly at work to transform the heart, mind and will of all believers toward transforming their character toward the character of Jesus Christ. God speaks though the Holy Spirit, who has inspired and illumined Scripture to be our supreme authority and infallible guide. I believe that the Gospel, the good news of salvation through Jesus Christ, cannot be understood apart from understanding salvation as redemption of God's good creation from the fallen state, and that the Old and New Testament together portrays God's unrelenting love for humankind and his desire for mercy, compassion, and justice.

The fundamental nature of the Triune God is deeply relational, defined by fellowship and mutuality. I believe that while the persons of the Trinity are undividable, I have had the experience that greater knowledge about each person of the Trinity has been part of my journey of faith. This growing understanding of the Triune God was part of my journey of exploring the wonder of creation, the depths of my sinfulness and neediness, the release found in repentance and the enormity of God's love for me. Having felt the deep sense of God's love for me and having understood my identity as a child of God; I have received the fullness of God's grace in my heart and I believe that this experience is open to all of humankind.

I affirm the basic tenets of Reformed theology in that we are saved from the consequences of our sins by grace through faith and that this faith is a gift given to us from our sovereign God. I believe that we are incapable of reaching past our sinful nature to obtain or earn our salvation on our own merits. I believe that God has a comprehensive plan for his creation and that God calls human beings to a special relationship and destiny which we are free to accept or reject. I believe that the Bible is supremely authoritative in revealing God's plans for the salvation of humankind.

Finally, I believe that the final eschatological goal of history will be the establishment of a new heaven and a new earth where those who are redeemed through the saving work of Jesus Christ will enjoy reconciliation with God, harmony throughout all of creation, and fellowship with each other. I believe that the establishment of this new community where humans enjoy reconciled fellowship, harmony in creation, and community with God is the ultimate eschatological goal for creation.

Critical Reading Response #1
By: Terrence Dwyer
February 1st, 2012
Text: Authority to Heal
Answers for everyone who has prayed for a sick friend
Author: Ken Blue
ST 502: Systematic Theology 2:
Christology, Soteriology, and Pneumatology
Professor: Dr. Marèque Steele Ireland

    In his extraordinary work Authority to Heal, author Ken Blue tackles head on the theological issues surrounding the ministry of healing in the church. He critically analyzes the common theological hindrances toward the ministry of healing and reveals them to be pastorally irresponsible, scripturally unsound, and undermining toward the healing ministry of the church. He then presents his theological arguments for the ministry of healing before concluding with a step by step guide for implementing a healing ministry into the life of a congregation. To sum up the premise of Authority to Heal is the assertion that "power from on high" is manifest as servants of the Most High pray (ATH p.54).

    In this essay I will show that Blue grounds his arguments for the ministry of healing in the Incarnation of God as revealed to us in Jesus Christ, the living Son of God, and that the ministry of healing is part of the ongoing work of the church in the eschatological Kingdom of God. In other words, through the resurrection of Jesus we see that it is God's will for our complete healing and restoration and through the ministry of Jesus we see that it is also God's will for His church to participate in this healing process until Christ returns. I will begin my review with a brief summary of Blue's common theological hindrances toward the ministry of healing and then I will review Blue's theological assertions regarding the Incarnation and the Kingdom of God and their implications toward the ministry of healing. I will conclude my review by exploring the implications of Blue's arguments for Christian ministry today before briefly touching on my own personal experiences with the ministry of healing.

    Having personally experienced two extraordinary spiritual healing episodes in my own life I have always been somewhat mystified that the ministry of healing has not been a more vital and visible ministry within the church. Blue begins and digs deeply here to root out the common theological hindrances toward the ministry of healing. Perhaps the greatest hindrance is the "notion that sickness is essentially good for us, and that it is sent to us to purify the soul and to build character" (ATH p.22). The theology of sanctification through sickness stems all the way back to the influence of Greek philosophy on the early church and the belief that the body was evil and the spirit was good. Greek philosophy believed that physical sickness in the body purified the soul which the early church found comforting in their persecution. We still believe this today as we misinterpret our sicknesses as our "cross to bear" for the Lord. While suffering may have merit we are never taught that sickness does. On the contrary, Jesus never tolerated sickness and his only response to sickness was to heal it (ATH p.28).

Blue also identifies "Divine determinism" as another major theological hindrance toward healing. When we believe that God controls all events we believe that God then decrees all pain and sickness. God has given us free will and through sin, accident, and stupidity much sickness has entered the world yet "God works for the good of those who love him and have been called according to his purpose" (Rom 8:28). When we believe that God pre-determines our sicknesses our prayers are undermined and they become passive and despairing (ATH 37). Blue also identifies "faith formula" thinking which is a human centered theology applied to healing that states that God will heal you if you have enough faith and God won't heal you if you don't. This theology also causes despair as failure to be healed always comes back to our lack of faith. "Subordinating the acts of God to the offerings of his creatures, even the offering of faith, is contrary to Biblical teaching." (ATH p. 47) Genuine faith understands that we live in a fallen world and our bodies are subject to death and decay until we are raised with Christ yet God has the power to heal anyone at any moment for God's own glory.

The last hindrance toward the ministry of healing identified by Blue is the secular world view that either God does not exist or God is not involved in creation. Medical science is the sole savior we turn toward when sickness comes to the utter exclusion of the living God. Too often the church is impacted by this secular world view which is dependent solely upon human effort when it comes to healing. Blue argues that Christian faith and medical science must not be polarized but must work together toward combating illness and bringing healing. Summing up our discussion to this point we have seen how the ministry of healing is deeply hindered by believing that sickness is sanctifying for the soul, by accepting sickness as a decree from God, by having presumptive faith versus genuine faith, and by believing in the secular world view to the exclusion of God.

For the remainder of his work, Blue makes compelling arguments for the ministry of healing by grounding his theological arguments in God's revelation of Himself through His Son Jesus Christ and in his theology that the ministry of healing is part of the ongoing work of the church in the eschatological Kingdom of God. Blue bases his theology of revelation argument in Jesus Christ being of one essence and being with the Father which reveals the character of God to us (ATH p. 72). "In Jesus, God has not just revealed His will but something of who He is in God's Self" (Ireland, Lecture 2). "Jesus participates by necessity in the essential nature of the one he reveals. He must be ontologically one with God and share in the divine essence which he exemplifies." (Grenz p. 264) Jesus informs us something of who God is. Jesus is not a complete revelation of God but through Jesus we can learn something of the will, character, and compassion of God among other things. Blue argues from Scripture that Jesus is dependent upon the Father's will and accurately reveals his will as Jesus acts exactly as his Father in heaven acts (John 5:19). Thus when Jesus is compassionate and heals the sick he reveals to us that God is compassionate and that it is God's will to heal the sick (ATH p. 74). Pannenberg might argue here that what is truth for one must be truth for all (Kärkkäinen p. 156) and in light of that I found quite interesting Blue's anecdotal evidence of dramatic healings for a woman of little faith and for a non-believing drug addict (ATH p. 46). It seems God is compassionate and desires healing for all his creatures. Jesus' compassionate ministry of healing was not just an expression of God's compassionate love toward his creation but it was also evidence of the advance of the Kingdom of God to which we will now turn.

Blue focuses his Kingdom of God theology on the obedience of Jesus Christ whose resurrection from the grave was the decisive victory in defeating death and Satan and inaugurating the Kingdom of God. Pannenberg highlight's this obedience of Christ in his doctrine of self-differentiation by stating that the Father's kingdom is dependent upon the Son and his obedience (Kärkkäinen p. 160). Christ came as the second Adam to heal the damage caused by the first Adam. Christ came to bring spiritual, physical, and relational liberation for all people and to reconcile, restore, and heal all of creation (ATH p.80-81). Kraus asserts that Jesus is the fulfillment and the revelation of God's intention for human life and that Jesus' obedience is what it means to be fully human (Kärkkäinen p. 168).

The healings that Jesus performed were not only symbolic of his kingly authority in the Kingdom of God but they were also means toward the advancement of the Kingdom. Jesus preached the Kingdom of God and healed the sick and he sent and commanded others to do the same.

Schweitzer contended that "everything about Jesus' preaching and ministry was eschatologically conditioned and therefore cannot be understood apart from it. The Kingdom meant an apocalyptical end-time transformation for Jesus" (Ireland, Lecture 4). Through the preaching of the Kingdom of God and the healing of the sick the Kingdom of God advances through time as the dominion of evil is driven back until the final coming of our Lord Jesus Christ when salvation will be complete and we will receive our fully resurrected bodies.

A dimension of the Kingdom of God which Blue perhaps under emphasizes is the restoration of the community of God. Through his atoning work, Jesus restores the eschatological community of God where the redeemed may fellowship with each other and with God in a redeemed creation (Grenz p. 350). We also learn from contextual theology that "the atonement was not just about spiritual salvation but about holistic healing in personal and communal dimensions" (Ireland, Lecture 5).

The implications of Blue's arguments for pastoral ministry today are extraordinary. Preaching the Good News of the Kingdom of God appears to be only partially fulfilling the commands of Christ and the work of the church in the Kingdom of God. We are also to be about the ministry of healing the sick to advance the Kingdom of God against the powers of evil. Blue gives an outline for pastors toward establishing a healing ministry within a congregation and his insight's here on obedience and subsequent authority to heal are brilliant. I am puzzled though by his lack of discussion on 1st. Corinthians 12: 8-10 regarding the specific gift of healing given by the Spirit to some within the church. Blue seems to infer here and even encourage that all are able to participate in the administration of the ministry of healing within the church which leads me to my personal experiences of healing.

My first extraordinary healing occurred when I was 28 years old and severely addicted to alcohol and very near suicide. I earnestly prayed alone to God for help with my addiction and I was instantly healed and the experience was very much like what is described as being released from spiritual bondage. I believe this experience affirms Blue's Scriptural argument that the Kingdom is advanced by over throwing the forces of evil. My second extraordinary healing however was quite different. I had torn my ACL and required surgery to repair it. A Nigerian faith healer friend of mine, who was known to have the gift of healing, laid hands on me and prayed and my torn ACL was instantly healed. I praise God and am grateful for both of these extraordinary healings but the second healing experience and the 1st. Corinthians 12: 8-10 passage led me to believe that certain healings required a person with the "gift of healing". As a result of reading this book by Ken Blue we are implementing a healing prayer service at Oakland City Church this coming Ash Wednesday February 22, 2012.

Critical Reading Response #2
By: Terrence Dwyer
February 16th, 2012
Text: Three Faces of Jesus
How Jews, Christians, and Muslims See Him
Author: Josef Imbach
ST 502: Systematic Theology 2:
Christology, Soteriology, and Pneumatology
Professor: Dr. Marèque Steele Ireland

In his work Three Faces of Jesus, author Josef Imbach seeks to review the status of Jesus among the three great monotheistic religions of Judaism, Christianity, and Islam in an attempt to find common ecumenical ground among these three religions through the person of Jesus. The authors' concerns are the polemics between these religions and given the unfortunate history of violence and intolerance against each other, he offers Jesus as a means toward finding some common dialogue toward some ecumenical unity. Imbach argues that the more one unquestionably affirms one's own beliefs the more foreign one is likely to find the religious practices and convictions of others. (TFJ p. 5) Imbach argues that perhaps a healthy questioning of certain tenets of one's faith and a closer examination of other religions will enable one to revise certain judgments and correct misunderstandings and thus foster an atmosphere of greater tolerance enabling better dialogue.

In this essay I will show that Imbach grounds his arguments for ecumenical unity through the person of Jesus from within the milieu of Classical Liberalism and Pluralist Theology. The result of which presents Christ as not divine but as more of a prophetic figure who is not the only mediator and where Christianity is presented as not the final religion. These Classical Liberalist views focus on the ethical dimensions of Jesus and deny his divinity and eschatology. Among other things these pluralist views also hold that the incarnation of Jesus is normative only for Christians. (Ireland, Lecture 7) I will briefly review what the author covers in his book and then present my critical analysis of some of the authors' Classical Liberalist and Pluralist Theologies before offering my concluding remarks.

Imbach begins his work by briefly reviewing the history of intolerance and persecution of the Christian church against the Jews and of the wars waged by the Christian Church against other faiths but principally against Islam. He even touches on the intolerance that the Christian Church has for dissenters within its' own members. Imbach concludes his review of intolerance by the church with the hope expressed through Vatican II's tectonic shift toward respect for human dignity and rights of freedom of conscience and freedom of religion which laid the groundwork for setting aside intolerance and for establishing an open dialogue between religions. The author brings the distinct view of the Roman Catholic theologian that he is into his work throughout and argues Christian polemics from a distinctive Roman Catholic perspective. Interestingly, Imbach has fallen out of favor with his faith and has apparently been banned from teaching in all Catholic Theological faculties worldwide for his 2002 work, Miracles, a 21st. Century Interpretation. As a result of this publication he was accused of not believing in the divinity of Jesus Christ and subsequently censored by the Congregation for the Doctrine of the Faith.

The author's review of Jesus in Judaism was for me personally, his most compelling work here. He reviewed Jewish history, the Talmud, and Jewish beliefs about Jesus but what was enlightening were his in depth reviews of the reclamation of Jesus within recent Jewish scholarship. Instead of writing Jesus off as a fanatic, recent Jewish scholarship has been rediscovering Jesus to be a "Jew among Jews". Rabbi H. G. Enelow stated, "Amongst all that is good and great that humanity has produced, nothing comes so near the universal as the claims and authority of Jesus. He has become the most charismatic figure in world history. The Jew cannot avoid being proud of what Jesus means for the world." (TFJ p. 36) Jewish philosopher Martin Buber said, "Jesus' message is Jewish through and through…that Christianity has seen and still continues to see him as God seems to me to be a fact of the greatest seriousness, which I must seek to comprehend, both for his and my sake." (TFJ p. 38) Jewish scholar Pinchas Lapide succinctly stated, "There can only be one universal bringer of salvation; so it follows that he who is so ardently awaited must be our mutual redeemer." (TFJ p. 43) The author concludes this section with a great question by Lapide who asks if the Jewish image of Jesus today could possibly serve as a model of tolerance for the Christian image of Judaism to take on a more Christian form.

In Imbach's brief review of Jesus in Islam we find no such dramatic change in thought toward Jesus as found in recent Judaism. Jesus is thought of highly as a prophet within the Muslim faith and both he and his mother Mary are revered. However, the differences between Islam and

Christianity remain significant. Muslims reject the Christian doctrine of redemption, the doctrine of the Trinity and the doctrine of the divinity of Jesus including his Son-ship and pre-existence. (TFJ p. 87) The author concedes that dialogue between Islam and Christianity can at least take place by acknowledging Jesus as a great spiritual and moral teacher who points humankind toward God and his life of poverty can be identified with certain themes of Islamic mysticism.

In his work the author also reviewed who Jesus is within Christianity by looking at the Christological titles ascribed to Jesus in Scripture, in Jesus' own claim as the Messiah, and in reviewing the arduous journey of the Christian Church in defining and clarifying the divinity and the humanity of the Messiah, Jesus Christ - The Son of God. Imbach also examined the different concepts of God within each of the three great religions including the doctrine of the Trinity within Christianity before concluding with his discussion and conclusions on salvation and revelation.

One of the arguments of the Classical Liberalist is that Christ is not the only mediator and Christianity is not the final religion and here Imbach does not disappoint. The author brings his Roman Catholic perspective to bear in his concluding chapter on salvation by comparing the path to salvation offered in the polemic teaching of the Council of Florence which stated that only Roman Catholics are saved vs. the openness of Vatican II which offers that no one, even those outside the church, are denied salvation. (TFJ p. 121) Imbach argues expansively that all people who try to follow their conscience and lead a good life are unconsciously linked to the church and are under the grace of salvation. The author then goes even further by presenting the arguments of the noted religious pluralist, Paul Knitter, who states, "No salvation outside the church has been superseded by the Christocentric – Christ as the only savior – which is now being replaced by a theocentric model where God reveals ways of salvation in religions." (TFJ p. 125) Imbach goes on to state that, "If God offers all mankind the chance of salvation, it means that this salvation cannot be attained in reality directly through the religions, but that the path of conscience and the ethical dimension of experience are to be defined theologically as the place where salvation is determined and as the substance of ways to salvation. In this respect the question of Jesus Christ's uniqueness is indeed relativized." (TFJ p. 125)

Another argument of the Classical Liberalist is that the incarnation of Jesus is normative for Christians only. Here Imbach argues that if Christians hold fast to the uniqueness of salvation through Christ alone as the literal only way to salvation that the Christian missionary should not wilt if conversion to Christianity does not take place. Instead, the Christian missionary should affirm those of other religions toward the observances and responsibilities of their own religious convictions and practices. (TFJ p. 126) The authors' argument implies that the incarnation of Jesus is normative for Christians only as he states that each religion offers its own pathway to salvation in God and that the Christian faith in Jesus is normative for Christians only.

Another argument of the Classical Liberalist is the denial of the transcendence of Jesus and in the eschatology of Jesus. Jesus repeatedly preached the Kingdom of God and while the author acknowledges such he essentially chooses to sidestep the eschatological implications of the teachings of Jesus Christ and of the Kingdom of God throughout his work. Albert Schweitzer stated that, "everything about Jesus' preaching and ministry was eschatologically conditioned and therefore cannot be understood apart from it. The Kingdom meant an apocalyptical end-time transformation for Jesus." (Ireland, Lecture 4) The author also diminishes the transcendence of Jesus by essentially equating Jesus with Moses and Mohammed as prophets of God. Imbach stated, "Finally, they are to be taken seriously because Muhammad knew, to the same extent that Jesus and Moses knew, that he was called by God, and because the message of each of these three figures is a deep experience of God." (TFJ p. 128) In these ways Imbach affirms the Classical Liberalist features of denying the transcendence of Jesus Christ and the implications of the eschatological teachings of Jesus Christ about the Kingdom of God.

In conclusion, I appreciate what the author is attempting to do here in his work, that being to find means for dialogue among the three great religions through the common ground of Jesus. The Christian faith has much to apologize for to both Muslim and Jew for our inexcusable intolerance and violence toward each. The search for common ground for open dialogue among us is noble and critically needed. I agree with the author in that looking to Jesus as the means toward finding this commonality is the key. However, I disagree with the authors' Classical Liberalist theological means of achieving this end by diminishing the divinity of Jesus Christ, his transcendence, his incarnation, his mediation, his work of salvation, and the eschatological implications of the Kingdom of God among other diminishments. On the contrary, it is through the supreme love of God in Jesus Christ and in his atoning work of salvation that we are able to rest in the grace and love of God and to love God in return and to love our neighbor as ourselves. It is through God's grace in the atoning work of Jesus Christ where the eschatological community of God is restored and where the redeemed may fellowship with each other and with God. (Grenz p. 350) The atonement was not just about spiritual salvation but about holistic healing in personal and communal dimensions. (Ireland, lecture 5) Indeed, Jesus Christ is our hope and our basis for communion with our Jewish and Muslim brothers and sisters.

Systematic Theology 2
Extra Credit Question #1
By: Terrence Dwyer, January 27th, 2012

Is the virgin birth essential to Christology? In other words, must we take the virgin birth as a key statement of belief? Why or why not?

The virgin birth is not the key pivotal truth in which we place our faith that saves us from sin and death and gives us our eternal salvation. That key pivotal truth in which we place our faith is in our living Lord Jesus Christ himself. The virgin birth is not the historical foundation upon which we make our saving confession of faith. Jesus claimed he was the Son of God and God affirmed this by raising Jesus from the dead. We place our saving faith in Jesus Christ and we can thus affirm the virgin birth of Jesus as an object of our faith as attested to by the Scriptures and affirmed throughout the long history and tradition of the church.

However, having said that, belief in the virgin birth has played an integral role in guarding the church throughout history against various heresies such as Docetism, Adoptionism, and Ebionitism. The Scriptures give significant witness to the virgin birth from the prophecy of Isaiah 7:14, to the NT texts in Matthew 1:18-25, Luke 1:26-35, John 1, 12-13. Additionally, early church history affirmed the virgin birth including early church fathers such as Ignatius, Justin Martyr, and others. The virgin birth was again later affirmed by the church in the Nicene Creed affirmed at the Council of Nicaea in 325 A.D. This is admittedly a very brief review of the history of the virgin birth within Scripture and within our church history and tradition. However, given this significant witness in Scripture and the significant affirmations throughout our church history, I would conclude that faith in the virgin birth is one of the key objects of our belief.

Systematic Theology 2
Extra Credit Question #2
By: Terrence Dwyer, February 25th, 2012

What is your position on predestination?
I affirm the doctrine of predestination citing significant Scriptural support in the New Testament and Old Testament as well as a long history of church tradition supporting and affirming the doctrine of predestination. Some of the main New Testament attestations for predestination are: Ephesians 1:11; 11 In him we were also chosen, having been predestined according to the plan of him who works out everything in conformity with the purpose of his will. Mark 13:20; 20 "If the Lord had not cut short those days, no one would survive. But for the sake of the elect, whom he has chosen, he has shortened them. 1 Corinthians 2:7; 7 No, we declare God's wisdom, a mystery that has been hidden and that God destined for our glory before time began. Romans 8:28-30; 28 And we know that in all things God works for the good of those who love him, who have been called according to his purpose. 29 For those God foreknew he also predestined to be conformed to the image of his Son, that he might be the firstborn among many brothers and sisters. 30 And those he predestined, he also called; those he called, he also justified; those he justified, he also glorified. Romans 9:17-23; Romans 9:17-23 17 For Scripture says to Pharaoh: "I raised you up for this very purpose, that I might display my power in you and that my name might be proclaimed in all the earth." 18 Therefore God has mercy on whom he wants to have mercy, and he hardens whom he wants to harden. 19 One of you will say to me: "Then why does God still blame us? For who is able to resist his will?" 20 But who are you, a human being, to talk back to God? "Shall what is formed say to the one who formed it, 'Why did you make me like this?'" 21 Does not the potter have the right to make out of the same lump of clay some pottery for special purposes and some for common use? 22 What if God, although choosing to show his wrath and make his power known, bore with great patience the objects of his wrath—prepared for destruction? 23 What if he did this to make the riches of his glory known to the objects of his mercy, whom he prepared in advance for glory.

One of the main Old Testament attestations for predestination is: Deuteronomy 7:6-8; 6 For you are a people holy to the LORD your God. The LORD your God has chosen you out of all the peoples on the face of the earth to be his people, his treasured possession. 7 The LORD did not set his affection on you and choose you because you were more numerous than other peoples, for you were the fewest of all peoples. 8 But it was because the LORD loved you and kept the oath he swore to your ancestors that he brought you out with a mighty hand and redeemed you from the land of slavery, from the power of Pharaoh King of Egypt.

Some of the church history and tradition affirming the doctrine of predestination has been the work of reformed theologian John Calvin, the Belgic Confession of 1561, the Westminster Confession of Faith of 1643 and the Council of Trent between 1545 and 1563.

It is a mystery that a loving God would chose to predestine some of creation for eternal salvation and predestine others of creation for eternal damnation. This seems to limit both God and God's plan of salvation and God's own revelation of himself to be a loving and merciful God. The overwhelming revelation in Scripture however seems to greatly affirm predestination as God's own prerogative to do what God wills for his creation.

Theological Reflection Paper
By: Terrence Dwyer, March 2nd, 2012
A Brief Theological Reflection on the Doctrine of Election
ST 502: Systematic Theology 2
Christology, Soteriology, and Pneumatology
Professor: Dr. Marèque Steele Ireland

Outline:
1. Introduction
2. The reason for writing this essay
3. Doctrine of election defined
4. John Calvin and the doctrine of election
5. Scripture supporting the doctrine of election
6. Jesus and the doctrine of election
7. Karl Barth and the doctrine of election
8. Scripture offering an alternative view
9. Conclusion
10. Bibliography

1. Introduction:
In this essay I will explore and argue for the doctrine of election as taught by John Calvin. I will begin by sharing my personal conversion experience which has greatly influenced my belief in this doctrine. I will then review the definition of the doctrine of election and touch on some of

the theological nuances within this definition. I will then briefly review Calvin's teaching on this doctrine while incorporating his exegesis supporting this doctrine. I will contrast Calvin's teaching with that of Karl Barth's teaching while incorporating Barth's supporting exegesis. The purpose of this essay is to achieve my hoped for conclusion from this investigation that the doctrine of election as taught by Calvin remains to be a sound theological doctrine for the church.

2. The reason for writing this essay:

Early in the evening of November 29th 1982 I came home from work and walked into my apartment and was immediately pinned to the floor with my nose pressed into the carpet. I was on my knees with my face planted into the floor within seconds of walking through the door and I was filled with the Holy Spirit. I had no idea what was happening to me but I immediately began cleansing my apartment of all sorts of nefarious materials and this Spirit quickly introduced me to Scripture and began teaching me about Jesus Christ and the ways of the Lord. At my point of conversion I didn't make a decision for God; God made the decision for me and provided me with the means to learn about him and to come to believe in him. God seemed to have elected me into his family for no other reason than God simply chose to do so. My reason for writing this essay is to explore the validity of my personal experience with a better theological understanding of the doctrine of election.

3. A theological definition of the doctrine of election:

The doctrine of election asserts that God has chosen from all of eternity those people who he chooses to bring to himself not based on anything of merit within those chosen. Those people chosen have no virtue or merit or faith that warrants such choosing by God they are simply unconditionally chosen by God's mercy to bring them to himself. God has chosen from all eternity to extend mercy upon those he has chosen and to withhold mercy from those he has not chosen. Those chosen receive the gift of salvation through Jesus Christ alone and those not chosen receive the just wrath of God for their sinfulness.

This definition is understood to be unconditional election which asserts that God's election of a person is not dependent upon anything inherent within that person. Our depravity is so complete in our sinful condition that we are unable to come to a saving knowledge of God apart from God first regenerating our souls. Thus God's choice in election is based solely upon God's own sovereign grace and not upon the foreseen actions of a person. This unconditional understanding of the doctrine of election is contrasted with the conditional doctrine of election which maintains that God chooses only those whom he foreknows will love him.

Finally, the definition of the doctrine of election must contemplate the order of God's decision regarding election known as Lapsarianism. Our definition includes the understanding of Supralapsarianism which contemplate God's timing of his decision to elect some and condemn others as occurring before the fall. This understanding is contrasted with the Infralapsarianism view which holds that God decided to save some and condemn others after the fall.

After my personal experience of conversion I was led by the Holy Spirit to Scripture where I found a God who appeared to be working out a divine plan through a series of choices and in particular his singular calling out of a chosen covenanted people. From the beginning of the Bible to the end we see stories of God working out his divine purposes through a continuous series of particular divine choices. Several noted theologians throughout history such as Augustine, Thomas Aquinas, and Martin Luther have taught various forms of the doctrine of election in their theologies. The theologian most noted for putting forth the doctrine of election is the reformed theologian John Calvin whose teaching on this doctrine we will now briefly review.

4. John Calvin and the doctrine of election:

John Calvin (1509 to 1564) was the noted French reformation theologian who broke from the Roman Catholic Church in 1530 and published his seminal reformed theological work, The Institutes of the Christian Religion in 1536. In this extraordinary work he wrote the following statement regarding the doctrine of election: "We say that the Lord once established in His eternal and immutable counsel whom He would take to salvation and whom He would leave in destruction. We say that He receives those whom He calls to salvation by His free mercy, without any regard for their own worth; on the contrary, that the entrance into life is closed to all those whom He wishes to give over to damnation and that this is done by His secret and incomprehensible but righteous fair judgment".

5. Scripture supporting the doctrine of election:

There are a number of Scripture passages which Calvin used to support this doctrine some of which we review here. In Malachi 1:2-3 we have an example of God electing one person over another in the case God electing Jacob over Esau. "I have loved you," says the LORD. But you say, "How have you loved us?" "Is not Esau Jacob's brother?" declares the

LORD. "Yet I have loved Jacob but Esau I have hated. I have laid waste his hill country and left his heritage to jackals of the desert." God chose Jacob over Esau before they were born without regard to how good or bad either one of them would be. Jacob having merited nothing by good works is accepted into grace and Esau having committed no offense is rejected by God. The Apostle Paul cites Malachi 1:2-3 in Romans 9:13 and he cites Exodus 33:19 when he further writes in Romans 9: 15-16 to explain; "For he says to Moses, "I will have mercy on whom I have mercy, and I will have compassion on whom I have compassion." So then it depends not on human will or exertion, but on God, who has mercy". God is just in choosing Jacob over Esau because neither deserved choosing thus God is just in choosing one over another because no one deserves to be saved. The salvation of anyone is wholly and entirely dependent upon the mercy of God.

Calvin continues to draw from Paul and from Romans in affirming the doctrine of election with Romans 9:22-23; "But who are you, O man, to answer back to God? Will what is molded say to its molder, "Why have you made me like this?" Has the potter no right over the clay, to make out of the same lump one vessel for honorable use and another for dishonorable use? What if God, desiring to show his wrath and to make known his power, has endured with much patience vessels of wrath prepared for destruction, in order to make known the riches of his glory for vessels of mercy, which he has prepared beforehand for glory". Proverbs attests to this as well in 16:4; "The LORD has made everything for its purpose, even the wicked for the day of trouble". Scripture affirms here the unconditional doctrine of election and God's sovereign will in being free to choose from all eternity to extend mercy upon those he has chosen and to withhold mercy from those he has created for that purpose.

6. Jesus and the doctrine of election:

The doctrine of election is also affirmed through the words of Jesus as we see in the Gospel of John 15:16; "You did not choose me, but I chose you and appointed you that you should go and bear fruit and that your fruit should abide, so that whatever you ask the Father in my name, he may give it to you". Later in John in the High Priestly Prayer of Chapter 17 Jesus prays for "those you have given me." Earlier in his ministry Jesus teaches the parable of the wheat and the tares where the sovereignty of God is displayed in choosing some out of his creation for salvation and where God's mercy and just wrath are contrasted in Matthew 13:40-43; "Just as the weeds are gathered and burned with fire, so will it be at the end of the age. The Son of Man will send his angels, and they will gather out of his kingdom all causes of sin and all law-breakers, and throw them into the fiery furnace. In that place there will be weeping and gnashing of teeth. Then the righteous will shine like the sun in the kingdom of their Father". Finally, we conclude our Scriptural affirmations for the doctrine of election with Ephesians 1:4-5; "Even as he chose us in him before the foundation of the world, that we should be holy and blameless before him. In love he predestined us for adoption as sons through Jesus Christ, according to the purpose of his will".

7. Karl Barth and the doctrine of election:

Karl Barth (1886 to 1968) was a noted Swiss theologian who has been referred to as the father of Neo-orthodoxy which is a 20th century Protestant theology which reevaluated many of the teachings of the reformation. Barth refocuses the doctrine of election from the destiny of individuals to the destiny of Jesus Christ. Barth argues that the object of the divine election of grace is not individuals but the one individual Jesus Christ who is the only person elected by God. Christ is the representative of the entire human race in this election and in Christ and through Christ all human beings are elected by God. Barth argued that the incarnation is proof that God is for humanity and not against it and in Jesus Christ the entire human race has been chosen for salvation. The role of the "called out" church in its being and doing is to represent God to others and others to God. "Through the Spirit's shaping of the ecclesial personhood of the church the Spirit is also at work to shape the personhood of all humanity in Christ".

8. Scripture offering an alternative view:

In his exegetical work Barth looks to John 1:1-2 as the basis of his belief that in the beginning in eternity Jesus was already the Elect Man as the eternal will of God. The entire human race was chosen for salvation in the Son of God in the Logos of Jesus Christ in the beginning in eternity. Another key passage Barth looks to is Ephesians 1:4 where Barth sees the main emphasis in the phrase "in Him". "God has chosen humanity "in Him" before the foundation of the world according to the good pleasure of his will for the purpose that we might be predestined unto the adoption of children by Jesus Christ himself". Barth asserts that the Biblical passages referencing election (mainly Romans 9 and Ephesians 1) must be read christologically revealing that it is God's will to save all of humanity.

9. Conclusion:

We have reviewed in this essay a God who is working out his divine purposes through a continuous series of particular divine choices. We have looked at the definition of the doctrine of election as a part of this divine will. We have reviewed and contrasted the theological teachings and exegesis of both Calvin and Barth regarding the doctrine of election. Calvin's doctrine "asserts the inescapable necessity of the working of the Holy Spirit" which rings true with my own personal experience of conversion. Barth may be reading more into John 1:1-2 than is really there. Is this passage really speaking about the Elect Man or is it speaking mainly of the pre-existence of the Word and the Deity of the Word? Barth's treatment of Ephesians 1:4 also limits God into having only one attitude toward man and that God cannot punish any sinful person eternally. Therefore, my conclusion based upon this brief review is that the doctrine of election as taught by Calvin remains to be a sound theological doctrine for the church.

Bibliography

Calvin, John. Institutes of the Christian Religion. Grand Rapids, MI: Wm. B. Eerdmans Publishing Co., 2009.

Grenz, Stanley J. Theology for the Community of God. Grand Rapids, Michigan: William B. Eerdmans Publishing Co., 2000.

Hausmann, William John. Karl Barth's Doctrine of Election. New York, NY: Philosophical Library, Inc., 1969.

Kärkkäinen, Veli-Matti. Christology: A Global Introduction. Grand Rapids, MI: Baker Academic, 2003.

McDonald, Suzanne. Re-Imaging Election. Grand Rapids, MI: Wm. B. Eerdmans Publishing Co., 2010.

Newbigin, Lesslie. The Open Secret: An Introduction to the Theology of Mission. Grand Rapids, MI: Wm. B. Eerdmans Publishing Co., 1995.

Nimmo, Paul T. New Perspectives for Evangelical Theology: Engaging with God, Scripture, and the World, Edited by Tom Greggs. New York, NY: Routledge, 2010.

Final Research Paper
By: Terrence Dwyer, March 15th, 2012
The Apostle Paul, Romans 9-11, and the Doctrine of Election
ST 502: Systematic Theology 2
Christology, Soteriology, and Pneumatology
Professor: Dr. Marèque Steele Ireland

Outline:
1. Introduction
2. The reason for writing this essay
3. The doctrine of election defined
4. Paul's anguish and our context
5. Paul's teaching on the doctrine of election in Romans 9 to 11
6. Calvin on Romans 9 through 11
7. Barth on Romans 9 through 11
8. Pannenberg on Romans 9 through 11
9. Newbigin on Romans 9 through 11
10. Conclusion
11. Bibliography

1. Introduction:
In this essay I will explore and argue that the Apostle Paul's letter to the Romans is one of the principal sources utilized by the church for the development of the theological doctrine of election. More specifically, I will look at chapters 9 through 11 as the area where Paul locates his teaching on this doctrine. I will begin with my reasons for writing this essay and then briefly offer a definition of this doctrine to support our discussion. I will then review Paul's dilemma and his teaching on election in chapters 9 through 11 as he wrestled mightily here with the integrity of the promises of God in light of Israel's rejection of God's saving promises. I will then review how arguments both for and against this difficult and divisive doctrine have been drawn from these three chapters. I will bring into our discussion the widely varying theological voices of Calvin, Barth, Pannenberg, and Newbigin and how each of them responded to Paul's teaching in these three chapters before concluding.

2. The reason for writing this essay:
In my theological reflection paper I argued for the doctrine of election as taught by the reformer John Calvin as I found his teaching concurred with my personal conversion experience in the Holy Spirit who chose me

for salvation and then gave me the means to learn about Jesus Christ. In that paper I contrasted Calvin's teaching with Barth's and I concluded in favor of Calvin's doctrine. In this essay I want to dig deeper to learn why Calvin and others drew the conclusions they did from Scripture but principally from these three chapters by Paul and why Barth and others looked at the same teaching by Paul and drew radically differing theological conclusions. The purpose of this essay then is to better understand Paul's teaching on election in Romans 9 to 11 and to review how four widely varying theological voices responded to this teaching within their respective theologies.

3. The doctrine of election defined:

To begin our review we offer the following definition for the doctrine of election. This doctrine asserts that God has chosen from all of eternity those people whom he chooses to bring to himself not based on anything of merit within those chosen. Those people chosen have no virtue or merit or faith that warrants such choosing by God as they are simply unconditionally chosen by God's mercy. All are fallen and depraved and are unworthy yet God has chosen from all eternity to extend mercy upon some and to withhold mercy from others. Those chosen receive the gift of salvation through Jesus Christ alone and those not chosen receive the just wrath of God for their sinfulness.

This definition is understood to be unconditional election which asserts that God's election of a person is not dependent upon anything inherent within that person. Our depravity is so complete in our sinful condition that we are unable to come to a saving knowledge of God apart from God first regenerating our souls. Thus God's choice in election is based solely upon God's own sovereign grace and not upon the foreseen actions of a person. This unconditional understanding of the doctrine of election is contrasted with the conditional doctrine of election which maintains that God chooses only those whom he foreknows will love him.

Finally, the definition of the doctrine of election must contemplate the order of God's decision regarding election known as Lapsarianism. Our definition includes the understanding of Supralapsarianism which contemplate God's timing of his decision to elect some and condemn others as occurring before the fall. This understanding is contrasted with the Infralapsarianism view which holds that God decided to save some and condemn others after the fall.

4. Paul's anguish and our context:

Paul was a Jew among Jews, an educated and devout Pharisee, who experienced a dramatic conversion and came to faith in Jesus Christ through the grace and mercy of God. Paul was called by God as an Apostle to the Gentiles to bring them to the obedience of faith. Paul struggled though as he experienced the success of his mission to the Gentiles where a people who weren't looking for the righteousness of God received it by faith while his own people who were chosen by God and who had sought after God's righteousness for centuries had rejected it. Paul was perplexed and anguished by this as God had shown mercy to the Gentiles but had apparently rejected his own chosen people Israel. If faith is a gift of grace from God then does this mean that God's Word had failed and that God's promises to Abraham and his descendants are invalid? For Paul, the very character of God was at stake here. God's faithfulness, trustworthiness, integrity, and righteousness were coming under question for Paul which he reconciled here in these chapters.

"1 I speak the truth in Christ—I am not lying, my conscience confirms it through the Holy Spirit— 2I have great sorrow and unceasing anguish in my heart. 3 For I could wish that I myself were cursed and cut off from Christ for the sake of my people, those of my own race, 4 the people of Israel". (Romans 9:1; NIV).

Romans 9 to 11 are arguably the most controversial chapters of Paul's letter as he concerned himself here with the future of Israel, the integrity and sovereignty of God, election, grace, and human responsibility. Our concern here is with Paul's teaching on election and this is the context within which Paul placed his teaching on this doctrine.

5. Paul's teaching on the doctrine of election in Romans 9 to11:

Paul was determined to find continuity between what God promised to Israel and what God was now doing through the Gentiles. He retells the story of Israel from the patriarchs (9:7-13), through the exodus and the wilderness journey (9:14-18), to their exile and their return (9:24-28), and finally to the coming of the Messiah (9:29). "At each point in the retelling of this story Paul shows that God chooses one person or one group and not another and that this pattern is part of God's righteousness to Israel." Paul combs through the Scriptures and retells the story of Abraham by stressing the choosing of Isaac over Ishmael and the choosing of Jacob over Esau. Here he recalls Malachi 1:3, "Jacob I loved, but Esau I hated". Paul seems to be wrestling with God as he experienced firsthand God's promises to the elder Israel now being handed to the younger Gentiles. Does this mean that God loves the Gentile Christians but hates unbelieving Israel?

Paul recalls Exodus 33:19; "I will have mercy on whom I have mercy, and I will have compassion on whom I have compassion." (Romans 9:15) Paul argues that God acts graciously in complete sovereign freedom to show mercy on whomever he chooses to show mercy and concludes, "16 It depends not on human will or effort but on the mercy of God." (Romans 9:16) Israel has been unfaithful to God in their rejection of the Gospel but God's promises concerning Israel's future blessings and hope are not due to Israel's faithfulness toward God but rest upon God's faithfulness alone. Those who receive God's blessings are therefore a matter of divine choice and not based upon human effort. Both those chosen for blessing and those who have been rejected are equally depraved, fallen, and under divine condemnation. Christ bore the wrath of God in the place of those whom God has granted mercy and those whom he has rejected and chosen to harden must bear the punishment which their sinfulness requires. "17 For Scripture says to Pharaoh: "I raised you up for this very purpose, that I might display my power in you and that my name might be proclaimed in all the earth." 18 Therefore God has mercy on whom he wants to have mercy, and he hardens whom he wants to harden." (Romans 9:17-18)

This seems unjust and unfair to our unregenerate mind and we question God's mercy on this but Paul immediately answers back:
"20 But who are you, a human being, to talk back to God? "Shall what is formed say to the one who formed it, 'Why did you make me like this?'" 21 Does not the potter have the right to make out of the same lump of clay some pottery for special purposes and some for common use?
22 What if God, although choosing to show his wrath and make his power known, bore with great patience the objects of his wrath—prepared for destruction? 23 What if he did this to make the riches of his glory known to the objects of his mercy, whom he prepared in advance for glory" (Romans 9:20-23)

Paul moves forward in the rest of chapters 9 and 10 combing through the Old Testament Scriptures to find that Israel's behavior is a fulfillment of the Scriptures. Paul quotes from Hosea, Isaiah, Joel, Psalms, and Deuteronomy to show that the righteousness of God provided in the Messiah would be rejected by God's chosen people and that the Gentiles would receive this righteousness. God's Word has not failed with respect to Israel but it has actually been fulfilled. Paul then moves on in chapter 11 to affirm that the promises of God to Israel will most certainly be fulfilled because God chose them and is committed to bless them and the world through them. Through divine election Paul is assured that God's sovereignty, faithfulness, trustworthiness, integrity, and righteousness all remain intact. Paul is assured that Israel's salvation rests upon the faithfulness of God and is not prevented by their unfaithfulness.

" 28 As far as the gospel is concerned, they are enemies for your sake; but as far as election is concerned, they are loved on account of the patriarchs, 29 for God's gifts and his call are irrevocable. 30 Just as you who were at one time disobedient to God have now received mercy as a result of their disobedience, 31 so they too have now become disobedient in order that they too may now receive mercy as a result of God's mercy to you. 32 For God has bound everyone over to disobedience so that he may have mercy on them all." (Romans 11:28-32)

We will turn now to review how certain theologians each addressed Paul's teaching on election in Romans 9 to 11 within their individual widely varying theologies.

6. Calvin on Romans 9 through 11:

John Calvin was a noted French reformation theologian who broke from the Roman Catholic Church in 1530 and published his seminal reformed theological work, The Institutes of the Christian Religion in 1536 in which he wrote the following statement regarding the doctrine of election: "We say that the Lord once established in His eternal and immutable counsel whom He would take to salvation and whom He would leave in destruction. We say that He receives those whom He calls to salvation by His free mercy, without any regard for their own worth; on the contrary, that the entrance into life is closed to all those whom He wishes to give over to damnation and that this is done by His secret and incomprehensible but righteous fair judgment".

There are a number of Scripture passages which Calvin used to support this doctrine but he draws principally from Romans 9 to 11 and especially from Romans 9 focusing on the election passages quoted above of 9:13, 9:15-16, and 9:20-23. Citing these verses Calvin concludes that Scripture affirms the unconditional doctrine of election and God's sovereign will in being free to choose from all eternity to extend mercy upon those he has chosen and to withhold mercy from those he has created for that purpose.

7. Barth on Romans 9 through 11:

Barth refocuses the doctrine of election from the destiny of individuals to the destiny of Jesus Christ and Barth insists that the election passages in

Romans 9 must be read christologically. Barth argues that the object of the divine election of grace is not individuals but the one individual Jesus Christ who is the only person elected by God. Christ is the representative of the entire human race in this election and in Christ and through Christ all human beings are elected by God. Barth argued that the incarnation is proof that God is for humanity and not against it and in Jesus Christ the entire human race has been chosen for salvation. The role of the "called out" church in its being and doing is to represent God to others and others to God. "Through the Spirit's shaping of the ecclesial personhood of the church the Spirit is also at work to shape the personhood of all humanity in Christ".

Some have accused Barth of being a "universalist" which is a charge he has not denied. However, Barth affirmed in his commentary on Romans 11 in Church Dogmatics that the expression "fullness of the Gentiles" from Romans 11 does mean the sum total of all Gentile individuals. Barth also goes on to affirm that the expression "All Israel" also from Romans 11 is the community of those elected by God in and with Jesus Christ both from the Jews and from the Gentiles.

8. Pannenberg on Romans 9 through 11:

Pannenberg focuses on the resurrection for his theology and his Christology. He agrees with Paul in the second Adam Christology and its' inclusion of all humanity in the work of Christ. (Lecture 5, Dr. Ireland) Pannenberg thus views Romans 9 to 11 through these particular theological lenses. Pannenberg supports and applauds Barth's connection of the doctrine of election to the election of Jesus for all of humanity and all of creation. Barth however speaks of the pre-existing election of Jesus for all of creation, Pannenberg places this election instead at the eschatological summation of all things. Pannenberg concurs with Barth that the election passages in Romans 9 are to be read christologically. However, Jesus' election is the summation of humanity and creation from the perspective of the end thus gathering all history and all creation into his own eschatological person. Pannenberg goes on to argue that the intention of God's elective activity in individual human history is not limited to a particular community or to isolated individuals. Individuals are chosen by God to exemplify the gracious intentions of God's love for all human beings.

9. Newbigin on Romans 9 through 11:

Newbigin's missional theology, much like Grenz, has a theology of community focus through which he views the doctrine of election in Romans 9 to 11. Newbigin agrees with Paul as he sees stories throughout the Bible of God working out his divine purposes through a continuous series of particular divine choices. Humanity in the Bible exists only in relationship and only in creation thus God's universal purpose of salvation is accomplished through the choosing of a particular people who are in human relationship with each other. For Newbigin, "salvation must be an action that binds us together and restores for us the true mutual relation to each other and the true shared relation to the world of nature." Our gift of salvation then does not come down to us like a shaft of light from above but it comes to us from our neighbor who has been called and chosen to be the bearer of the blessing from God. (Romans 10:14-17) The blessing is intended for all but it is accomplished by way of election through choosing, calling, and sending out the bearer of the blessing to all.

10. Conclusion:

In conclusion we have dug deeper into the doctrine of election in this essay and we now have a better understanding of the teachings of Paul specifically within Romans 9 to 11 regarding this doctrine. We saw how Paul wrestled here with not only the promises of God to his chosen people Israel but also with the very righteousness of God. We learned how through divine election God's promises to Israel remain intact in spite of their unfaithfulness to God. Paul was assured that Israel's salvation rested upon the faithfulness of God and not upon the works or the faithfulness of his chosen people.

We then heard from four widely different theological voices and how they each responded to the teaching of Paul in Romans 9 to 11. Calvin focused on the sovereignty of God within these passages and developed a theology of unconditional election which affirmed and magnified the sovereignty of God. Barth focused his theology on Jesus Christ and the person of Christ who was the only elected person of God and the entire human race stands elected through Jesus Christ. Pannenberg focuses his theology on the resurrected Jesus Christ but places Jesus' election at the eschatological summation of all things. Newbigin places his emphasis on the community of God and sees election as the only alternative for God to deliver salvation but through community.

Finally, I like Paul can only marvel here at the depth of the riches and wisdom and knowledge of God. How unsearchable are his judgments and how inscrutable his ways. For from him and through him and to him are all things. To him be glory forever. Amen. (Romans 11: 33 & 36)

Bibliography

Bradshaw, Timothy. Pannenberg, a Guide for the Perplexed. New York: T&T Clark International, 2009.

Calvin, John. Institutes of the Christian Religion. Grand Rapids, MI: Wm. B. Eerdmans Publishing Co., 2009.

Grieb, A. Katherine. Paul's Theological Preoccupation in Romans 9-11 Between Gospel and Election, Edited by Florian Wilk and J. Ross Wagner. Tubingen, Germany: Mohr Siebeck 2010.

Hausmann, William John. Karl Barth's Doctrine of Election. New York, NY: Philosophical Library, Inc., 1969.

Kärkkäinen, Veli-Matti. Christology: A Global Introduction. Grand Rapids, MI: Baker Academic, 2003.

McDonald, Suzanne. Re-Imaging Election. Grand Rapids, MI: Wm. B. Eerdmans Publishing Co., 2010.

Newbigin, Lesslie. The Open Secret: An Introduction to the Theology of Mission. Grand Rapids, MI: Wm. B. Eerdmans Publishing Co., 1995.

Nimmo, Paul T. New Perspectives for Evangelical Theology: Engaging with God, Scripture, and the World, Edited by Tom Greggs. New York, NY: Routledge, 2010.

Pannenberg, Wolfhart. Human Nature, Election, and History. Philadelphia: The Westminster Press, 1977.

ST503 Systematic Theology 3
Reading Response: #1
By: Terrence Dwyer, June 21st, 2010

Lumen Gentium or "Light of the Nations" is one of the principal documents issued by Vatican II and it discusses the sociological characteristics of the church and the work of the Holy Spirit. This document issued by Pope Paul VI on November 21, 1964 sets the stage for the Decree on the Apostolate of the Laity issued a year later which addresses the issues of structure, hierarchy, and order within the church. The Lumen Gentium declares that Christ is the "Light of the Nations" and that Vatican II was gathered together in the power of the Holy Spirit to proclaim the Gospel to every creature to bring the light of Christ to all people. To carry out the will of God, Christ inaugurated the Kingdom of Heaven on earth and revealed to us the mystery of the Kingdom. When the work of Christ was finished, the Holy Spirit was sent in order that the Spirit might continually sanctify the church and all those who believe would have direct access through Christ in one Spirit to the Father. The Kingdom of God, now present in mystery, grows visibly through the power of the Holy Spirit in the world.

In the building up of Christ's body, various members and functions have their part to play. There is only one Spirit who gives different gifts for the welfare of the church. This is the one church of Christ, which in the creed is professed as one holy, catholic and apostolic church. This church is called to communicate the Gospel of salvation to all mankind. Thus, the church needs human resources to carry out its mission. The baptized, by regeneration and the anointing of the Holy Spirit are consecrated as a holy priesthood to do good works which God has predestined them to do. Therefore, all Disciples of Christ should present themselves as living sacrifices, holy and pleasing to God to bear witness to Christ and to the hope of eternal life which is in them. Though they differ from one another, the common priesthood of the faithful and the ministerial are interrelated; each one in their own special way is a participant in the one priesthood of Christ. The Holy Spirit distributes special graces among the faithful of every kind and through these gifts makes them fit and ready to undertake the various tasks which contribute toward the renewal and building up of the church. All the faithful, scattered throughout the world are in communion with each other in the Holy Spirit since the kingdom of Christ is not of this world.

The Decree on the Apostolate of the Laity was issued by Pope Paul VI on November 18, 1965 shortly before Vatican II closed three weeks later on December 8, 1965. This decree was a long awaited and historic document issued by Vatican II as it was the first time in the history of the Catholic Church that a church council issued a Papal Decree recognizing and affirming the role of the laity within the church. Finally, almost 450 years after Martin Luther called for the priesthood of all believers; the Catholic Church through Vatican II finally recognized and affirmed the priesthood of the laity.

The Vatican acknowledged and affirmed the role of the laity stating that the apostolate of the laity was derived from their Christian vocation and was indispensable in the mission of the church and that the church could never be without it. Modern times in fact demanded that the role of the laity be broadened and intensified. The church was founded for the purpose of spreading the Kingdom of Christ throughout the earth for the glory of God to enable all people to share in God's plan of salvation. All activity of the mystical body directed to the attainment of this goal is called the apostolate which the church carries on in various ways through her members. Within the church there is a diversity of ministry but oneness of mission. The laity derives their right to be an apostolate from their union with Christ the head of the church.

Vatican II also went on to embrace and encourage the laity by stating that the mission of the church is not only to bring mankind the message of salvation but it is also to permeate and improve the whole range of the temporal world as well. It is the laity that carries out this mission of the church by exercising their gifts in the world as well as in the church. It is the apostolate of the laity that announces to the world the grace of Christ through their word and actions. The laity is to work to renew the temporal order and make it increasingly more perfect such is God's design for the world. The apostolate of the laity therefore is to take on this task of renewing the temporal order guided by the light of the Gospel and the mind of the church. The laity is everywhere and always to seek justice and to offer acts of mercy and love thus spreading the light of Christ.

Vatican II also went on to highlight the various fields of the laity such as church communities, individuals, groups, associations, the family, the young, the social environment, national and international spheres among others. The council also went on to especially recognize and affirm the increasingly active role of women in the life of the Church and encouraged their growth.

ST503 Systematic Theology 3
Reading Response: #2
By: Terrence Dwyer, June 22nd, 2010

The "marks" of the church are the visible signs of the nature of the church. They are the attributes of the church that are visible to the world and distinguish the church from the world. The early church went to great lengths to outline these distinguishing marks in their early creeds. These creeds developed out of the practical necessity of the early church to identify to themselves what they believed in so that they could also express to others what they believed. The four distinguishing marks noted by the early church were that the church was one, holy, catholic and apostolic church as expressed in their early creed and finally ratified in the Nicene Creed of 325 A.D.

Holiness was the first mark attributed to the early church. This mark of holiness was derived from the presence of the Holy Spirit within the church not from the moral quality of holiness of the believers. Another distinguishing mark of the early church was that of unity. The church described itself as being "catholic" which is derived from the Greek "kata holos" meaning through or according to the whole. This implies wholeness and unity within the church and refers to the whole of believers spread throughout the known world. Another distinguishing mark of the church is that of being "one". There is only one church headed by Jesus Christ to which all believers belonged through faith and by the power of the Holy Spirit. Another distinguishing mark of the church is that it is apostolic in that its' members adhere to the original apostolic teaching and to the teachings of their legitimate successors.

It is interesting to note here regarding early creed formation, that the Apostle Paul seems to be quoting an early church creed in 1 Cor. 15:3-4 when he says, "that Christ died for our sins in accordance with the Scriptures, that he was buried, that he was raised on the third day in accordance with the Scriptures..". Paul most likely picked this early creed up from the apostles in Jerusalem during an earlier visit there.

The main challenge presented to the church throughout history has been one of unity. Through the centuries the church has seen many heretics, schisms, sects, cults, divisions, etc. develop from outside and from within the church disturbing the unity of the church. In the Middle Ages Popes sought to solidify the power and authority of the Papal office over the church. Schisms within the Papacy developed, were briefly alleviated and then Papal striving for power and authority returned. In the 1500's the Reformation began to greatly divide the church between Roman Catholic and Protestant with the Protestant Reformation movement further splintering into sub groups of Protestants such as Lutherans, Calvinists, Church of England, and Anabaptists. The Catholic Church argued that the Protestant movement could not be of the one true church because of the lack of unity among the Protestant believers. The Protestant believers argued the one true church was unified through faith and not through visible unity. Zwingli argued that the church consists not in outward rites and ceremonies, but rather in truth and unity of the Catholic faith. The Protestant's also argued that there is no other head of the church but the Lord Jesus Christ. In the modern church the mark of unity is also a mark that is strongly desired by the church with the ecumenical movement becoming increasingly prevalent in the early 20th century. The Protestant Ecumenical movement formed the World Council of Churches in 1948 which included 145 churches from 44 countries. The Roman Catholic Church in Vatican II issued in their "Lumen Gentium" document from the Council, among many other things, recognition that many elements of sanctification and truth are found outside the visible confines of the Catholic Church itself. The Council also invited both Protestant and Orthodox leadership to the Council as observers which was an extraordinary step of affirmation by the church.

ST503 Systematic Theology 3
Reading Response: #3
By: Terrence Dwyer, June 23rd, 2010

The main points characterizing Lesslie Newbigin's missional ecclesiology are that the church is missional, ecumenical, and dynamic. The church is essentially missional in nature in that it is striving to preach the Gospel to all people and even to the ends of the earth, to beseech all people to be reconciled to God. Newbigin describes this beautifully when he says that the nature of salvation is governed by its' source which is a love that reaches out after all people and goes to all lengths to recover one lost sheep. He goes on to say that it belongs to the very heart of salvation that we cannot have it in fullness until all for whom it is intended have it together. Therefore, the church is missional in nature in striving for the Gospel message of salvation to be obtained by all.

Secondly, the missional church is ecumenical in its unity in spreading the Gospel message. Newbigin is a great defender of Christian unity and brilliantly describes the three divisions that we find in within Christianity today. Newbigin describes that we are grafted onto Christ in three main ways: 1st, by hearing the Gospel and believing, 2nd, by sacramental participation, 3rd, by receiving and abiding in the Holy Spirit. Newbigin describes the three divisions within the church as over emphasizing one of these three to the detriment of the other two. He describes the Protestant approach as emphasizing hearing the Gospel and believing, the Catholic approach as emphasizing the sacraments and the Pentecostal approach as emphasizing the experience of the Holy Spirit. The church needs to wholly embrace all three in unity in its mission.

Thirdly, the church is dynamic in its mission as it is eschatological in nature. The people of God are pilgrims who are on the move, hastening to spread the Gospel to the end of the earth so that all people are reconciled to God in the fullness of time so that we may be all gathered to into one to meet our Lord. Newbigin also describes the tension that the missional church experiences as it often finds itself witnessing in hostile non-Christian cultures and yet at the same time the church must tend to those within the church who have answered the call to Christ. Finally, the missional church needs to adapt and be relevant to the current culture it finds itself in.

In answering the two questions from McGrath regarding what ways does Newbigin think the kingdom is present now and in what way does it remain to be fulfilled; we may have partially answered these above but will reiterate here. Newbigin believes that the kingdom is only partially present now in the church and will not be fully present until the fullness of time when Christ comes again. In the meantime, the missional church has been given the charge to spread the Gospel to the ends of the earth and indeed every person to thereby bring about the fullness of time when our Lord will return and the kingdom will then be fully present.

ST503 Systematic Theology 3
Reading Response: #4
By: Terrence Dwyer, June 24th, 2010

Reading Metropolitan Anthony of Sourozh's, "The Hierarchical Structures of the Church", reminded me of reading Vatican II's "The Apostolate of the Laity" and Luther's writings about the priesthood of all believers. Sourozh makes a similar call in this writing when he states that we must recapture the holiness and the dignity of the laity. We must recover the notion that the laity includes the clergy.

He lays the foundation for his discussion by outlining what the church is. He describes the church as a living organism and a body which is both human and divine. It is human in that we are human and Christ humbled himself by participating in our humanity, and the church is at the same time divine in that Christ is the head of the church and the Holy Spirit directs and resides within the church. He goes on to say here that in Christ and in the Holy Spirit, we are called to become adopted sons and daughters of God and even to be the only Son of God as a whole body.

Initially, Sourozh's discussion on the Icon of the Trinity startled me a bit as he seemed to be calling us to become an image of the Holy Trinity itself and saying that this is what we are called to be. Upon further reflection, I see that Sourozh is using the imagery of the icon to describe that we must grow toward the perfection of the Trinity in all our being and that the Lord Jesus is our model. Through the Holy Spirit we must grow in our relationships, in our love and in our holiness as we grow toward this image. He quoted St. Ephraim of Syria who eloquently described this process as one where God places the perfect image of God within the core of every person and the purpose of life is to dig deeper and deeper until we reach this point and bring it to the fore. He concludes his discussion here by reminding the church of our imperfections and frailties and that our temptation is to structure the church upon a hierarchy of the worldly principles submission and enslavement. He calls the hierarchical structure of a Pope a heresy and reminds us that the true structure of the church was modeled by Christ who says, "If anyone wants to be first, let him be a servant of all" (Mark9:35).

Sourozh then brings in his discussion on the holiness and the dignity of the laity which is very similar to the call of Luther and the priesthood of all believes and of Vatican II and the Apostolate of the Laity. He concludes by calling for a hierarchy of humility and a hierarchy of service within the structure of the church where there is no dominion or power. He admits that structure is necessary for proper stewardship and that there is giftedness toward leadership and ministry within the church but that the attitude of the people in these positions must be one of humble service because Christ is in our midst as the one who serves. We are called to servants as he is a servant. The towel for the washing of feet is our symbol. He says eloquently that our role as ministers is to be masters guiding the whole of creation into the fullness of unity with God, not to dominate.

Rev. Terrence S. Dwyer

ST503 Systematic Theology 3
Reading Response: #5
By: Terrence Dwyer, June 25th, 2010

Liberation theology believes in the future of God, in God's promises and in a final righting of all wrongs. Liberation theology began as primarily a Roman Catholic movement originating in Latin America. The yearning for liberation is deeply rooted within both the Old and New Testaments and liberation theology is centered on this biblical theme of liberation and freedom. It is a response to oppression and violence committed in word and deed and recognizes Christian values. Since sin has entered the world, we would all have driven to despair if God had abandoned his creation. But God didn't abandon us to ourselves; he promises us liberation through the death and resurrection of Christ. From this hope we as Christians draw our strength to act resolutely in the service of love, justice and peace throughout the world. The Gospel message is a message of freedom and is a liberating force.

The eschatology of liberation theology then is that the Kingdom of God is not simply a personal transformation of the individual soul but it is also has a historical dimension in the relationship between people and the overall structure of society. The eschatology of this liberation theology then seeks to overcome the dichotomy between the world and the world to come. Theologian Leonardo Boff says, "The historical process anticipates and paves the way for definitive liberation in the kingdom. Thus human forms of liberation acquire a sacramental function. Liberation theology is the opposite of a pessimistic religiosity. The sacramental nature of this theology deeply resonates with me and gives me new meaning to the social justice work that I have done over the years. Your comments yesterday about your Orthodox approach to daily life as having a sacramental reverence deeply resonated with me as well. Thank you.

Gustavo Gutierrez from Lima, Peru is one of the major theologians of liberation theology. He says that Biblical eschatology is the driving force of salvation history and is radically oriented toward the future. Eschatology is thus not just one more element of Christianity, but the very key to understanding the Christian faith. The elimination of misery and exploitation therefore can be understood as a sign of the coming kingdom. I so appreciate liberation eschatology because if gives meaning to the good works that I feel so compelled to do as a follower of Jesus Christ.

In reading through the feminist perspective on liberation theology I was struck by the feminine perspective on the book of Revelation and also by the thoughts of feminist theologian Rosemary Radford Ruether. She beautifully articulates that it is our main responsibility to give shape to a community on earth that is interconnected in love, so that it can also be handed onto our children. Our responsibility is to use our temporal life to create a just and good community for our generation and for our children. As a father, this resonates deeply with me and left me wanting to read more of the feminist perspective.

Christian eschatology in the universal context is the idea that Christian faith has to be asserted within the context of many competing worldviews, and religions, and that these contexts need to be taken into account in the expression of our faith which is termed process theology. Theologian John B. Cobb, Jr. writes about process theology in his book, "Christ in a Pluralistic age". He states that Christ is present in all things and without Christ there is no hope for a better future. Our task then is to bring this hope to this world through the power of the Holy Spirit. Theologian John Hick addresses the eschatology of the Christian faith among the world's major religions in his work, "Death and Eternal Life". In his work he argues for a universal salvation.

Emerging Churches
Creating Christian Communities in Postmodern Cultures
By: Eddie Gibbs & Ryan K. Bolger
A supplementary reading review
By: Terrence Dwyer, July 12th, 2010
Fuller Theological Seminary
ST503: Systematic Theology 3: Ecclesiology & Eschatology
Professor: Dr. Eve Tibbs, Ph.D.

Introduction
The modern church is in rapid decline yet the hunger for all things spiritual has perhaps never been greater. The church is responding in the form of emerging churches which are a fresh, new expression of church into the post-modern culture of today. These churches have sprung up throughout Western culture in recent years and have taken on a wide variety of forms and expressions. The authors interviewed over fifty emerging church leaders in the USA and UK in an attempt to discern what it is that makes up the emergent church.

Current Culture

There has been a significant and steady decline in population of the major denominations in both the USA and the U.K. The decline began in the 1960's and continues unabated to today with church attendance in the USA down to 40% while in the U.K. it has eroded to 8% of the population. For populations under the age of 30 the reported weekly church attendance is 1% in both countries. For the Western church to survive the 21st century it must incarnate the Gospel within the current culture.

We in the West are currently in the midst of a huge cultural shift from modernity to post-modernity and from Christendom to post-Christendom. Since the conversion of the Roman emperor Constantine in 313 AD until the midpoint of the 20th century, the church occupied a central position within Western societies otherwise known as Christendom. Modernity began prior to the Renaissance and survived until the 20th century. Modernity represented a period of order and tradition and separated the secular from the spiritual. We are now in an age of pluralism, radical relativism and a merging of the spiritual and the secular.

There is much more transition going on in the world today than just these two significant shifts. Some of these are the economic transitions of globalization and the shifts in technologies and information based economies which the authors do a good but brief job of covering in the text. It is clearer to me after reading this text that to minister today in Western culture requires one to be trained as a missionary to this new emerging culture. One must understand the incarnational demands of the Gospel and the surrounding cultural context within which to minister.

What is an Emerging Church?

Emerging churches remove modern practices of Christianity, not the faith itself. Western Christianity has wed itself to the modern culture which is in decline. Theologies given birth within modernity will not transfer to post-modern cultures so emerging church practices seek to find ways to embody itself into the post-modern culture. Essentially the goal is to be more like Jesus and less evangelical and to state more what the church is for rather than what the church is against. The emerging church is a new and a fresh expression of church to a new and emerging culture. Some of the attributes of the emerging church are such things as: kingdom theology, focus on the inner life, friendship & community, justice, earth keeping, inclusivity, creativity and the arts, and a holistic spirituality.

Through their research of interviewing over fifty emerging church leaders throughout the USA and the U.K., the authors identified nine patterns or practices that are common to these emerging churches. The first three are core practices and the following six are derived from the three core practices. These nine practices are highlighted here as follows:

Identifying with the Life of Jesus

I enjoyed the quote in the text from Emerging Church leader Joe Boyd of Apex, Las Vegas who said, "I read the Gospels over and over and nothing I was doing on Sunday was what I thought Jesus would be doing if he were here". This quote speaks loudly regarding how disconnected the church has become from the incarnation of the Gospel. Emerging churches seek to rectify that disconnect by drawing closer to Jesus and his way of ministry within culture. The issue is to discern what aspects of Jesus' life was his participation in culture and what aspects can be translated into other cultures as expressions of the kingdom. I felt that the authors could have elaborated more here on this issue. They simply said that Jesus served and forgave others as did the early church and thus emerging churches seek to practice serving and hospitality. This leaves me wanting a bit more depth on what aspects of Jesus' ministry are culturally transferrable. However, the good news is that the kingdom of God is here and the mission of God is alive in the world and emerging churches seek to draw close to Christ and in doing so draw close to the mission of God in the world.

Transforming the Secular Realm

Transforming the secular realm is about the destruction of the sacred/secular split of modernity. The modern period created a secular space and relegated spiritual things to the church. Post-modernity is about the sacredness of all life and emerging churches seek to give all life over to God in worship. Psalm 24:1, "The earth is the Lord's and everything in it". Emerging churches seek to end secularity by overcoming linearity, print culture, systemization, and the visible/invisible through creating whole-life spirituality in the realm of society. In other words, emerging churches break down the walls modernity put up between the secular and the religious and merge the two into one. This is the Gospel incarnate as it is intended to be.

Living Highly Communal Lives

Emerging churches seek to live out their corporate lives in accord with the practices of the kingdom of God as expressed by Jesus in his ministry. They commit to a community that follows Jesus with all other loyalties and commitments secondary. The emerging church is a mission focused community of people and a way of life as followers of Christ and not so much concerned about a meeting place or a physical location. Space is given within the community for each individual member of the community to participate and to express their gifts.

Welcoming the Stranger
Emerging churches develop their hospitality, welcome and grace so that they may offer unconditional love and acceptance to anyone believing that at the heart of the kingdom practice of Jesus is the practice of inclusion. Emerging churches don't seek to tell people what to think or offer answers or apologetics. Then humbly introduce Jesus without any evangelical agenda and they admit that they "see through a glass darkly" themselves. The focus is to create welcoming cultures of the kingdom and allow God to do the work. They do not target people or have an agenda but rather they seek to love all those whom God brings to them.

Serving with Generosity
Emerging churches serve others with abundant generosity expecting nothing in return. They have no strategy or agenda to hook and convert others as they seek to simply show others that the kingdom of God is within them and near them. They are genuinely committed to be in relationship with those whom they serve.

Participating as Producers
Another great line from this remarkable book is from an emerging church leader at Vaux who said, "We sat each week surrounded by some of the brightest talents in film, TV, theater, art, social work and politics who were made to watch in silence because they didn't play the guitar or preach. It just seemed such a waste". Emerging churches seek to remedy this by including all members and producing participants in the worship. The idea is for members of the community to cease being spiritual consumers and to participate as spiritual producers. Emerging churches seek to put the priesthood of all believers into practice.

Creating as Created Beings
Jesus invites us to join him in the kingdom work of redeeming of the world. Emerging churches therefore make space for creativity and imagination to thrive in this redemptive work. God created us to be creative and to partner with him in creating something beautiful which inspires others to turn toward God.

Leading as a Body
Emerging churches seek to lead together as a body through servant hood and consensus building in collaboration with each other. It demonstrates to others the presence of the kingdom and God's order. I thought the authors could have done more here as this form of governance

is a Congregational governance model which they did not mention and they did not adequately discuss some of the pitfalls of this form of governance.

Taking Part in Spiritual Activities

There is a hunger for spiritual practices in the post-modernity culture which emerging churches are seeking to address by returning to the spiritual practices of old. Emerging church leaders are uncovering some of the ancient spiritual practices of the early and medieval church and are incorporating them into their worship.

Conclusion

I found this to be an extraordinary text which has dramatically altered my modern orientation toward ministry while at the same time affirmed my post-modernity ministry visions and desires that I have had for such a long time but had no apparent avenue for expression. This text and the realization of the emergent church movement give me the affirmation of those dreams and it gives me the language that I needed to express them. I am deeply grateful for having read this text and I look forward to reading more from these authors and others on the emerging church movement.

Bibliography

Bolger, Eddie Gibbs and Ryan K. Emerging Churches. Grand Rapids, Michigan: Baker Academic, 2005.

Rev. Terrence S. Dwyer

ST503 – Final Exam – Systematic 3 – Dr. Tibbs – Summer 2010
By: Terrence Dwyer, July 8th, 2010

Summarize each of the classical "notes" of "marks" of the church.

In our Nicene Creed we profess our faith in a church that is one, holy, catholic and apostolic. We regard these as four essential attributes of the church and we refer to them as the "notes" or the "marks" of the church. They are called the marks of the church because they are the markings or the visible signs of the attributes of the church. These four attributes distinguish the church from other religious bodies or assemblies. However, these four marks were not always used to describe the essential nature of the church but developed over time.

Holiness was the first mark attributed to the church and was found in our earliest attempts at establishing our creeds of belief. Creeds developed in the early church, within the first three centuries, out of the necessity of Christians to be able to tell others what they believed in. The second mark attributed to the early church was that of unity and unity was closely connected to and dependent upon holiness. The church is one through the unifying power of the Holy Spirit just as the church is holy through the power of the Holy Spirit. The church's holiness is not derived from the high moral quality of its members but from the presence of the Holy Spirit who unifies the church and gives the church its holiness. The Holy Spirit is seen as uniting believers to one another and to God in the body of Christ. As Paul says in 1 Cor. 12:13; "For in one Spirit we were all baptized into one body-Jews or Greeks, slaves or free-and all were made to drink of one Spirit."

The term catholic also describes a distinguishing mark or attribute of the church and it is derived from the Greek "Kata holos" meaning according to the whole. The term catholic refers to entire body of believers spread throughout the whole world implying wholeness and unity with each other under the lordship of Jesus Christ and the unity of the Holy Spirit as opposed to sectarian, dissident, and heretical groups. The term catholic then became another distinguishing mark of the church.

The early church also believed that the unifying function of the Holy Spirit was exercised through the office of bishop who maintained unity within the church and who worked to protect the church. The unity of the church was maintained through a continuous apostolic succession from the original Apostles. This unbroken apostolic succession distinguished the true church from the heretical and the term apostolic thus became another distinguishing mark of the church.

By the fourth century then the church was described by these four traditional marks of one, holy, catholic and apostolic through the creation of the Nicene Creed accomplished at the Councils of Nicaea (325AD) and Constantinople (381 AD). These four classical marks of the church are perceived to be interdependent. The church was one because it was holy and it was holy through the power of the Holy Spirit who unified the church. The church was apostolic because it was unified in its obedience to the bishops who were successors to the original Apostles. The church was catholic because it was apostolic and had been sent throughout the whole world and yet remained whole and united together through the Holy Spirit.

The protestant reformers of the 16th century rejected the idea that the one, holy, catholic and apostolic church referred to the visible church headed by the Pope. The church of the four marks they insisted was to be found where the gospel is properly preached and the sacraments rightly administered. It was problematic however, for the reformers to claim oneness and unity as they broke away from the Catholic Church but the reformers distinguished between visible unity under the Pope and unity of faith under Christ. Roman Catholic apologists pointed to the wide variety of Protestant churches as an indication of the disunity of the Protestants and therefore they could not be the true church of Christ.

The mark of unity continued to be an issue for the modern church as well and there has been a growing ecumenical movement among Protestant churches in the 20th century as they worked toward joint cooperation in certain areas such as missions. There has even been reconciliation between Catholics and Protestants beginning with Pope John the 23rd inviting Protestants to Vatican II and calling them "our brethren in Christ". This Vatican Council went so far as to acknowledge that all who have been justified by faith in baptism are incorporated into Christ and therefore have the right to be called Christians and are accepted as sisters and brothers in the Lord by the children of the Catholic Church.

Examine various approaches to the intermediate state.

The intermediate state refers to the state of the soul of a person between death and the resurrection. There are various approaches regarding the intermediate state but it is difficult to determine the validity of any one approach as there is little Scriptural support for any of these various approaches.

A) The Traditional Doctrine regarding the intermediate state is that the soul enjoys a foretaste of the eternal condition. The Old Testament view is that all initially go to Hades or to Sheol regardless of their state of grace. The Old Testament meaning of Sheol is unclear as there is little written about it. Sheol however, is not seen as the repose of the essential person after death nor is it a place of bliss. The New Testament view is that the unrighteous go to Hades or to Gehenna while the righteous go to paradise. A critique of this view is that this view holds that the soul exists without the body and is a disembodied soul the state of eternal life? If so then this view seems to conflict with the theology of a bodily resurrection.

B) Purgatory is the Roman Catholic belief that the dead go to a place where they experience certain degrees of suffering in order to purge them of their sins before their entry into heaven. This idea of a temporary punishment was promoted by Thomas Aquinas and his concept of penal suffering. Aquinas also put forward the idea of an intermediate state for the righteous of the Old Testament to await the coming Messiah which he called "limbus patrum". Aquinas also described an intermediate state for infants who die before receiving baptism called "limbus infantium". These beliefs were made official doctrine at the Council of Florence in 1439 AD and reaffirmed at the Council of Trent (1545 AD to 1563 AD). The Scriptural support for this view is 2 Maccabees 12:43-45;"Therefore he made atonement for the dead, so that they might be delivered from their sin" and Matt. 12:32; "Whoever speaks a word against the Son of Man will be forgiven, but whoever speaks against the Holy Spirit will not be forgiven, either in this age or the age to come". The Protestant critique of this view is that the Biblical support is not strong and the idea of a Purgatory undervalues the finished work of Jesus Christ.

C) Death as an Entrance into Eternity: This view proposes that there is no intermediate state at all but that at death the eternal body is immediately given for eternity. This view was promoted in medieval times by Pope Benedict XII. A newer view is held by Evangelicals who believe that death places us in a realm where we receive our eternal body and that this is a foretaste of ultimate destiny. Pannenberg criticizes this view in that this view seems to conflict with the resurrection of Christ as the anticipatory resurrection of all believers.

D) Instantaneous Resurrection: Another version of the above view that death is an entrance into eternity is the view of an Instantaneous Resurrection. This view is supported in Scripture by Paul in 1 Cor. 15:51-52; "We shall not all sleep, but we shall be changed, in a moment, in the twinkling of an eye, at the last trumpet." And 2 Cor. 5 can be interpreted to support either an intermediate state or an instantaneous resurrection with an immortal body given at Christ's return. This view is also supported in Luke 23:43; "I tell you the truth, today you will be with me in Paradise." However, this was not intended to describe the state of the soul after death,

but to support the fact that even in death we remain in God's love.
E) Soul Sleep: In this view of the intermediate state the adherents believe that the soul enters into unconsciousness and sleeps after death while it awaits the final state. This view was promoted by Pope John XXII in the 13th century and was also supported throughout history by Martin Luther, the Anabaptists, by the Socinians of the 16th century and is supported today by the Adventists and the Jehovah Witnesses. The critique of this view is the same critique of the traditional view. The soul exists without the body and is a disembodied soul the true state of eternal life? This view conflicts with the theology of a bodily resurrection.

Difficulties in determining the intermediate state can be seen in Luke 16:22-23 where we see the poor man had died and was carried by the angels to Abraham's side. The rich man also died and was buried and found himself in torment in Hades and he saw Abraham and Lazarus together. It seems here that both the righteous and the unrighteous are in the same place and are we to interpret this literally or figuratively? However, even in death we remain in God's love and our salvation is not complete at death but at the second coming of Jesus Christ. Therefore the issue of the intermediate state is not a primary issue.

Examine arguments for and against universalism.
The word Universalism is derived from the Greek word "apokatastasis" meaning restoration. The idea being that all will be restored or saved. Universalism affirms universal salvation and it denies the belief in eternal punishment. Universalists believe that ultimately all humans are somehow in union with Christ and that in the fullness of time they will gain the release from the penalty of sin and be restored to God.

The arguments for Universalism:
A) The divine love of God as a loving God would not torture his creation.
B) The complete triumph of Christ as the existence of hell would mean there is a place where he is not Lord as death and sin would continue to rule in hell.
C) God desires that everyone is to be saved and he is unrelenting in pursuing the wayward. This is affirmed in Scripture is 1 Tim.2:4; 4:10, and 2 Peter 3:9.
D) Christ's atonement is intended for all. This is supported in Scripture by 2 Cor.5:19, Titus 2:11, Heb. 2:9 and John 2:2.
E) God will bring all creation into its fullness in Christ. Affirmed is Scripture by John 12:32, Eph. 1:10, and Col. 1:16-23.
F) Final restoration of all persons to God. Supported in Scripture by

Acts 3:19-21 and Phil. 2:9-11.
G) There are two supporting arguments for universalism from Paul's writings and they are: Rom. 5:12-21 where all were tainted by sin through Adam's disobedience which brought condemnation to all and Jesus' victory brought life to all. Also in 1 Cor. 15:20 Just as in Adam all die, so in Christ all live.
H) God intends punishment as education and healing and eternal punishment is not just as it does not correct anything. Also, universalism does not deny the urgency to turn to God.
I) Finally, Origen believed that even the evil one would be saved and reformed theologian Karl Barth said to hope for universalism but do not teach it.

Arguments against universalism:
A) The exegesis of Universalist theory is theology unsound as the Scripture does not seem to allow for a second chance at salvation as Scripture seems clear in its admonition for faith and for a choice for salvation. See Scripture verses below:
B) God has limited himself by giving his human creation freedom of choice. This freedom of choice would be rendered moot and meaningless by universalism as God would ultimately not be respecting our freedom of choice.
C) We cannot be sure that humans would respond to God's love after death.

Scripture verses that go against universalism are:
Matthew 22:13 (New International Version)
13"Then the king told the attendants, 'Tie him hand and foot, and throw him outside, into the darkness, where there will be weeping and gnashing of teeth
Luke 13:25-29 (New International Version)
25Once the owner of the house gets up and closes the door, you will stand outside knocking and pleading, 'Sir, open the door for us.' "But he will answer, 'I don't know you or where you come from.' 26"Then you will say, 'We ate and drank with you, and you taught in our streets.' 27"But he will reply, 'I don't know you or where you come from. Away from me, all you evildoers!' 28"There will be weeping there, and gnashing of teeth, when you see Abraham, Isaac and Jacob and all the prophets in the kingdom of God, but you yourselves thrown out. 29People will come from east and west and north and south, and will take their places at the feast in the kingdom of God.

Romans 6:21 (New International Version)
21What benefit did you reap at that time from the things you are now ashamed of? Those things result in death!
Philippians 1:28 (New International Version)
28without being frightened in any way by those who oppose you. This is a sign to them

that they will be destroyed, but that you will be saved—and that by God.
Philippians 3:19 (New International Version)
19Their destiny is destruction, their god is their stomach, and their glory is in their shame. Their mind is on earthly things.
1 Thessalonians 5:3 (New International Version)
3While people are saying, "Peace and safety," destruction will come on them suddenly, as labor pains on a pregnant woman, and they will not escape.
2 Thessalonians 1:8-10 (New International Version)
8He will punish those who do not know God and do not obey the gospel of our Lord Jesus. 9They will be punished with everlasting destruction and shut out from the presence of the Lord and from the majesty of his power 10on the day he comes to be glorified in his holy people and to be marveled at among all those who have believed. This includes you, because you believed our testimony to you.

Summarize the origins and leading ideas of Latin Liberation Ecclesiologies.

Latin Liberation Ecclesiology refers to a theological movement developed in the Catholic communities in the late 1960's in Latin America where it still continues to be prominent. Theologian Gustavo Gutierrez was the first to write about Liberation theology ("A Theology of Liberation"- 1971) which emphasized the Scriptural theme of liberation which is understood as overcoming the oppression of poverty and political oppression. Latin Liberation theologians attempt to unite their theology with their sociopolitical concerns. Liberation theology emphasizes the responsibility of the church to bring justice to the poor and the oppressed, particularly through political activism. Some Protestant theologians became involved in the movement but it is seen largely as a movement within the Catholic Church calling for a new commitment on the part of the church to the poor and the marginalized. The congregational movement came about in response to the oppressive political regimes within Latin America and due to the acute absence of ordained Roman Catholic priests.

In 1968 the Second General Conference of Latin American Bishops met in Medellin, Columbia and debated how to apply the teachings of Vatican II in Latin America especially in light of the pressing issues of justice, peace, and poverty among their people and the responsibility of the church toward addressing these needs. They issued an extraordinary document calling for sociopolitical change in the areas of justice, peace and poverty and they called for changes within the church to better effect change within these areas.

Leonardo Boff is recognized as one of the most significant liberation theologians. He understood Vatican II's "Lumen Gentium" as opening up new ways of thinking about the church in its actualizing the Kingdom of God. He demanded institutional reform within the church which led to the recognition of Basic Ecclesial Communities which were primary centers of Christian community and evangelism. They were not recognized by the church as traditional churches but they were recognized as a new ecclesiality. These BEC's did not meet in churches but they met in meeting halls and they elected lay leadership. There were no rigid rules or titles but they were small congregational pioneers for social justice within the Catholic Church and within their Latin American communities. These BEC's were grassroots communities for purposes of effecting scripturally based sociopolitical change within their communities. These communities studied the Word, prayed together, cared for the sick, taught people to read and looked after the poor among other ministries.

Liberation theologians were admonished by the Vatican in the 1980's for using Marxist's concepts and for emphasizing orthopraxis over orthodoxy as well as rejecting the hierarchical structure of the church. However, the church did praise their ideal of justice, their rejection of violence, and the responsibility of Christians toward the poor and the oppressed.

Latin Liberation theologians stressed that the church needed to elevate the Word and laity instead of clergy and sacrament. The clergy and sacrament are not to cripple the Word and laity but they are to be in balance. Vatican II stressed the priesthood of all believers and the Latin Liberation movement put it into action in part due to the absence of ordained priests. They saw their local Evangelical brothers and sisters in their community doing church and the Catholics opened up to the movement of the Holy Spirit within their community. They too realized that they too had unmediated access to God through the power of the Holy Spirit.

The arguments for the ecclesiality of these para-churches are the priesthood of all believers, the same baptism, same faith, and that the church comes into being when people become aware of the call of salvation in Jesus Christ and come together in community to profess that faith and seek to live as Christ's disciples.

Liberation theology has also found representation among marginalized groups in North American society such as women, African Americans, Hispanics, Native Americans, and Asian Americans. There are still BEC's in Latin America today and social justice concerns are still a major issue there today.

A Comparative Review of the Post-Modern Emerging Church Movement
With the Theology of Mission of Lesslie Newbigin
By: Terrence Dwyer, August 10th, 2010
Fuller Theological Seminary
ST 503: Systematic Theology 3: Ecclesiology and Eschatology
Professor: Dr. Eve Tibbs, Ph.D.

Introduction

There has been a significant and steady decline in population of the major denominations in both the USA and the U.K. The decline began in the 1960's and continues unabated to today with church attendance in the USA down to below 40% of the population while in the U.K. it has eroded to 8% of the population. For populations under the age of 30 the reported weekly church attendance is only 1% of the population in both countries. For the Western church to survive the 21st century it must seek to incarnate the gospel within the current culture.

We in the West are currently in the midst of a significant cultural shift from modernity to post-modernity and from Christendom to post-Christendom. Since the conversion of the Roman emperor Constantine in 313 AD until the midpoint of the 20th century, the church occupied a central position within Western societies. Modernity began prior to the Renaissance and survived until the 20th century and represented a period of order and tradition. We now are in an age of pluralism, radical relativism and a merging of the spiritual and the secular. There is much more transition going on in the world today than just these two significant shifts. Some of these are the economic transitions of globalization and the shifts in technologies and information based economies as well as global climate change.

The modern Western church is in rapid decline yet the hunger for all things spiritual has perhaps never been greater. One of the ways that the church is responding and reacting to this decline is in the form of "emerging churches" which are a fresh, new expression of church into the post-modern culture of today. These churches have sprung up throughout Western culture in recent years and have taken on a wide variety of forms and expressions. Emerging churches remove modern practices of Christianity but not the core of the faith itself. Western Christianity has wed itself to the modern culture which is in decline in our post-modern era.

245

Theologies given birth within modernity will not transfer to post-modern cultures so emerging church practices seek to find ways to incarnate itself into the post-modern culture. Essentially the goal is to be more like Jesus and less evangelical and to state more what the church is for rather than what the church is against. The emerging church is a new and a fresh expression of church to a new and emerging post-modern culture.

Lesslie Newbigin (1909-1998), a Church of Scotland missionary to India for almost forty years, was one of the most respected and significant theologians of the twentieth century. Newbigin argues that the dichotomy between the private and the public world is fundamental to Western culture, and that if there is to be an effective missionary encounter of the gospel with this culture, the understanding of this dichotomy is a prime requirement. The main points characterizing Lesslie Newbigin's missional ecclesiology are that the church is missional, ecumenical, and dynamic. The church is essentially missional in nature in that it is striving to preach the gospel to all people and even to the ends of the earth, to implore all people to be reconciled to God. Secondly, the missional church is ecumenical in its unity in spreading the gospel message. Thirdly, the church is dynamic in its mission as it is eschatological in nature.

We will seek in this paper to compare and contrast these three key points of the missional theology of Lesslie Newbigin with the reactionary expressions of the emerging church into post-modern Western culture. The emerging church has admittedly not yet developed their own deeply thought through system of theology; they simply strive to follow Jesus as they feel led by the Holy Spirit. However, emerging church leaders do look to theologians N.T Wright, John Howard Yoder, David Bosch, and Lesslie Newbigin among others, for their understanding of Jesus, the gospel, the kingdom and the mission of God in the world. We will seek to compare and contrast here in this brief review the certain core emerging church expressions with the distinct missional theology of Lesslie Newbigin.

The Missional Church

Newbigin argues that the church is essentially missional in nature in that it is striving to preach the gospel to all people and even to the ends of the earth, to implore all people to be reconciled to God. Newbigin describes this wonderfully when he says that the nature of salvation is governed by its' source which is a love that reaches out after all people and goes to all lengths to recover one lost sheep. Therefore, the mission is not ours but it is God's mission. He goes on to say that it belongs to the very heart of salvation that we cannot have it in fullness until all for whom it is intended have it together. Therefore, the church is missional in nature in striving for the gospel message of salvation to be obtained by all.

Newbigin teaches us that the missional church proclaims God's kingship over all of human history and over the whole cosmos. Mission is concerned with nothing less than the completion of all that God has begun to do. Mission is also the very presence of God in the incarnation and kingship of Jesus Christ who introduces the kingdom of God and in the church. Mission is also something that is done by the Holy Spirit, who is himself the witness, who changes both the world and the church and who always, goes before the church in its missionary journey.

Emerging churches look to Jesus as the one who initiated the work of the kingdom and their hope is to point to the kingdom through their communal practices in postmodern culture today. Karen Ward of Church of the Apostles in Seattle says, "We focused on the humanity of Jesus and lost all the categories from church history. The culture gets that Jesus was for the marginalized and the oppressed. It is only the church that needs to be trained to look at Jesus again. 95% of the non-churched have a favorable view of Jesus so Jesus is not the problem. It is the church they dislike because they do not see the church living out his teachings". Emerging church leaders say that the church was telling the story of modernity and baby boom aspirations rather than the radical message of the kingdom of God.

The current Western church is normally structured as a "come to us" church model where people come to a place to receive spiritual products. The service is built around the consumption of these experiences. The visitors expect to be served and are consumers. Over time, members come to believe that church represents programs and services done to them rather than participants who are all invited and expected to contribute. The experiences of community and service vary widely from church to church. This "come to" structure ceases to be missional in that the church is asking those outside the faith to come into their world instead of those within the church serving in the world of those outside. That is precisely what the emerging church seeks to do by serving others in the world outside of the church. Joe Boyd, an emerging church leader of Apex, Las Vegas said, "I read the gospels over and over and nothing I was doing on Sunday was what I thought Jesus would be doing if he were here". This quote speaks loudly regarding how disconnected the church has become from the incarnation of the gospel. Emerging churches seek to rectify that disconnect by drawing closer to Jesus and his way of ministry within culture which again is what Newbigin describes as the essential missional nature of the church. One unique example of an emerging church's missional incarnation would be "i-church". "i-church" is an on-line Christian community for people who want to explore Christianity and have questions of faith but are not able to or are not yet ready to belong to a local congregation. The web pastor supports key volunteers and provides pastoral support for individuals along with teaching the Scripture. This is an example of a non-traditional, emerging church that is seeking to move outward into the world to serve the needs of others and to spread the hope of the gospel into their world. Other examples are emerging church café's and clubs where these new expressions of church are seeking to cross over into secular space to share the hope of the gospel of Jesus Christ into these traditionally secular spaces. I believe that essentially the emerging church, in all its many forms, is a true expression of Lesslie Newbigin's theology of the missional church.

The Ecumenical Church

Secondly, Newbigin argues that the missional church is ecumenical in its unity in spreading the gospel message. Newbigin is a great defender of Christian unity and he accurately describes the three divisions that we find within Christianity today. Newbigin says that we are grafted onto Christ in three main ways: 1st, by hearing the Gospel and believing, 2nd, by sacramental participation, 3rd, by receiving and abiding in the Holy Spirit. Newbigin describes the three divisions within the church as over emphasizing one of these three to the detriment of the other two. He describes the Protestant approach as emphasizing hearing the gospel and believing, the Catholic approach as emphasizing the sacraments and the Pentecostal approach as emphasizing the experience of the Holy Spirit. Newbigin argues that the church needs to wholly embrace all three of these approaches in unity in its mission.

I believe that it is in this area of ecumenical unity where the emerging church is still working through their ecclesiology. The emerging church expression is a combination of both the Protestant approach in emphasizing the hearing of the Gospel and the Pentecostal approach in emphasizing the experience of the Holy Spirit. However, it is in the area of sacramental participation where the emerging church admittedly fails. In the leaving behind of the practices of the traditional Western church, emerging churches often also leave behind the practices of the sacraments of the church which Newbigin says are essential as part of our grafting onto Christ. How does one reverently or even appropriately practice the sacrament of the Eucharist in a pub or a café? These are issues that the emerging church still needs to come to terms with as they develop their ecclesiology over time.

That being said, there is a real desire among the leaders of the emerging church movement to reach back in time to the early church for their liturgy and for their spiritual practices and disciplines. They are looking backward in an attempt to retrieve practices that sacralize all space, to a time when all of life was holy. These ancient practices serve as a resource for the emergent church from a time when the church did not practice the Western heresy of secularism. Examples of ancient practices that they are incorporating into their liturgies are such practices as "lectio Divina" and chanting.

The Dynamic Church

Thirdly, Newbigin argues that the church is dynamic in its mission as it is eschatological in nature. The people of God are pilgrims who are on the move, hastening to spread the gospel to the end of the earth so that all people are reconciled to God in the fullness of time so that we may be all gathered together into one to meet our Lord. Newbigin also describes the tension that the missional church experiences as it often finds itself witnessing in hostile non-Christian cultures and yet at the same time the church must tend to those within the church who have answered the call to Christ. Finally, Newbigin says that the missional church needs to adapt and be relevant to the current culture it finds itself in.

Taking Newbigin's last point first regarding the dynamic church, it is clear that the emergent church is a direct result of the church seeking to adapt and to be relevant to the current culture that it finds itself in. The emergent church is seeking to incarnate itself into Western culture to humbly serve the needs of the people and to bring to them the gospel of Jesus Christ.

The process of making disciples once someone comes to believe in Christ is an area where the emerging church still leaves much to be desired. Emerging church expressions in general are good at introducing people to the gospel of Jesus Christ but then attending to a person's spiritual growth and maturity after receiving the gospel is often beyond the resources available to some emergent churches. Certain emergent churches however, are addressing this very issue by choosing to remain small so that they can minister to the spiritual growth of their members.

Newbigin asks, "How is it possible that the gospel should be credible, that people should come to believe that the power which has the last word in human affairs is represented by a man hanging on a cross?" He goes on to suggest that the only answer, indeed the only hermeneutic of the gospel, is a congregation of men and women who believe it and live by it. Emergent churches, in their communal expressions of church, are seeking to live out this very call of Newbigin to be visible congregations communally living out the gospel in secular space.

Conclusion

In conclusion, the emerging church movement does appear at their core to be living out the missional theology expressed by Lesslie Newbigin with perhaps the exception of the practice of the sacraments within certain emergent church expressions. Newbigin describes three key areas of missional theology for the church. The first is that the church is essentially missional in nature in that it is striving to preach the gospel to all people the world over. Secondly, the missional church is ecumenical in its unity in spreading the gospel message. Thirdly, the church is dynamic in its mission as it is eschatological in nature. We compared the emerging church movement to Newbigin's theology and saw that this new expression of church was indeed missional and dynamic but only partially ecumenical. As the emerging church movement develops, incorporating the sacraments and developing disciples will be areas that will need to be addressed by these church leaders.

Newbigin says, "We are witnesses not of our religious experiences, but of Jesus Christ, his incarnation, ministry, death, and resurrection. We cannot keep silent about this because it is truth that concerns every human being so it must be told to every human being. That obligation remains till the end of time."

It is the emerging church movement that is actively and creatively seeking to fulfill this obligation by making itself relevant to current Western culture in a wide variety of church expressions in order to share the gospel of Jesus with those within the culture that would never dare set foot inside a church and who may otherwise never hear the gospel articulated.

Bibliography

Bolger, Eddie Gibbs and Ryan K. Emerging Churches. Grand Rapids, Michigan: Baker Academic, 2005.

Kärkkäinen, Veli-Matti. An Introduction to Ecclesiology. Downers Grove, Illinois: IVP Academic Press, 2002.

McGrath, Alister E. Theology, the Basic Readings. Malden, MA: Blackwell Publishing, 2008.

Newbigin, Lesslie. Foolishness to the Greeks. Grand Rapids, MI: William B. Eerdmans Publishing Company, 1986.

Newbigin, Lesslie. The Gospel in a Pluralist Society. Grand Rapids, MI: William B. Eerdmans Publishing Company, 1989.

Newbigin, Lesslie. A Word in Season, Perspectives on Christian World Missions. Grand Rapids, MI: William B. Eerdmans Publishing Company, 1994.

Newbigin, Lesslie. The Open Secret. Grand Rapids, Michigan: William B. Eerdmans Publishing Company 1995.

Percy, Louise Nelstrop and Martyn. Evaluating Fresh Expressions, Explorations in Emerging Church. London, UK: Canterbury Press Norwich, 2008.

ABOUT THE AUTHOR

Rev. Terrence S. Dwyer, MDiv, MBA is an ordained Presbyterian Minister in the PC USA and works for Kaiser Permanente as an acute care and Palliative care chaplain in Oakland and Richmond, CA. Rev. Dwyer serves the San Francisco Presbytery as a pulpit supply preacher and lives in Oakland, CA.

Made in the USA
Lexington, KY
04 March 2017